8-CIRCUIT
ASCENSION

Some Other Titles from Falcon Press

Antero Alli
The Eight-Circuit Brain: Navigational Strategies for the Energetic Body
Eight-Circuits of Consciousness (video)
Angel Tech: A Modern Shaman's Guide to Reality Selection
Experiential Astrology: From the Map to the Territory

Christopher S. Hyatt, Ph.D.
Undoing Yourself with Energized Meditation and Other Devices
Secrets of Western Tantra: The Sexuality of the Middle Path

Christopher S. Hyatt, Ph.D. with contributions by Wm. S. Burroughs, Timothy Leary, Robert Anton Wilson et al.
Rebels & Devils: The Psychology of Liberation

Steven Heller
Monsters & Magical Sticks: There's No Such Thing As Hypnosis?

Peter J. Carroll
The Chaos Magick Audios
PsyberMagick

Phil Hine
Condensed Chaos: An Introduction to Chaos Magic
Prime Chaos: Adventures in Chaos Magic

Joseph Lisiewski, Ph.D.
Kabbalistic Handbook for the Practicing Magician
Ceremonial Magic & the Power of Evocation

Israel Regardie
The Complete Golden Dawn System of Magic
The Golden Dawn Audios

Denny Sargent
Naga Magick: The Wisdom of the Serpent Lords
Tantra for All: The Path of Nath Tantrika

Gregory Peters
Yogini Magic: Sorcery, Enchantment & Witchcraft of the Divine Feminine
New Aeon Tantra: Secrets of Typhonian Magick & Western Tantra

**For up-to-the-minute information on prices and availability,
please visit our website at
originalfalcon.com**

8-Circuit Ascension

A Guide to Metaprogramming the Multidimensional Self

by
Douglas S. Wingate &
Rachel Turetzky, Ph.D.

Foreword with
David Jay Brown

THE *Original* FALCON PRESS
TEMPE, ARIZONA, U.S.A.

International Standard Book Number: 978-1-61869-624-3
ISBN: 978-1-61869-625-0 (mobi)
ISBN: 978-1-61869-626-7 (Epub)
Library of Congress Control Number: 2025931523

First Print Edition 2025
First eBook Edition 2025

Logo Design/Cover Image by Rachel Turetzky and Rob Randolph
Cover Design by Douglas Wingate

The paper used in this publication meets the minimum requirements of the American National Standard for Permanence of Paper for Printed Library Materials Z39.48-1984

Address all inquiries to:
The Original Falcon Press
1753 East Broadway Road #101-277
Tempe, AZ 85282 U.S.A.
(or)
PO Box 3540
Silver Springs NV 89429 U.S.A.
website: originalfalcon.com
email: info@originalfalcon.com

Dedication

We dedicate this book in tribute and with the utmost reverence and gratitude to the original developers of the 8-Circuit Model of Consciousness:

Dr. Timothy Leary, Robert Anton Wilson, and Antero Alli

— and —

the OG Metaprogrammer:
Dr. John C. Lilly

Acknowledgements

We would like to thank our publisher, Nick Tharcher. We're beyond honored to be included as part of the original 8-Circuit Model lineage through The Original Falcon Press, along with our forebears, Dr. Timothy Leary, Robert Anton Wilson, and Antero Alli. We also extend this acknowledgement to the founder of The Original Falcon Press, Dr. Christopher S. Hyatt (decd.), to whom we also owe a debt of gratitude for his intellectual influence and brilliance (e.g., *Undoing Yourself with Energized Meditation and Other Devices*—read it, do it).

Many thanks to those with whom we've shared a preliminary copy of this book and who took the time to read and review our work: David Jay Brown, Grant Morrison, Michael Mithoefer, MD, Heather Berlin, PhD, MPH, Stefan Kasian, ND, PhD, David Shoemaker, PsyD, Michael Patterson, Gregory Peters, Gabriel Kennedy, Danielle Herrera, Baal Kadmon, Zappy Zapolin, Coby Michael, and Zach West. Your time and glowing appraisals have been appreciated beyond measure.

A huge thank you to Rob Randolph for his awesome work on our logo/sigil!

Shout out to the leaders and innovators in the burgeoning 8-Circuit Model community who are developing novel and diverse applications of the model: Mariana Pinzón, Zach West, Gabe PropAnon Kennedy, RU Sirius, James Heffernan, Dr. Stefan Kasian, Laurent Huguelit, Richard Rasa, Mike Gathers, Cole Vasquez, Rodrigo Abdo, and all of the other contemporary pioneers of the 8-Circuit Model.

And we'd like to honor the thinkers, authors, teachers, rebels, and brilliant minds who have influenced and inspired us over the years—too numerous to list.

"If I have seen further than others, it's because I have stood on the shoulders of giants."
— Sir Isaac Newton —

Dr. Douglas S. Wingate's Acknowledgements

I'd like to express a great amount of gratitude to those who have helped support, educate, guide, influence, and motivate me over the years without which this work would not be possible. A special thank you to the incredible Dr. Rachel Turetzky and David Jay Brown for bringing me on this ride with them.

To those who have taught me so much over the years: Ken Glowacki, Joe Coletto, Bob Quinn, Brandt Stickley, Lonny Jarrett, Heather Zwickey, Hong Jin, Zhenbo Li, Feng Zheng, Zhaoxue Lu, Satya Ambrose, Eric Stephens, Mitch Stargrove, Regina Dehen, Robert Kaneko, Martin Kidwell, Michael Berletich, Yan Lu, Susan Hare, Molly Fitzpatrick, Dessa Bingley, Beth Howlett, Tracy Thorne, Crystal Sheldon, Kimber Savage, Ed Chiu, David Eisen, Forrest Cooper, Guohui Liu, Leslie Monarch, Aaron Lee, Christine Sanmiquel, Fengli Lan, Alexandra Dimitrova, Ted Carrick, Ayla Wolf, Adam Klotzek, David Traster, Marvin Berman, Glen Zielinski, Bruce Wojciechowski, Poney Chiang, Jim Chialtas, Anna Goldfarb, Robert Yao, Master Liu He, Jeffrey Yuen, Tran Viet Dzung, Tal Sharabi, Erica Zelfand, Gina Gratza, Nate Howard, Tom Eckert, Will Van Deveer, Keith Kurlander and my incredible colleagues at the Integrative Psychiatry Institute and 7 Gates Sanctuary.

I cannot express enough love and appreciation to those who have been there through thick and thin over so many years and are truly family: my sister Pam, my brother Jason, Allison, Clint, Jesse, Jerry, Isaiah, Levi, Sabs, Angie, and Aaron.

Thank you to my child who has been a continual source of inspiration since the day you were born.

Lastly, to both of my parents, Dave and Jeanette Wingate, both no longer with us, but who were unending sources of love and support which continues to resonate and inspire me.

Dr. Rachel Turetzky's Acknowledgements

I would first and foremost like to acknowledge and thank my visionary co-founders of 8-Circuit Ascension/The Institute of Applied Metaprogramming, Dr. Douglas Wingate and David Jay Brown. These are two of the most brilliant minds and beautiful souls that I've had the pleasure and privilege to connect with in this life. Their genius and tenacity have been paramount to the writing of this book and the manifesting of this vision.

I acknowledge and honor the many spiritual teachers and guides (both incarnate and discarnate) who I have met along this convoluted path that I traverse. In particular, I would like to credit Anthony Eufemio and Jason Farrell (americanconjure.com, Instagram @americanconjure) for their profound influence on my psychospiritual/magickal development, and for their roles in introducing me to the 8-Circuit Model of Consciousness.

I've been blessed with some of the most brilliant, inspiring, and supportive teachers and mentors that I've had the privilege to work and study with on my professional journey: The Multidisciplinary Association for Psychedelic Studies (MAPS)/Lykos Therapeutics, Dr. Rick Strassman, Alchemy Community Therapy Center (formerly called Sage Institute), Dr. Heather Berlin, Hermetic Order of the Golden Dawn, Builders of the Adytum, Antero Alli, Marianne Wells Yoga School, Integrative Wellness Academy, Mariko Zervos-Batyr & Rick Batyr, and my dissertation committee: Dr. Juliet Rohde-Brown, Dr. Susan Guy, and Dr. Jose Sanchez. I am humbled, strengthened, and nurtured by these connections and experiences.

Infinite gratitude to my family for their support: Linda Pepe, Dr. Elliott J. Turetzky (decd.), Dominick & Carla DelCarpine (decd.), John & Christina Pepe, Eric & Renata Turetzky, Giordan Lasane, Emily Turetzky, Lois Schneider, John W. Pepe (decd.), Roberta Sidelman, and Nicholas Minerva & family.

I have the most amazing network of friends and meaningful acquaintances that would take pages to list. Those listed here I consider family, and have supported me immensely through our connection: Rebecca Jalinos & family, Eva Andresen, Mary Neary, Ruby Rose Boehme, Julie Turner & family, Dr. Michael Lamm & family, Robert Valasek ("Capt'n Frizzo" decd.), Charlie Mohr, Mike Russo & Melissa Wilbur, Jason & Marissa Ferrara & family, Robert & Michael Mezynski (decd.), John Beneduce ("The Manimal"), Frater EC (decd.), Nikki Masih, Dennis Yabut, Mike Stanley, Dr. Joseph Lodespoto, Elizabeth & Cody Briggs, my cohort at Pacifica Graduate Institute ("The Whales"), Phil Silverman (decd.) & Donna Rice, Mike LaMothe, Charles Finkelstein, Evan Taylor, Claire Nicole & Janet Smith, Sara Phinn Huntley. Special thanks to Steven Franzen.

And to the best friend I've ever known... I would be absolutely lost without my soulmate and greatest teacher—my most amazing cat, Zephyr. He has been with me through all of the turbulence that comes with following one's dreams and taking the path less traveled. Thank you for your unconditional love and tolerating my chaotic lifestyle, my sweet shaman.

CONTENTS

BOOK III:
TRANSMIT

FIGURES

TABLES

PREFACE

"Think for yourself. Question authority." This is the iconic mantra that most people associate with Dr. Timothy Leary (1920–1996). Leary was infamous for his controversial advocacy of free thought, and his flamboyant counterculture escapades, including psychedelic research and advocacy. Leary's potential threat to the Establishment was so influential that President Richard Nixon and his administration dubbed Leary, *"the most dangerous man in America."* In response to this threat, the Nixon administration set out to arrest him, damage his reputation, and criminalize psychedelics; they were successful on all counts. Leary spent three years in prison from 1973–1976. Psychedelics were then classified as Schedule I drugs, (which the U.S. government considers the most dangerous, allegedly having no medical or therapeutic value, and a high potential for abuse) under the Controlled Substances Act of 1970. Under this classification, psychedelics were stigmatized, and became increasingly difficult to study. Moreover, Nixon-era propaganda and fallacious studies were reported in the media regarding the adverse and dangerous effects of psychedelics. Unfortunately, this *did* damage Leary's reputation and legacy, and to this day, his notoriety often obscures his genius and his many great intellectual contributions outside of the aforementioned counterculture dynamic.

One such contribution was his development of the 8-Circuit Model of Consciousness (8-CM)—an adaptable "meta-model" into which myriad other models can be plugged into and organized in a meaningful way. This framework can be used as an effective tool to understand the many diverse facets of consciousness, including but not limited to:

- the developmental history of consciousness encoded in the DNA of all life, and its increasing complexity as it evolved into the nervous systems of invertebrate reptiles, vertebrate mammals, and through to modern humans
- its application in understanding historic and contemporary individual and cultural/collective psychology
- personality development throughout the human lifespan
- intergenerational/transgenerational trauma
- psychological, psychospiritual, and psychosomatic healing practices (Western, Eastern, indigenous, etc.)
- the use of psychedelics, meditation, and other mind-altering techniques to initiate a change in consciousness
- the future evolution of human consciousness
- spiritual, mystical, and parapsychological experiences

This meta-model influenced a lineage of great thinkers who expanded upon it, including Robert Anton Wilson (*Cosmic Trigger*, *Prometheus Rising*) and Antero Alli (*Angel Tech*, *The Eight-Circuit Brain*), and several other more recent authors, including one of the authors of this book, Dr. Douglas Wingate (2016), James Heffernan (2017), Laurent Huguelit (2013), and Mike Gathers (2020). This model has a subculture following outside of mainstream academia (e.g., self-proclaimed psychonauts, occultists, metaprogrammers, and others who have stumbled upon this gem); however, with so many applications on both professional and personal levels, this model deserves proper recognition and use in the mainstream, which brings us to the story of how this book came to be.

Dr. Rachel Turetzky has been studying and practicing various forms of witchcraft, magick, and other esoterica for over 30 years, and discovered the 8-Circuit Model in her early exploration of occult literature. She had the good fortune to participate in a course on the model, and study it under the guidance of Antero Alli. While pursuing her graduate studies in the field of psychology—during which she was able to get involved in psychedelic research—she observed the lack of an adequate framework that could bridge conventional, contemporary psychology with what, at the time, was considered more fringe and "woo-woo" ideas relating to non-ordinary states of consciousness. As psychedelics became increasingly mainstream (starting around 2017), she recognized the 8-Circuit Model of Consciousness as this bridge, and resolved to write a book on this topic. She shared this vision with friend and author, David Jay Brown (who was a good friend of both Leary and Wilson, and who has shared many inspiring stories and memories about them both) upon their first in-person meeting in March 2020, and he enthusiastically shared this vision. (Although David has been limited in his capacity to co-author this book due to time constraints, he is still very much a part of this vision as a colleague and consultant.) They began brainstorming ideas for this book and thoroughly researched other works already written on the 8-Circuit Model. This led them to the work of Dr. Douglas Wingate, and upon connecting, *8-Circuit Ascension* was formed.

Dr. Wingate has been meditating and studying Eastern philosophy and medicine for many years in addition to Eastern and Western esoteric practices and traditions. He was introduced to the 8-Circuit Model in his teens upon discovering Robert Anton Wilson's book *Prometheus Rising,* and later studied the model directly from him and Antero Alli through Wilson's *Maybe Logic Academy.* In 2016, he published his first book, *Circuits & Shen: Models of the Evolution of Consciousness & Chinese Medicine,* in which he explores how the model has been applied and integrated into his Chinese Medicine practice. Dr. Wingate is also among the first cohort of licensed psilocybin facilitators in the state of Oregon. As Dr. Turetzky is also trained in psychedelic-assisted psychotherapy, together Drs. Wingate and Turetzky have developed a protocol to utilize the 8-Circuit Model of Consciousness in various applications, including: psychotherapy; life-coaching; acupuncture and other somatic body/energy work; and psychonautic/psychospiritual guidance, healing, and development.

With the so-called "psychedelic renaissance" upon us, we feel the time is right for this model to be brought out of the fringes, back into academia, and even into the mainstream where it can be of great benefit to many. In *Book I: Absorb,* we explicate Leary/Wilson's 8-Circuit Model. Further, we

provide evidence for the model as it correlates to neuroanatomy, and we discuss various applications related to psychology (e.g., evolutionary development, lifespan development, transpersonal psychology, and parapsychological phenomena); non-ordinary states of consciousness (e.g., psychedelics,
meditation, lucid dreaming, and psi); psychotherapy (with emphasis on psychedelic-assisted psychotherapy); metaprogramming, and hedonic engineering. (Metaprogramming is the intentional programming or re-programming of beliefs, habits, and thought patterns through the action of
applied metacognition—thinking about or reflecting on how and why one
has certain thought or behavior patterns and the development of the ability
to consciously alter these for one's benefit. Hedonic engineering refers to
methods of using incoming sensory signals and somatic sensations as a
means of experiencing heightened pleasure for pleasure's own sake.) At the
end of each chapter we provide metaprogramming exercises for developing
and balancing each circuit. In *Book II: Integrate,* we offer a guide for practitioners and psychonauts who wish to utilize this model in their psychospiritual healing and development work. In the final section of this book, *Book
III: Transmit,* we share our vision of how the widespread application of this
model can potentially facilitate individual and collective human evolution.
Lastly, as some terms may be unfamiliar or unclear in their specific uses
throughout this text, we provide a Glossary of terms in the back of this
book.

Foreword

A Conversation with David Jay Brown

You knew both Timothy Leary and Robert Anton Wilson (RAW) personally. Could you offer your unique experiences with them, especially as they may relate to the development of, or application of, the 8-Circuit Model?

David: I spent a lot of time hanging out with both Tim and Bob back around the turn of the last century. I went to a lot of parties at Tim's place in Beverly Hills during the 1990s, and gatherings at Bob's places in LA and Capitola. I was especially close with Bob; I saw Bob around once a week for around 17 years. Although I was really influenced by the 8-Circuit Model—

I found it to be a far more inclusive model than anything proposed by the psychological theorists I studied in school—it wasn't something that I discussed with them a lot, or that really came up much in conversation. Nonetheless, it certainly influenced me. I used the 8-Circuit Model as the primary model for understanding all my initial psychedelic experiences, and it seemed to resonate uncannily well.

I was mystified as to why Bob reversed the order of Tim's 6th and 7th circuits in his book *Prometheus Rising,* and asked both Bob and Tim about this. Bob told me that it seemed to him that the metaprogramming circuit incorporated the neuro-genetic circuit, and that it was programmable from a higher circuit within the brain, like the other lower circuits. Tim told me that he thought that with each higher circuit, the processing center was smaller and more central—so that for the 5th circuit it's the body, for the 6th circuit it's the brain, for the 7th circuit it's the DNA code, and for the 8th circuit it's the nucleus of the atom. Tim's sequence always made more sense to me.

In one of my interviews with Tim, the first one in 1989, I asked him to explain the basic intention behind why he created the 8-Circuit Model of Consciousness and what it expresses. He replied:

> *"In the late 1950s and 1960s, a group of a hundred or so select psychologists and philosophers discovered the brain. That is, they discovered how to navigate and explore the brain, just like Magellan and Columbus did for the outer geography of the planet earth. People like Aldous Huxley, Alan Watts, and Albert Hofmann used psychoactive vehicles to move around in the brain. One of the major philosophic tasks of the late twentieth century is mapping the different islands or hemispheres or continents in the universe of the brain. I remember Huxley used the metaphor of the fire antipodes of the brain, or the mind, like Australia being discovered by Captain Cook. This is the first task of the psychedelic philosopher. So, over the years I've produced dozens of sketch maps of the circuits or the levels of consciousness. These were crude words to build up a vocabulary or a cartography of inner space. I don't use the notion of eight circuits now as much as I did, but that's why I did it."*

The use of the term one's "belief system" as one's "BS," which RAW was known to use throughout his works and lectures, has been attributed to you. Could you share how this came about and any personal thoughts about the importance of awareness around one's own BS?

David: I find it really interesting how commonly used the term "belief system" has become. I'm pretty sure it was a term originally coined by John C. Lilly in his book *Programming and Metaprogramming the Human Biocomputer,* and just a few decades ago, pretty much only psychedelic people used it. I think it takes a certain kind of circuit-6-metaprogramming-insight to even understand what a belief system is, as most people simply confuse their BS with reality.

I first used the abbreviation BS for belief system in the Introduction for my book *Mavericks of the Mind,* and it was truly heartwarming that Bob credited me almost every time he used the abbreviation in his own books and lectures. However, this abbreviation was initially the idea of a Marvel comic book writer that I used to hang out with in LA years ago—Allyn Brodsky said it to me on a phone call once.

When I was in college studying anthropology, the term "cultural relativism" was used similarly to how people use the term "belief system" these days—to imply an understanding that what we are all taught to believe as children—through our parents and our culture—is just one perspective or configuration out of an infinite array of possibilities. Taking conscious control over this normally unconscious process, and being able to "try on" different belief systems, so to speak, can do wonders to promote empathy and a better understanding of the world.

Do you feel there has been much change to, or needed updates to, the model since Leary and Wilson's works? Do you feel the model holds up since its introduction?

David: I don't think that the 8-Circuit Model requires any major revisions or updates, and that new discoveries in neuroscience, evolutionary psychology, genetics, and quantum physics only add details and insight to the model. I think it's remarkable, not only how well it holds up to new discoveries in psychology and neuroscience, but also how well it's predicted the trajectory of cultural evolution since its inception.

When the 8-Circuit Model was first developed in the 1970s, it seemed that the leading-edge cultural movement in California was immersed in a hedonistic 5th circuit consciousness, with hot tub parties, massage therapy, Yoga, etc. During the 1990s and the early part of the 2000s it seemed to be moving into the 6th circuit, as computers, virtual reality, artificial intelligence, and the Internet took off. These days, with popular interest in lucid dreaming, the scientific study of the death process, and research at Imperial College, London into extended-state DMT (where intravenous DMT is administered over time to keep people in the DMT space/state for hours rather than minutes), we're beginning to see Circuit 8 consciousness entering our culture.

In this book, we discuss Dr. Stanislav Grof's perinatal matrices and propose "Circuit Zero" to address this stage of prenatal and perinatal consciousness development and experience. This may open up even broader questions and concepts such as reincarnation, cycles of birth and death, valence shells in chemistry, etc. What are your thoughts on this and whether it's a factor worth bringing attention to?

David: I think this is a really valuable idea worth pursuing further. Bob tried to bring together some of Grof and Leary's ideas in his books, like the similarities between Leary's Circuit 7 and Grof's "phylogenetic consciousness." I personally found it rather perplexing trying to find a good correspondence between Grof's Basic Perinatal Matrix stages and the 8-Circuit Model, as they both seem to model the psychedelic experience well, but in different ways.

The idea of a circuit zero seems important to me. While the 8-Circuit Model explains much of the psychedelic experience as activations of the "higher"—5th, 6th, 7th, and 8th—circuits, it doesn't seem to incorporate the central insight of the mystical experience—the revelation that we're all one consciousness; that prior to having an 8-circuit mind, you were a bubble of pure awareness—what some people call a "soul"—and which may incarnate through an evolutionary or developmental sequence.

I'd love to hear your perspective on the significance of the number of circuits (8), and their relation to cycles and patterns in nature and other realms outside of this particular model.

David: It seems to me that great power of the 8-Circuit Model comes from its expression of the Law of Octaves. In chemistry, the Law of Octaves states that every eighth element has similar properties when the elements are arranged in the increasing order of their atomic masses. You can see this as the pattern of the rainbow in the visible light spectrum projected through a prism—red, orange, yellow, green, blue, indigo, violet, white—and is observable throughout nature. It's evident in the musical scale—Do, Re, Mi, Fa, Sol, La, Ti, (higher) Do. It's the developmental sequence that every living and cosmic thing goes through throughout its existence. F. Lanier Graham explores this phenomenon in *The Rainbow Book*. Once you understand that this basic pattern is everywhere in nature, it becomes obvious that it applies to the evolution of consciousness itself. Many mystical and divination systems intuitively incorporate this understanding, and both Bob and Tim tried to outline many of the parallels between the 8-Circuit Model with the Periodic Table of Elements, Astrology, the Tarot, the Kabbalah, etc.

Chapel Perilous: any comments on your own experiences navigating it, or possible words of wisdom you'd like to share?

David: Well, I've certainly spent my share of time there, and I've been there more than once. I agree with Bob and Antero's perspective that it's a rite of passage of sorts, and it can mark important transitions and growth in one's life. I like adding the mythic dimension to these experiences—in the Holy Grail mythology, with the Knights of the Round Table, every seeker of the Grail has to enter Chapel Perilous, where their virtue and sanity is tested. That's the original use of the term, before Bob used it in *Cosmic Trigger*. This makes it sound so much more noble, so much more respectable, romantic, and fun than just saying I went fucking crazy and didn't know what the hell was real anymore. But feeling the full weight and confusion from having one's reality shattered seems to be a necessary transitional stage for many people to bridge the higher and lower circuits. As for navigating it, I don't think much helps more than love, so you don't emerge paranoid from the experience.

In some of our previous conversations, you had mentioned having an interest in writing a book on the 8-Circuit Model material. Why did you want to write a book on the material, and what do you feel makes it worthy of doing so?

David: Timothy Leary's books *Exo-Psychology, The Game of Life,* and the *Intelligence Agents* were three of the most influential books I've read, along with Bob's *Prometheus Rising* and Antero's *Angel Tech.* I read these books while I was studying psychology and neuroscience in college and graduate school, and from them I learned more that helped explain my own experiences than any of my psychology classes.

I've long wanted to do a book that carried these ideas forward, and more efficiently mapped out the brain anatomy and neurological processes that correspond to each of the eight circuits, as well as their imprinting and re-imprinting. It seems that our understanding of neuroscience allows for a sophisticated mapping of where and how the circuits operate in the brain. I think that the practical applications in psychotherapy are extremely valuable, and that this model holds the potential to open up new forms of treatment and guide future research.

You've written extensively on lucid dreaming. How does this fit into the context of the 8-Circuit Model? Another topic you've written extensively on is psychedelics. What is your perspective in terms of psychedelics as they relate to the 8-Circuit Model? With the recent resurgence and growing cultural interest, research, decriminalization, and pending legalization or rescheduling of psychedelics in select places, do you feel the 8-Circuit Model might have something to offer this paradigm shift?

David: I think that the 8-Circuit Model is one of the most valuable tools for helping us to work with the great potential of psychedelics, and for understanding altered states of consciousness—like lucid dreaming or awareness beyond one's body. In my book *Dreaming Wide Awake* I discuss the many similarities among lucid dreaming, psychedelic adventures, and out of body experiences—which all correspond to aspects of the meta-physiological or 8th circuit of consciousness. The 5th, 6th, 7th, and 8th circuits seem to model the spectrum of psychedelic consciousness observable from light cannabis experiences to heavy DMT journeys quite well.

I think that understanding psychedelic mind states, and the exploration of other worlds or realities through lucid dreaming or extended state DMT studies, within the context of the 8-Circuit Model, adds philosophical insight into where we're going as a species, as well as practical considerations for our future scientific research. For example, the 8-Circuit Model suggests that the beings that we encounter in DMT hyperspace are genuine independent entities and not the imaginary products of a hallucinating mind. Also, understanding which of the three stages of a particular circuit that one is in—reception, integration, or transmission—is also an important aspect of the model, with regard to its relationship to understanding psychedelic mind states.

Do you have any other thoughts on the future direction and applications of this model?

David: I worked with MAPS for five years. I'm beyond delighted to finally see these valuable psychedelic medicines being made available to more people, to help heal the psychopathologies and psychological ills of the modern world. It's a godsend that these sacred substances are no longer being demonized, criminalized, ridiculed, or ignored, and are finally being made available to people with depression, PTSD, obsessive compulsive disorder, drug addiction problems, terminal illness, etc. However, I'm really looking forward to the psychedelic research that seeks to improve human performance, and push beyond the boundaries of what seems possible.

I suspect that the 8-Circuit Model will be adopted by more and more psychotherapists, psychologists, and others in the mental health field simply for its practical value, and I suspect that our growing understanding of neuroscience will help us to map out the circuits and processes in the brain better. I see the future, post-pathology, psychedelic research heading into five important directions: developing a science of increasing pleasure, enhancing creativity, improving telepathy and psychic phenomena, developing an experimental theology, and exploring contact with other intelligent entities through DMT. These areas of research seem to roughly correspond to the four higher circuits of the mind. I also think that the relationships among psychedelic mind states, ecological awareness, and Circuit 7, neuro-genetic consciousness, needs to be explored more.

Do you have any suggestions for those who are new to utilizing this model (both professionally and personally)?

David: In Bob's book *Prometheus Rising* and Tim's book *The Game of Life*, they both offer dozens of exercises for activating each of the circuits, so that you can experientially understand them. Tim's classic books on the subject make learning about it really entertaining, with fun visual images and humor. Part of what I enjoyed so much about Tim's, Bob's, and Antero's book about the 8-Circuit Model was the style of the books that incorporated both images and text in a way that simultaneously activated the left and right hemispheres of the brain. The books were especially fun and insightful when I read them high or tripping.

Is there anything else you feel is important or of interest to discuss that we haven't touched upon yet?

David: I think that the traditional psychological theories, from Freud, Adler, Erikson, Jung, etc., all work pretty well when people are just activating their lower circuits. It's when people start activating their higher circuits through Yoga, psychedelics, or other transformative experiences, that the conventional academic models fail to explain much of the phenomena. It's like how Newtonian physics works well for certain phenomena, but then fails at subatomic levels, and requires Einsteinian or quantum physics to explain what's happening. Contemporary academic models of the mind basically address the lower circuits. The huge wave of interest in psychedelic mind states, and research in their potential, is causing many people to see the inadequacy of the current models and the need to adopt a more visionary and inclusive one.

§ § §

David Jay Brown is the author of 19 books, including *Dreaming Wide Awake; The New Science of Psychedelics;* and *The Illustrated Field Guide to the DMT Entities.* For more about his work see:

davidjaybrown.com

BOOK I: ABSORB

Chapter 1

History of the 8-Circuit Model

"The brain is not a blind, reactive machine, but a complex, sensitive biocomputer that we can program. And if we don't take the responsibility for programming it, then it will be programmed unwittingly by accident or by the social environment."
— Dr. Timothy Leary

The 8-Circuit Model of Consciousness (8-CM) was first described by Timothy Leary, Ph.D. in *Exo-Psychology* (1977, which was later revised and published as *Info-Psychology*, 1987), and further described in *Game of Life* (1978). Leary initially approached the 8-Circuit Model from the perspective of the current and projected biological evolution of species on our planet. Within each of the eight circuits, he described three stages that encompassed a full development. First is the reception stage, where you are able to take in new forms of information. You then need to develop the ability to integrate this information into your nervous system for it to be useful—the second stage. In the third stage, after the information has been fully assimilated (updated and modified to adapt to new information that does not fit into the pre-existing paradigm; Siegler, 2005), you are then able to transmit this information into the external environment. These are essential components of any intelligent learning process.

The following chapters in *Book I: Absorb* discuss each circuit in great depth, but here is a brief overview of the circuits to provide a basic foundational understanding of the model:

THE LOWER CIRCUITS:
PERSONAL EGOIC HUMAN DEVELOPMENT

Circuit 0: Prenatal and perinatal experiences and influences (Grof's "Basic Perinatal Matrices"); this circuit is a new addition identified by the authors, and not included in the original 8-Circuit Model of Consciousness

Circuit 1: Basic needs, survival, physical security/safety, attachment style (Freud's "oral stage"; Bowlby's "attachment theory"; Dr. Jean Piaget's "sensorimotor stage")

Circuit 2: Emotional needs, role in social hierarchy/territorial politics, power dynamics in relationships (docile/submissive versus assertive/dominant); autonomy versus. dependence (Freud's "anal stage"; Piaget's "pre-operational stage")

Circuit 3: Logic, symbolic thought, language/semantics, writing, dexterity, mathematics, development of representational mental maps, cognitive processes, executive functions (Piaget's "concrete operational stage")

Circuit 4: Social groups, cultural norms, tribal behaviors, religious/other rites of passage into adulthood, sexuality, morality/superego development, social proscriptions/prescriptions (puberty/adolescence; Piaget's "formal operational stage")

THE UPPER CIRCUITS:
NON-ORDINARY STATES OF CONSCIOUSNESS (NOSC)/
TRANSPERSONAL EXPERIENCES

Circuit 5: Pleasure for the sake of itself, ecstatic states (e.g., as attained through yoga, cannabis, ecstatic dance, tantric sex)

Circuit 6: Questioning of your identity and the influences of conditioning on personality and sense of self, metaprogramming (the conscious and intentional deprogramming and reprogramming of the self in accordance with more internally/transpersonally-defined constructs of personality/psychospiritual identity and individual will (e.g., Crowley's concept of the Holy Guardian Angel [HGA]), conscious and intentional self-transformation and self-actualization

Circuit 7: Archetypes, epigenetics, synchronicity, inter-generational hereditary/genetic memory encoded in DNA, astral plane/astral projection, experiences with non-physical/discarnate entities, paranormal/psi experiences, telepathy, accessing past lives, Akashic records, and what depth psychology refers to as "psychoid space" (i.e., unconscious processes that are a synthesis of instinct and spirit)

Circuit 8: Non-dual states, ego dissolution, dream states, near-death experiences (NDE), oneness with the universe or "God"

We contend that the 8-Circuit Model of Consciousness remains a scientifically-supported, psychological model that is widely applicable to human development and regulation as its genesis lies in the foundations of neuroscience and biochemistry. In chemistry, the generalization made by the British chemist J.A.R. Newlands in 1865 was that, if the chemical elements are arranged according to increasing atomic weight, those with similar physical and chemical properties occur after each interval of seven elements. This became known as the Law of Octaves, and is the basis for the Periodic Table of Elements. The law also applies to the color spectrum of the rainbow and the musical scale. Many processes in the universe follow this distinctive pattern—from the life cycles of stars to the healing of wounds in the body—and we propose it may apply to psychospiritual development as well.

It was Leary's stroke of brilliance to apply this law to ancient mystical systems, evolutionary theory, and the development of the brain and consciousness—including non-ordinary states—in an attempt to unify science and spirituality. Robert Anton Wilson further developed this theory, initially referencing it in his work *Cosmic Trigger* (Wilson, 1977), and making it the key focus of his later text *Prometheus Rising* (Wilson, 1983), in which he fleshed out details and brought more attention to it through his own counterculture audience. Antero Alli (1987) has subsequently helped to transform the theory into a practical tool for understanding, managing, and reorganizing the different parts of oneself. Later, Alli (2009) furthered this theory in his *verticality* approach that divides and correlates the lower (personal) and upper (transpersonal) circuits, as well as further developing praxis for the application of the model.

Now, with renewed cultural interest and acceptance of psychedelic medicines and their potent therapeutic potential, it seems necessary to shine new light on Leary's 8-Circuit Model to encompass contemporary approaches to psychedelic practices, be they clinical, personal, relational, transpersonal, or whatever the intention. The updated version of the model as presented in this book is influenced by the model used by the Multidisciplinary Association for Psychedelic Studies (MAPS) and Sage Institute in their psychedelic-assisted psychotherapy protocols (MDMA and ketamine, respectively); holistic, integrative, wellness life-coaching; psilocybin facilitator training offered in Oregon; the Yale Manual for Psilocybin-Assisted Therapy of Depression (Guss et al., 2020); and various other approaches to working with psychedelics and psychospirituality that the authors have studied and worked with.

We assert that the 8-Circuit Model has stood the test of time, and that it becomes increasingly more relevant as knowledge and research advances in neurochemistry, neuroanatomy, and the function of neural circuits/networks. We also suspect that much of the reason for the power of the 8-Circuit Model stems from its being based on the law of octaves, which describes how all energetic systems evolve in the universe. Leary's application of this idea to the evolution of consciousness and the development of the individual has provided a rubric, a meta-model, through which we are able to map a wider range of the human experience and its potential. In this book we explore how neuroanatomical, molecular, atomic, and quantum structures fall within the eight circuits. We suspect (and hope) that this will continue to be evolved by others as clinical use, research, and the general accessibility of psychedelic medicine also evolve.

We provide instructions on how to induce imprint vulnerability and metaprogramming exercises for activating and balancing each circuit throughout this text. We describe how various psychotropic plants, fungi, amino acids, and nootropics fit in this context within their correspondences with the circuits.

Finally, we explore the utility of this model for various fields of study. Most importantly, perhaps, we propose that this model can be of value in engineering—or accelerating—cross-cultural and transgenerational heal-ing, and potentially further the forward momentum of humanity and our individual and collective consciousness.

If by the end of this book you find our approach of value, and would like to learn more, we offer workshops and a certification course. You can find more information on these resources at the end of the book.

Before diving into the model and the individual circuits, it is helpful to become familiar with some related terms and concepts found throughout this text.

COMPLEXITY VERSUS HIERARCHY

While we use terms such as "lower" or "higher" circuits throughout this text, this does not imply any form of hierarchy among them. While the per-sonal egoic stages in circuits 1–4 tend to develop linearly, once established they become important facets of Self that remain in play and are accessible to those aware of how to do so. While the upper circuits that encompass non-ordinary and transpersonal states may become activated without the same linearity—depending on your experiences—they, along with the first four circuits are placed in order of increasing complexity and broadness in scope. With the first four circuits, your sense of self, reality, and the world expand into larger, more complex arenas of navigation. Circuits 5–8 further expand your worldview to include species, ecological, transcendent, and unitive consciousness—each encompassing a wider facet of awareness.

"Psychological evolution is best explained as an expansion of identity, as one moves from egocentric to ethnocentric to worldcentric to kosmocentric." (Khamsehzadeh, 2022:292)

"The way one can track evolution is by seeing the increase of complexity— of interconnection and organization taking place—within the cosmos." (Khamsehzadeh, 2022:268)

According to Dr. Peter Russell (1995:90), complexity seems to have three characteristics:

- Quantity/diversity: "The system contains a large number of different elements"
- Organization: "The many components are organized into various interrelated structures"
- Connectivity: "The components are connected through physical links, energy interchanges, or some form of communication. Such connectivity maintains and creates relationships and organizes activity within the system."

Dr. Terence McKenna (1975) believed that the two fundamental forces in the cosmos were habit and novelty. This bears similarity to the morphic fields of Dr. Rupert Sheldrake (1981) which hold the memory of a species, wherein habit always strives to maintain patterns. Novelty breaks patterns, brings in complexity, and moves evolution forward. Dr. Jahan Khamsehzadeh (2022:274) contends that psychedelics may act as "novelty generators."

Neuron Model of Intelligence

This book is laid out in the form of the neuron model of intelligence. Transmission of signals and communication within the human nervous system occur in three primary stages:

1) **Reception of signal**—this occurs at the dendrites of neurons where information is received from another neuron
2) **Integration/consolidation/interpretation of signal**—this occurs along the axon of the neuron where it becomes coherent and travels throughout the nerve cell
3) **Transmission of signal**—this occurs at the synapse of the neuron where the signal is passed onto the next neuron

Leary (1994) laid out three sub-phases within each circuit of consciousness that coincide with absorption, integration, and transmission phases—the circuits that were essential for effective functioning and increasing intelligence. In accordance with this neuron model, this book is laid out in three sections:

1) **Absorption:** foundational explorations of the individual circuits
2) **Integration:** potential methods of approaching and working with the individual circuits and interrelations among them
3) **Transmission:** how can this information and the approaches within be used beyond just the individual to (perhaps) allow for collective healing and engineering a better future

Reality Tunnels

This is a term initially used by Leary to describe the breadth, or lack thereof, of a model of reality relative to those available.

"The gene-pool politics which monitor power struggles among terrestrial humanity are transcended in this info-world, i.e., seen as static, artificial charades. One is neither coercively manipulated into another's territorial reality nor forced to struggle against it with reciprocal game-playing (the usual soap opera dramatics). One simply elects, consciously, whether or not to share the other's reality tunnel." (Leary et al., 2006:93)

Mental constructs of reality may be self-limiting in which a type of "tunnel vision" develops either consciously or unconsciously, filtering out aspects of reality that may not neatly fit within this "tunnel." Wilson (1986) relates this to discrepancies between the concepts of Dr. Harold Garfinkle (1967) who used the term "emic reality" to describe internal perception, while using "etic reality" to describe the external event "out there."

"Idolatry is my label for that stage of semantic innocence in which the inferential and metaphoric nature of models and reality-tunnels is forgotten or repressed or has not yet been learned; the stage of innocence or arrogance in which...'emic reality' is confused with...etic reality." (Wilson, 1986:16)

This concept is explored further in the discussion of neuro-relativity in Chapter X. As a reality tunnel becomes established, it may calcify over time, and become more rigid and resistant toward conflicting information. This includes what is known as "confirmation bias" (Peters, 2022), or "reality bias," in which you actively seek or hold onto information that reinforces a particular reality tunnel or belief. Wilson (1983) refers to a phase attributed to Dr. Leonard Orr as "Orr's Law" which states *What the 'thinker' thinks, the 'prover' proves"*—that is, the mind seems capable of processing limitless thoughts, concepts, and ideas; however the individual tends to form *reality tunnels*, and the thoughts within this tunnel are those of the "thinker"; and once established, another facet of the mind continually expends energy "proving" this model of reality to be true.

This phenomenon does not stay contained within the individual. Cases of "mutual contagion" or "peer contagion" are well documented (especially among adolescent populations; Dishion & Tipsord, 2011). Cases of mass hysteria have been documented throughout history (Bartholomew, 2011). Societal factors may work to further reinforce reality tunnels, ranging from familial transmission, direct peer reinforcement, and online algorithms that filter out or present certain sets of reaffirming information in accordance with personal biases.

Dr. Marten Scheffer and colleagues explore the notion of "belief traps," describing "neuronal attractors" that may play into this tendency toward belief system reinforcement:

> *"Neurobiological measurements have revealed abrupt and widespread shifts in neural activity in the prefrontal cortex as animals adjust their 'world view' in response to changes in their experimentally controlled environment, such as altered task-reward rules.... As brain activity converges toward one of the attractor states representing the alternative beliefs, neural activity shows a rapid decrease in variability and a quickly diminishing influence of newly arriving information...in this case, corresponding to strong commitment to a decision, belief, or action. The presence of such resilient states is important, as it allows the brain to maintain short-term memories that are resistant to distraction.... Upon a stimulus, the firing rates of competing pools of neurons initially increase together (because of stimulus ambiguity or noise), but at some point, the activity of one of the pools suddenly rises (due to accumulating evidence in favor of one choice) while the others are rapidly suppressed (due to*

winner-take-all competition caused by the feedback inhibition). The choice is thus determined by which of the alternative attractors wins the competition and reaches a stable attractor state." (2022:5)

The term "semantic memory" is used to describe the web of concepts and their properties. When beliefs become activated—or "primed"—this activation spreads to neighboring concepts, increasing the chance that associated concepts will be retrieved and can be modeled as *"a contagious spread of activation in a network of correlated attractors"*(Lerner et al., 2012). Thus, semantic priming acts to make certain sets of information easier to process, while making them more easily believed than other incoming information—sustaining and self-reinforcing existing beliefs.

"The human understanding when it has once adopted an opinion...draws all things else to support and agree with it."
— Francis Bacon, 1620

IMPRINTING

The concept that life-events at particular stages of development set patterns that tend to resonate throughout your lifetime, is called "neurological imprinting." This seems to happen within very narrow windows in a person's development, with what occurs within this window "hard-wiring" itself into the person's nervous system and psyche. This establishes a "belief" about a particular aspect of the world which, without significant self-work, remains unlikely to readily change.

"Critical periods" of development refers to a specific timeframe within which a child "must" acquire certain skills, because if this does not happen, the child cannot easily attain these skills outside this time frame (Bruer & McDonnell, 2011). Critical periods are narrow periods during which particular input to the individual is expected (imprint vulnerability). On the other hand, "sensitive periods" are an

"opportunity for certain types of learning, but they are not so rigidly tied to specific ages or passage of time... During a sensitive period, if there is a

lack of opportunity for a certain type of learning, it is not gone forever (as it is for critical periods)." (Galván, 2017:93)

Dr. Bruce Perry uses the phrase "neuroarcheology" to describe the impact that events and experiences can have on the developing brain. According to Perry,

"The neuroarcheological perspective…simply posits that the impact of a childhood event (adverse or positive) will be a reflection of (1) the nature, intensity, pattern and duration of the event, and (2) that the resulting strengths (e.g., language) or deficits (e.g., neuropsychiatric symptoms) will be in those functions mediated by the neural systems that are most rapidly organizing (i.e., in the developmental 'hot zone') at the time of the experience." (2001:2)

TREADMILLING

Alli introduced the concept of "treadmilling" into the 8-Circuit Model. This is an instance in which a person becomes stuck within the narrow confines of operating from one particular circuit.

"Treadmilling can occur by: 1) any failure to sufficiently integrate your experience, 2) any lack of communication from not linking experiences with others, 3) any excessive inertia from absorbing more data than there is time or energy to assimilate and communicate." (Alli, 2008:42)

Alli emphasizes the importance of effective integration of circuit material, and says that material which cannot be properly integrated or "digested" becomes stuck or "constipated."

SHOCKS & ANCHORS

Another significant contribution by Alli is that of building descriptions of the vertical relationships between the lower and upper circuits. Circuits 1–4 provide stabilizing "anchors" for upper circuit dynamics that may become too chaotic or disorienting, while circuits 5–8 may act as stimulating "shocks" toward development, evolution, or reprogramming within the egoic circuits. These relationships are:

Circuits 1 & 5: relationship of safety and security anchors; ecstasy and bliss shocks

Circuits 2 & 6: relationship of power and control anchors; uncertainty and freedom shocks

Circuits 3 & 7: relationship of sanity and communication anchors; unity and synchronicity shocks

Circuits 4 & 8: relationship of community and belonging anchors; impermanence and death shocks

— Antero Alli, 2008:44

Shocks risk excessively shaking the foundation of or destabilizing the anchors of circuits 1–4, which may result in a loss of your sense of purpose or context. For instance, a sudden Circuit 7 experience may "shock" the nervous system into a vastly more complex state than it was in before, and may cause a perceived destabilization in your Circuit 3 models of compartmentalization and rationalized, logic-based models of reality. This may result in feeling like you are losing your grip on the Circuit 3 anchor of sanity; you may feel like you are losing your mind. In a sense, you very well may be, at least the mind as you had previously experienced it within the limitations of pre-transcendent consciousness.

METAPROGRAMMING

One purpose of this text is to explore approaches that have the potential to alter detrimental or rigid imprints, belief systems, or the effects of their impact. Exploring these negative imprints, and working to alter them—a process called "re-imprinting" or "metaprogramming"—may not prove straightforward or linear. As neural myelination and pruning in the brain strengthen certain neural patterns and beliefs, states of disequilibrium that drive learning (Piaget, 1964) may be required for the re-patterning of that which may no longer serve you. You must be at a place psychologically that allows you to become both vulnerable and flexible, and allows you to process and assimilate the information. Metaprogramming is explored in greater detail in Chapter IX.

Psychedelic Science & Use

The word "psychedelic" is derived from Greek terms meaning "psyche/soul/mind" and "to manifest"; or together, to mean "mind-manifesting." Wilson argues that any chemical that gets into the brain changes consciousness to some degree, that *"all of our ideas are psychedelic"* (Wilson, 1983:36), and any significant changes in routine act in a psychedelic manner. An example he uses is the consciousness-altering experience you may experience by changing from a vegetarian diet to an omnivorous diet or vice versa. *"Thus, potatoes, like LSD, are 'psychedelic'—in a milder way"* (Wilson, 1983:35).

"Psychedelics can give a lived experience of complexity." (Beiner, 2023:55)

That considered, many of the not-so-mild psychedelic substances and their effects on the human nervous system are explored throughout this book. Both authors have received formal training and have worked with psychedelic substances in clinical settings. It warrants emphasizing that we are not advocating for indiscriminate psychedelic use. Psychedelics do not seem appropriate for everybody, even in legally sanctioned scenarios, and information in this text is not meant as, or to be taken as, any kind of medical advice or open advocacy for such substances.

"Psychedelics open the doors of perception, but it is up to us to step through."
Beiner (2023:233)

Exploring what happens under these substances and related non-ordinary states of consciousness may lend insight into the vast spectrum and potential of the human experience. Although modern neuroscience helps to reliably demonstrate various phenomena, we anticipate that there may be those who claim this to be reductionistic—that spirituality cannot be reduced to biochemistry and neural activity. We also suspect there may be some who relegate the implications of this material and their broader interpretation to the realm of unsubstantiated metaphysics. Our goal is to present existing research and a broad set of reports of human experience, and to discuss how to use that information to initiate change or healing—not that what is presented is all there is to say or experience or understand. The 8-Circuit Model of Consciousness acts as a *map*—a model we have found particularly useful in navigating and working with this spectrum of experiences—but we make no claims that it is the only useful model. We invite you to proceed with what Wilson called "catmas"—a counterpart to *dogmas* (rigid absolute beliefs); catmas, rather, are relative meta-beliefs that remain flexible and open to revision in the face of more information, and can be applied so long as they remain applicable.

> *"The map is not the territory"*
> — Alfred Korzybski

CHAPTER II

CIRCUIT O (C-O): VALENCE JUMPING: THE PRENATAL & PERINATAL MATRICES

"I carry from my mother's womb a fanatic heart."
— William Butler Yeats

Prenatal and perinatal development, as well as consciousness, are not well-addressed in previous material on the 8-Circuit Model of Consciousness. We are not sure why this is so. We speculate that despite Dr. Stanislav Grof's material on the perinatal matrices (1975, 1985), existing neurobiology had little information to offer at that time. In Leary's bio-evolutionary perspective (1994), this pre/perinatal state would fall into the biosurvival receptivity of Circuit 1. We are going to look at this separately from the Circuit 1 material as an opportunity to explore it in more depth. There has been an increased understanding of neural development, and the broad influence this phase has on subsequent development. It also brings up some interesting philosophical implications around topics such as reincarnation, past lives, etc.

The greater part of neural development actually occurs during the prenatal period at an average rate of about 250,000 nerve cells per minute throughout pregnancy (Ackerman, 1992). Many die off soon after birth, which makes prenatal brain development a critical period. Therefore, we would be remiss to underestimate the importance of the prenatal period in terms of its influence on brain development (Fox & Schonkoff, 2011:8–14).

As the fetus remains in a passive state of receptivity, interacting only within the confines of the womb, each experience is to some degree filtered through the direct environment; i.e., the mother's nervous system. Thus, this developmental environment seems highly influenced by the mother's experiences during this time. Maternal health and lifestyle are cited as two critical factors. Factors such as diet, exposure to stress, drug and alcohol misuse, dependence on prescribed drugs, and pollution all shape fetal development, with likely effects into adulthood (Fitzgerald et al., 2020; Gerhardt, 2015).

Research by Dr. Michael Meaney (2001) on the influences of maternal behavior on neural growth, has shown an influence on gene expression. For instance, a poor maternal die—high in processed foods and lacking in protein and essential fatty acids (EFAs)—may cause direct effects on gene expression (epigenetic changes) in the fetus, resulting in susceptibility to lifelong conditions such as diabetes, obesity, heart disease, and reduced lifespan. The myelination process becomes interrupted due to insufficient nutrients required to form healthy neurons. Where EFAs are lacking in the diet, myelination does not occur effectively; this results in a slower transmission of signals between neurons (Prado & Dewey, 2014:269).

Early life adversity also plays a critical role in neural development by altering DNA methylation patterns. This may be associated with an increased risk for psychopathology (Conkbayir 2021; McGowan & Kato, 2008; McGowan et al., 2009;). Dr. Ian Weaver et al., (2004) showed that early life adversity altered the offspring's DNA methylation patterns in the hippocampus; this affects the development of the hypothalamic-pituitary-adrenal (HPA) axis and related hormonal responses to stress through tissue-specific effects on gene expression.

FIRST TRIMESTER

In the first month, the embryo forms the neural plate. The neural plate will curve into the neural tube, which will close and eventually develop into the nervous system (the brain and the spinal cord). Around week six, the first electrical brain activity begins to occur. Once the neural tube closes, it will curve and bulge into three sections, commonly known as the forebrain, midbrain, and hindbrain (Conkbayir, 2011:51).

Second Trimester

The brain directs the diaphragm and chest muscles to contract, thereby allowing for the first sucking and swallowing reflexes (Conkbayir, 2011:52). By the end of the second trimester, the baby's brainstem is almost entirely developed. The ridges and valleys of the brain's texture (the gyri and sulci, respectively) begin to form, leading to the thickening of the cerebral cortex and myelination. The most significant period of myelination occurs from mid-gestation to age two years (Conkbayir, 2011:269).

Here the fetus demonstrates conscious movement through purposeful actions. As development continues, these actions become more sophisticated. This can include facial expressions (smiling or frowning) in response to soothing or startling noises, or pushing its elbows or legs to change position within the womb. This movement readies the infant to be close to and interact with mother after birth, and is instrumental to an infant's initiating relationships and being an active partner in preverbal conversations with caregivers (Conkbayir, 2011:289).

Third Trimester

At this stage, the brain nearly triples in weight. The previously smooth brain further creates more sulci and becomes "bumpier." During this phase, the cerebellum (at the base of the brain) grows faster than any other region (Conkbayir, 2011:52). Neuronal axons and non-neural brain cells (glia) are produced from glial progenitor cells, and become integrated into neural circuits (Doi et al., 2022).

GROF'S MODEL OF
BASIC PERINATAL MATRICES (BPM)
(GROF, 1975)

Here we explore Grof's work as it relates to reports of individuals re-experiencing prenatal and perinatal experiences while under the influence of psychedelics.

Matrix	Phase	Experience
Matrix I	Gestation prior to labor	Oceanic oneness; heavenly unless there is trauma in which case it can be experienced as "poisonous womb"
Matrix II	Labor prior to cervix opening	One is in hell, frustrated, and in despair
Matrix III	Cervix has opened	Passion and anger, animalistic themes—"Through tooth and claw, one must survive"
Matrix IV	Delivery	Ego-death, conquered tribulations, liberation

Table 1: *Grof's Basic Perinatal Matrices*
(Khamsehzadeh, 2022:207)

PERINATAL MATRIX I (BPM I):
PRIMAL UNION WITH THE MOTHER

Grof relates this matrix to the original condition of intrauterine existence, during which the child and mother form a symbiotic unity. In the absence of noxious stimuli, these are ideal conditions for the child: security, protection, and satisfaction of all needs. These experiences are associated with a blissful, undifferentiated, oceanic state of consciousness.

"Its basic characteristics are transcendence of the subject-object dichotomy, exceptionally strong positive affect (peace, tranquility, joy, serenity, and bliss, a special feeling of sacredness, transcendence of time and space, an experience of pure being, and a richness of insights of cosmic relevance" (Grof, 1975:105).

These descriptions sound a lot like material covered later in this text on Circuit 8: the unitive consciousness of being "in touch with infinity," "ineffable" and paradoxical experiences of being "contentless and yet all-consuming." These descriptors included a great sense of awe, humility, and "oceanic ecstasy" in which everything is as it should be. Grof recognizes the similarities, stating they *"seem to be closely related to, if not identical with, the transcendental experiences characterized by Dr. Walter Pahnke's mystical categories (1963) and those for which Dr. Abraham Maslow coined the term 'peak experiences'"* (Grof, 1975:107).

In Grof's observation of LSD psychotherapy sessions, people have reported re-experiencing their own conception and various stages of fetal development. Experiences from these sessions also suggest that the child may be able to experience and distinguish noxious stimuli on a primitive level, establishing either a "good" or "bad" womb. He states that sometimes the type of interference can be identified, such as physical disease of the mother, or emotional upheaval by the mother (e.g., anxiety, aggression, attempted abortion, etc.) At other times they may be re-experienced as vague visual disturbances such as being blurred by an ugly film. Sometimes they may be re-experienced with physical symptoms akin to the flu, or nausea similar to a hangover.

PERINATAL MATRIX II (BPM II): ANTAGONISM WITH THE MOTHER

The second perinatal matrix relates to the first clinical stage of delivery in which the perfect oceanic state of Matrix I ends abruptly. Chemical changes alter the milieu within which the developing fetus has been held so comfortably. Uterine contractions then begin to physically disrupt the fetus' environment. There is physical discomfort; there is threat and emergency. The cervix has not yet opened, and there is no way for both child-bearer and child to escape this bombardment of pain. Physical symptoms typical of Matrix II involve extreme head and body pressure, ringing in the ears, excruciating pain in various parts of the body, breathing difficulty, significant cardiac distress, and rushes of hot and cold.

In observations of LSD re-experiencing, this matrix is described as characteristic spiritual experiences of "no exit" or "hell"—feeling claustrophobic and torturous. It may feel hopeless and endless. A striking visual darkness coupled with ominous colors is frequently reported. Elements of this matrix may be experienced in several different levels. The deepest levels relate to the concepts of hell with unbearable physical, psychological, and metaphysical suffering as depicted in various religions. More superficially, one may become preoccupied by negative bias toward the world and one's placement within it. The world becomes seen as an apocalyptic place of terror and suffering, of wars and disasters.

It is common for those re-experiencing this dynamic to experience great empathy for and identification with the victimized, downtrodden, and oppressed in the present or the past. Life may feel meaningless, seeming absurd, monstrous, or even futile. A great existential crisis may occur in which the only certainty of life becomes that it seems destined to end.

One may also feel as though they are losing a grip on their sanity or mental control, with similarities to the experience of Chapel Perilous explored in Chapter VII. Despite all of this, there remains a desperate need to find meaning in life. This is likened to the attempts of the fetus to find a way out of the painful womb state.

PERINATAL MATRIX III (BPM III): SYNERGISM WITH THE MOTHER

The third perinatal matrix relates to the second clinical stage of delivery in which uterine contractions continue, but the cervix has opened, and the difficult and complicated process of propulsion through the birth canal occurs.

> *"For the fetus, this involves an enormous struggle for survival, with mechanical crushing pressures and frequently a high degree of suffocation. The system is no longer closed, however, and a perspective of termination of the unbearable situation has appeared. The efforts and interests of the mother and child coincide; their joint intense striving is aimed at ending this often painful condition." (Grof, 1975:125)*

During the conclusion of this stage, the child can come into contact with various kinds of biological material, such as blood, mucus, urine, and feces. A typical cluster of physical manifestations regularly accompanying BPM III seems to confirm the relationship of this matrix to the biological birth trauma. These can include: enormous pressure on the head and body; choking, suffocation, and strangulation; torturous pain in various parts of the body; severe cardiac distress; alternating chills and hot flushes; profuse sweating; nausea and projectile vomiting; increased bowel movements; urge to urinate, accompanied by problems of sphincter control; and generalized muscular tension discharged in various tremors, twitches, shaking, jerks, and complex twisting movements.

In the LSD-induced re-experiencing of this stage, it may be experienced as either a reliving of the elements of the actual biological situation, a symbolic form of the death-rebirth struggle, or both. Grof states that the underlying theme of this phase seems to be the encounter with death, and further delineates four distinct experiential aspects within:

• **Titanic:** A struggle or painful tension appearing beyond what any human can bear; an immense buildup of energy and its subsequent explosive release, which may be felt as streaming currents of energy throughout the body. It may be experienced as *"a wild, ecstatic rapture of cosmic proportions that can be referred to as 'volcanic ecstasy'"* (Grof, 1975:127) with which Grof draws a correspondence to Nietzsche's *"Dionysian element in man"* (Grof, 1975:135). This is in contrast to the "oceanic ecstasy" of Matrix I.

• **Sadomasochistic:** Said to be a prominent and constant feature, *"The sequences of scenes accompanied by enormous discharges of destructive and self-destructive impulses and energies"* (Grof, 1975:129) involving tortures and cruelties of all kinds.

• **Sexual:** Excessive sexual excitement that experiencers describe as resembling the first part of sexual orgasm with a progressive increase in tension throughout the entire organism rather than being localized in the genital area.

• **Scatological:** This seems to belong to the final stage of the death-rebirth struggle, immediately preceding birth or rebirth.

"Its essential characteristic is an intimate encounter with various kinds of biological material, identified as mucus, sweat, products of putrefaction, menstrual blood, urine, and feces.... The deepest motivational force for these deviations appears to be the association between the contact with such biological materials and the termination of the agonizing experience of birth." (Grof, 1975:130)

PERINATAL MATRIX IV (BPM IV):
SEPARATION FROM THE MOTHER

The fourth and final perinatal matrix relates to the third clinical stage of delivery in which the agonizing experiences culminate, the propulsion through the birth canal ends, and the apex of the tension and suffering buildup is followed by sudden relief and relaxation. The infant is no longer being suffocated and deprived of oxygen, but becomes able to take the first breath from the world outside the womb. This completes the physical separation of the child from the mother.

There are now many new factors the child must tend to for themselves that had previously been tended to by the oceanic environment of the womb—there are temperature changes, loud noises, intense lights, and tactile sensations that are not all pleasant. These are nothing compared to the experiences of Matrices II and III, but still demand a great deal of acclimation. Physical manifestations typical of the fourth matrix can include prolonged withholding of breath, suffocation, and increasing muscular tension, followed by sudden inspiration, relief, relaxation, and feelings of perfect physiological well-being.

In Grof's work with LSD, people re-experiencing this matrix may have a concrete, realistic reliving of their biological birth, sometimes involving specific characteristics or details of the birth that were verified by those present at or privy to the circumstances of their birth. This may range from smells, anesthetics used, lighting in the delivery room, to birth position or difficulties.

The manifestation of BPM IV on a symbolic and spiritual level constitutes the death-rebirth experience—it represents the termination and resolution of the death-rebirth struggle. Suffering and agony culminate in an experience of total annihilation on all levels—physical, emotional, intellectual, ethical, and transcendental. The individual experiences final biological destruction, emotional defeat, intellectual debacle, and utmost moral humiliation (Grof, 1975:139).

The perception of the environment has a certain primary quality; every sensory stimulus—be it visual, acoustic, olfactory, gustatory, or tactile—appears to be completely fresh and new, and at the same time, unusually exciting and stimulating (Grof, 1975:140).

This is ego-death. It may be accompanied by feelings of being cleansed or purged with an atmosphere of *"liberation, redemption, salvation, love, and forgiveness"* (Grof, 1975:138). Much like Matrix I (as well as Circuit 8), there may be a sense of cosmic unity with everything.

REACTIVE CONSCIOUSNESS

Dr. Jenny Wade, in her holonomic theory of the evolution of consciousness (1996), describes "reactive consciousness" as a perinatal stage at its most simplistic form. Everything experienced by the baby is an extension of itself, and reactions to the environment are determined by "exocepts". Exocepts are described as a type of genetically programmed, unconscious reaction of the motor system whereby there is no conscious recognition of these movements as they are purely automatic. It is postulated that rather than the experience of pleasure and pain, at this stage things are even more vague and simplistic, registering more as states of equilibrium or disequilibrium.

Reactive Consciousness	
Primary Motivation	Cessation of discomfort
Ultimate Value	Maintaining comfort?
Attitude Toward Life	None—unaware of life
Perception of Death	None—unaware of death
Self-Boundaries	None
Perception of Temporality	Timeless present
Concept of Other	Adult humans or visual patterns suggesting human features responded to differently than other environmental features at a preconceptual level
Locus of Control	Purely reactive to both internal and external states
Level of Abstraction	Abstractions do not exist. Rudimentary or universal template for 3-D spacialization of visual and auditory cues may organize perception. Physical objects may appear to be bounded spatially, and to a very limited extent, temporally
Options for Actions	Reaction only to avoid noxious stimuli
Correct Opinion	None—choice is not possible

Table 2: *Wade's Holonomic Theory: Reactive Consciousness*

Chapter III

Circuit One (C-1):
Survival, Safety & Comfort

Vegetative-Invertebrate Circuit (Leary)
Oral Bio-Survival Circuit (Wilson)

"The single most important issue for traumatized people is to find a sense of safety in their own bodies"
— Bessel van der Kolk

"Safety is not the absence of threat, it is the presence of connection."
— Gabor Maté

Basic means of survival are initially the only drives we have. Beyond anything else, an organism must establish how to regulate itself enough to survive. As the world seems to grow and expand one's perceptions, new needs and drives develop, but the most basic needs never become unnecessary or subsumed. They continue to exist in the background of every moment of our lives—ever-present and ever-influencing the directions we move in. Should these become neglected, they will find a way to scream forth with the force of a wailing infant needing tending.

A wide range of patterns of illness can develop as a reaction to unmet physical and emotional needs. In the case of the first circuit, these pathologies tend to manifest in the more core elements of self. Concerns tend to be more somatic in nature, with the body and sensory/proprioceptive system tending to take the brunt of things. There is a good reason for this; they are the first components of our existence to develop, preceding the development of any awareness of "Self."

The newborn mind does not seem to experience itself as separate from the primary caregiver. To the child, both child and caregiver remain extensions of the same entity and simply happen to inhabit two separate places in space. It is largely for this reason that if a primary caregiver is not present—physically or emotionally—the loss to the child is experienced as total; it is crushing and world-shattering. This results in a loss of self on top of lacking the external experience of love and nurturing. It could be argued that no other trauma exists that creates such a deeply rippling effect through the psyche. These sorts of situations continue to influence and play out throughout the rest of one's life.

When exploring emotional trauma, it is not uncommon to come to an epiphany that below the immediate concern, the root of the problem stems from a lack of relationship, presence, or nurturing from the primary caregiver at a very young age. This can often also apply to a good number of other concerns they have dealt with throughout life.

The first circuit is imprinted within the first six months of life, and may even be impacted prenatally if conditions are influential enough. During this time, the world the child interacts within is very small, and the relationship to the maternal figure is a paramount factor in determining whether the child will take on a "positive" or "negative" imprint. This imprint primarily concerns issues of safety and receptivity to interactions with the immediate environment.

The child imprints a general "forward-back" program of trust versus suspicion—either forward toward things felt as safe, cuddly, nurturing, or sociable; or backward away from experiences felt as dangerous, noxious, cruel, or destructive (Wilson, 2020:127). On Dr. Timothy Leary's Interpersonal Grid (below, 1957), the "forward" imprint coincides with sections D & E (found from the center of the diagram outward), which encompasses qualities found in the "Aggressive-Sadistic" outer portion of the diagram. The backward imprint coincides with positions L & M on the grid that encompasses the "Cooperative-Overconventional" outer portion of the diagram with traits of lack of curiosity and aversion to new experiences (neophobia).

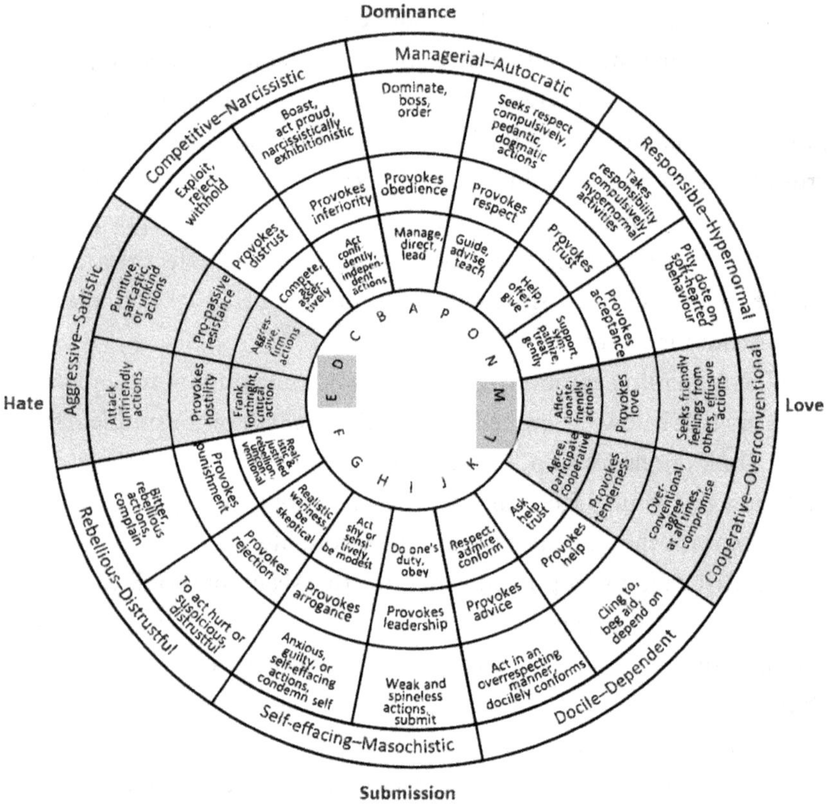

Figure 1: *Dr. Timothy Leary's Interpersonal Grid:*
Forward-Backward Imprint

This period of development coincides with Dr. Lev Vygotsky's (1978) sensorimotor stage (0–2 years), in which infants learn mostly through trial and error, initially relying on reflexes, and eventually changing or controlling actions to adapt to the world (Galvan, 2017:118). It is suspected that mirror neurons in the brain might play an important role in early childhood development (Conkbayir, 2021:15). Mirror neurons fire while observing an action as if the person themself were performing the action. Both the mirror neuron system and non-mirror neuron mechanisms have been shown to achieve understanding of action. Dr. Mine Conkbayir, a specialist in early childhood education, says, *"from birth, an infant is primed for socialization; this might manifest when an infant imitates their caregiver"* via the mirror neuron system (Conkbayir, 2021:15).

When a child feels safe and secure, their social engagement system (face, eyes, mouth, and middle ear) and heart work cohesively, allowing the child to interact with others. Facial expression, eye contact, tone of voice, and hand movements are the means by which interactions, connections, and processing the emotions of others can occur (Conkbayir, 2021:73). Experiments strongly suggest that human infants are naturally empathetic, helpful, generous, and informative (Warneken & Tomasello, 2006). Mike Gathers (2020:16) cites one key point to be taken away from understanding biosurvival consciousness: that we are relational creatures. More sophisticated prosocial behavior—such as reciprocity—seems to emerge later in childhood, however.

CO-REGULATION & DEVELOPMENT OF
SELF-REGULATION

During this developmental period, your entire existence revolves around meeting basic survival needs, as well as the tactile exploration of the world around you. Objects and people are assessed through the sensory system—specifically, the child's ability to touch and taste. The most fulfilling of all of these needs is the mother-child bond during the act of breastfeeding. The infant is not only receiving essential nourishment, but sensory fulfillment via stimulation of bodily warmth. The two are close enough to hear both heartbeat and breath, while experiencing the oral sensation of mouth to breast. Here, two beings are co-regulating one another's nervous systems. The child is dependent on this co-regulation as their ability for self-regulation has yet to fully develop. This form of interaction, of course, was the rationale for Dr. Sigmund Freud's coining this earliest stage of development as the "oral stage." At this stage, the mouth acts as a primary means of assessment as any parent who has yelled, "Don't put *that* in your mouth!" can certainly attest. This is simply how the young child evaluates its surroundings; the mouth is a sensory organ just like hands and feet, able to determine shape, size, etc. Is it safe to touch? Is it safe to taste/eat? Is it something pleasant to be approached and explored further, or is it unpleasant and to be avoided? This last question is imperative to the first circuit. The safer and more nourishing the infant's environment is, the more positive the neurological imprint tends to be, and the more expansive their overall view of the world they tend to develop.

As this imprinting occurs prior to the development of any formal language, these early sensory experiences are processed by the child at a somatic level. As such, these experiences remain unconscious and automatic—they are only felt. As infants are unable to form a linguistic means of processing, experiences deeply impact the entire body and psyche. The psyche remains a direct extension of the body at this point, and as with the relationship to others, the two are not experienced as separate; everything seems to be experienced as one undifferentiated entity. For this reason, we will see that methods of addressing this circuit focus highly on the body and direct tactile experience.

The emotional wellbeing and development of an infant requires consistent regulation, affection, and support from primary caregivers to help them manage and express their feelings (Thompson & Goodvin, 2005). Conkbayir (2021:48) lists a number of factors that allow for healthy brain development at this stage:

- A healthy pregnancy
- Giving unconditional love
- Eating healthily
- Avoiding toxic stress
- Finding healthy ways to cope with stress (this includes parents)
- Comforting the child when they are upset
- Never humiliating the child
- Abundant opportunities for play
- Sharing books and reading together regularly

- Lots of social interactions
- Praising child's efforts
- Being outdoors in nature
- Regular exercise
- A stable and predictable home life

Shanker, Hopkins, and Davidson (2015:9) argue that the most important discovery that scientists have made about the early years of development is that by co-regulating, a child more readily develops their ability to *self-regulate.* Babies are wholly dependent on their caregivers to help regulate their emotions (Conkbayir, 2021:135) until the ability to self-regulate begins in infancy within the mother-infant dyad through relationship, attunement, bonding, and effective communication (Conkbayir, 2021:146).

Whitebread et al. (2016:4) emphasized a central, leading role of child-led play in the development of self-regulation and executive functioning skills. Dr. Peter Gray draws a line between a decline in the ability to play and the development of psychopathology later in life:

"The reduction in play opportunities is associated with increased risk of pathologies in children, adolescents and young adults: anxiety, narcissism, feelings of helplessness, depression, and suicide. This can be correlated with feeling of loss of control that children develop regarding their lives." (Gray, 2011:448)

Dr. Stuart Shanker (2018) has identified five key domains of self-regulation:

- Biological: excessive visual stimulation, noise; insufficient exercise; having to be too still; cluttered classroom; illness
- Emotional: intense emotions (both positive [over-excitement] and negative [fear and anger]); anxiety; change in routines; excitement
- Cognitive: difficulty in processing certain kinds of information (organizing thoughts, time constraints, interruptions)
- Social: Difficulty in understanding the effect of their behavior on others, and in understanding social cues; bullying

- Prosocial: Difficulty in coping with others' stress; feelings of injustice; being late; empathy/sympathy

The state of arousal and the amount of stimulation provided or sought out by the young child also has a direct effect on behavior and the ability to develop self-regulation:

- **Overstimulation** can inhibit executive functions like [self-regulation], inhibitory control, working memory, planning, problem solving, concentration and learning; leaves little space for self-talk; can cause hyperactivity; sensory overload; children with neurodevelopmental differences (like ADHD and autism) are particularly vulnerable. This can lead to a state of hyperarousal which is related to being easily startled, hyper-vigilant, angry, and irritable; shouting or screaming, hitting, suffering from panic attacks, engaging in self-destructive behaviors, or finding it difficult to concentrate and sleep (Conkbayir, 2021:113).
- **Understimulation** can cause passivity in children; can lead to self-limiting behaviors; does not ignite children's innate curiosity; the brain is experience-dependent—a lack of quality experiences can impact cognition; children will not be stretched or challenged (Conkbayir, 2021:171).

Understimulation can lead to a state of hypo-arousal, which is related to disassociation, zoning out; flatness of affect; feeling empty, numb or dead inside; general lethargy; hypervigilance; disconnection between thoughts, feelings, and behaviors; and a separation between the mind and the body. With this, engagement, joint problem-solving, and co-regulation of emotional state are more difficult to achieve (Conkbayir, 2021:112–113).

Due to the importance of this necessary co-regulation mechanism, if the child is met with a response of isolation (being left to "cry it out"), the instinctual psychological need of the child goes unmet. Brain imaging has shown that the experience of relational pain—like that caused by rejection and isolation—looks very similar to the experience of physical pain (Siegel,

2012:32). (The effects of social isolation are explored further in Chapter VI.)

In regards to early life biosurvival consciousness, Conkbayir offers the following advice: *"The key is equipping children to prevent their panic button from being activated in the first instance"* (Conkbayir, 2021:96).

Dr. Shanker (2020) also outlines five steps in promoting self-regulation:

• Read the signs of stress and reframe the behavior
• Recognize the stressors
• Reduce the stress
• Reflect and enhance stress awareness
• Respond

COMPENSATORY IMPRINTING

The biological drives for nourishment, comfort, and security are so strong that in the absence of an effective source, the child will seek out and establish a surrogate source. This surrogate may be another person, or even a member of a different species, or an object. This was observed by Dr. Konrad Lorentz in his studies of imprinting in animals (Hess, 1958; 1973), and explored in relation to the 8-Circuit Model by Wilson (1983). When a young animal is removed from its mother shortly after birth, they will seek out a proxy maternal figure, creating a bond to that replacement that allows for the necessary sense of security. This ranged from adoption by a maternal figure of another species to imprinting and bonding to inanimate objects (such as a gosling imprinting a ping pong ball or a giraffe imprinting a jeep). In the cases of imprinting to inanimate objects, while there is no active reciprocation of affection, the animal received the closest they were able to develop to a relationship, and would thus feel comforted/regulated in its presence.

A human child may form the same compensatory imprint in the form of a favorite toy they want to take everywhere, a blanket that they are never seen without, or some similar "comfort item." The object becomes even more likely to become imprinted if it has, or at one time had, some associative memory or sensory experience—such as a smell—that reminds them of their mother or a historically nurturing figure. The body's primary initiative is to be felt deeply, and it will go to great lengths in an attempt to make sure that it is achieved.

ADVERSE CHILDHOOD EXPERIENCES (ACEs) & EARLY LIFE NEGATIVE IMPRINTS

Wilson cited a 1968 public health study in which 85% of the population had one or more signs that could be related to a negative first circuit imprint. Most symptoms relating to the first circuit are somatic on account of the physical body acting as the primary processor of information. Some of these symptoms included dizzy spells, heart palpitations, wet palms, and frequent nightmares. This is a staggering statistic! Moreover, considering how long ago the study was, there seems a real possibility that that statistic has only grown as socio-economic demands have increased the number of mothers who go to or return to work soon after giving birth. Increased rates of divorce or single-parent households can also interfere with consistent mother-child interaction and other factors related to socio-economic status. This is not to say that a father, grandparent, or other loving figure cannot play the role that meets the child's need for nurturing and unconditional love. If the child has initially imprinted the mother, however, the impact of changes within this stage are significant. In cases of transference, the bond will never be as strong or emotionally fulfilling as it would be if the relationship with the initial mother/imprint were maintained.

Birth trauma, traumatic events during imprint vulnerability, or traumatic child-rearing conditions can also create this type of negative imprint. A 1997 study on adverse child experiences (ACEs) by the Centers of Disease Control and Prevention (CDC), showed more than half of those in a large-scale study of over 13,000 individuals reported some significant adverse and potentially destabilizing effect in young childhood (Felitti et al., 1998). A systematic review published in 2020 found *"almost two thirds of youth experience significant adverse events no matter where they reside across the world"* (Carlson et al., 2020). The World Health Organization estimates that child maltreatment is responsible for almost 25% of mental health syndromes

(Conkbayir, 2021:62). A degree of awareness around this impact has grown, with some attempts to ameliorate it, including around the birthing process (e.g., the rising use of midwives, prolonging the time before the umbilical cord is severed, or water birthing). The vast majority of the birthing practices in the United States, however, remains less than optimal for the newborn's overall development.

Dr. Vincent Felitti identified 10 ACEs, in three categories, that underpin the above-mentioned CDC study:

- **Abuse:** emotional, physical, or sexual
- **Neglect:** emotional, physical
- **Household challenges:** abuse/violence, substance abuse, mental illness, parental separation/divorce, incarcerated parent/relative

This study did not include other adverse experiences such as bullying, community violence, natural disasters, war, displacement, poverty/economic hardship, oppression, and racism, *"each of which is likely to exert pervasive neglect effects on the child and their family"* (Conkbayir, 2021:88).

These life events affect more than just neuropsychological development. Trauma can manifest as psychosomatic symptoms, including tightness in the chest and difficulty breathing; chest pains; migraines and stress headaches; back pain; fatigue; limb pain; ulcers; gastrointestinal disturbances (e.g., IBS); and insomnia. In children ages 0–3, these may look like irritability; difficulty in soothing; separation anxiety (clinginess); constricted play, exploration, and mood; increased startle response; new fears/general fearfulness; eating disturbances; sleep disturbances and/or nightmares; developmental regression; language delay; aggressive behavior; sexualized behavior; talking about the traumatic event; and reacting to memories and trauma triggers.

Cumulative effects of ACEs are considered significant risk factors for several of the leading causes of death in adults. These include COPD, asthma, obesity, kidney disease, stroke, coronary heart disease, cancer, diabetes, and substance abuse (CDC, 2020), as well as poor general health, sleep disturbances, increased absences from school, learning difficulties,

ADHD, autism spectrum disorder, and violent and suicide-related behaviors (Kiota et al., 2018). Individuals who have six or more ACEs have shown risk of early mortality, potentially dying up to twenty years earlier than an individual who has no ACEs (Brown et al., 2009). Since pathologies tend to develop as a response to unmet innate needs, the unavailability for parents to meet a child's emotional needs may be the greatest source of neuroses in our species (Wilber, 1994).

NEOPHILIA

Those whose needs are sufficiently tended to, imprint a positive first circuit perspective, tend to have a greater capacity to explore the world with confidence, bravery, and natural inquisitiveness. Those who imprint negatively tend more toward timidity, fear of new situations, and withdrawal. Thus, they may see the world as a harsh, hostile, and frightening place. Other people may be perceived as dangerous or to be avoided. Later in life, this can manifest as rigid ideologies about particular groups of humans.

Various brain regions and functions become active or more prominent throughout development. Their progression seems to microcosmically mimic the larger scale evolution of life on Earth ("ontogeny recapitulates phylogeny"). At the earliest stage, the most basic instinctual drives for survival are at the forefront, with "guttural" reactionary responses to the environment determining the course of action. This is a pre-linguistic stage, where reactions are *felt,* unlike higher order experiences that are analyzed and filtered prior to initiating a proper response. At the first circuit, everything is a knee-jerk response to the immediate moment. The portion of the brain from which these in-the-moment instincts seem to derive is often referred to as the "reptilian" brain, or "R-complex." This consists mostly of the brainstem, cerebellum, and components of the autonomic nervous system (ANS). These brain structures regulate the body's automatic functions and drives, including the basic functions of eating, excreting, and maintaining sleep/circadian rhythms (which is the reason some say that "all a baby does is eat, sleep and shit"). Each of these, of course, are essentials to life. Six primary patterns of behavior are associated with the R-complex:

- Routinization of motor operations
- Isopraxis: self-imitation or like-manneredness
- Tropism: positive or negative responses to thoughts
- Repetition: reinforcement of somatic experiences
- Reenactment: mimicry of sensory input
- Deception of others to benefit oneself

Other autonomic functions—including hormonal regulation of temperature, growth rate, and metabolism by the neuroendocrine system—also fall within the purview of this circuit. A particularly heavy first circuit imprint can affect glandular function in a way that may remain throughout one's lifetime. Wilson notes that these individuals tend to develop a viscerotonic or endomorphic body structure which, at its extreme, tends to display as a rounder, gentler body structure. They may be on the heavier side, never seeming to lose their "baby fat" or they continue to have a so-called "baby face."

The tendency for the body to retain or convert more of its nutritional intake to be stored as fat is a means of holding onto survival resources within the body. Should you be placed in a situation of scarcity, or where basic food needs may not be met, you have assurance of stored emergency resources, and thus, are more likely to survive. Those with a heavy first circuit imprint may take this storing function into other aspects of their adult life, including a potential to cling to people or material possessions. This is often in the hope that these external means will offer a sense of survival security or the fulfillment of an internal longing, a (sometimes very vague) sense of emptiness, or feeling as though something is missing within. Such a person becomes fixated on food, shelter, and self-preservation, gathering beyond necessity. An extreme example would be the hoarder who seems unable to part with things whether they continue to serve any functional purpose or not.

Over-consumption by any means, whether physical possessions or eating, can be an attempt to fill this felt void or means of dealing with a negative imprint. This also applies to comfort-eating when you experience an emotional state impacting the first circuit. Concerns relating to the body such as body image, situations with a compromised sense of security, situations where you do not feel nurtured or nourished, or where integrity or self-worth may feel compromised all may fall into this compulsion.

Imprints can also impact your sexuality later in life. The tendency for people to satisfy an oral impulse sexually stems from the first circuit. Kissing, gratification from performing oral sex, or bringing the breast to mouth, or even feeling comforted by round objects, all of which the brain subtly associates with the breast and being nurtured by a maternal figure, fall into this impulse. Fetishization of Circuit 1 behavior or components can occur with strong circuit imprinting.

Money is another aspect of modern civilization that intimately ties into our survival mechanism. Money acts as the means of acquiring many of the things needed to ensure survival (food, shelter, adequate clothing, etc.). It is for this reason that there is a direct association between your capacity to have and earn money and the ability to live. Because of this, those with ready access to money may tend to feel more secure—that their survival is ensured and less likely to be compromised; they may not even consider these matters knowing their needs are tended for. Those with no guarantee of enough funds to take care of essential needs are much more likely to be anxious, stressed, worried, or fearful that these needs may no longer be available at some point, and cause a direct threat to survival. This continual lack of security can cause deep fear or existential panic, and require immediate attention. If these basic needs are not met or are perceived to be at risk, the anxiety over these matters does not allow for focus on other circuits. Survival is paramount and takes precedence. A stable and healthy first bio-survival circuit allows for the foundation to develop the "higher" circuits.

As the body acts as the primary mechanism of this circuit, a negative imprint can also result in a negative perception of your own body. "Body trashing," "not feeling comfortable in one's own skin," or perception that the body is "bad" in some sense can all come about. People may also actively ignore the body's needs for nourishment or to be felt deeply. With enough negligence, physical pathology can develop, or one may become accident prone in a type of self-fulfilling prophecy of their body working against them. A healthy first circuit recognizes and listens to the needs of the body and the fundamental role it plays in growth and development.

Body language—the ways we utilize our bodies—is directly interpreted by others, and often communicates more information than verbal exchange. If your body projects an air of safety or confidence, this gets picked up by others, and can make them feel at ease. This is a reason for healthcare practitioners, psychotherapists, or anyone working with people to have a well-grounded biosurvival circuit while interacting with patients/clients.

"All behavior is communication."
— Mine Conkbayir

Alli (2014) describes the body as the physical manifestation of the subconscious. This sentiment is also explored in detail in the book *Jung and Reich: The Body as Shadow* by John P. Conger (1998) in which the ideas of Dr. Carl Jung's collective unconscious are compared with the psychosomatic work of Dr. Wilhelm Reich. Reich wrote of muscular holding patterns within the body, stemming from unconscious emotional blockages or emotions that are not processed, addressed, or expressed properly.

Reich's life work covered a great deal of ground over a wide range of topics. One of his significant contributions was a theory of how we unconsciously displace unpleasurable emotions or suppressed impulses by tensing up or restricting movement and blood flow to muscles. This displacement acts as an avoidance mechanism of instinctual physical responses to stimuli. An example would be the inclination to lash out aggressively with biting in cases of intense anger. Because this is a socially unacceptable response, one may reroute this charged energy into tensing the masseter muscles in the jaw (which are used in this action), along with the muscles in the front of the neck that are used to hold the head back. This attempt to hold back these impulses may develop into jaw disorders.

EXPANSION & CONTRACTION

Reich postulated that life—and the universe—act within a general principle of pulsation in which things continually cycle between states of expansion and contraction. This parallels the imprinting of the first circuit in which the child imprints a tendency toward moving forward out into the world, or a tendency toward withdrawal, with the world generally seen as a threat. Reich emphasized the breath as a key factor in emotional health. It sums up your ability to freely expand and contract toward and away from the external world. He said of pathology, *"If you can't understand someone's irrational behavior, start by observing their breathing."* By changing your breath, you may bring about change, both emotionally and neurologically.

Consciously altering, or rather, bringing your breath to a more natural rhythm is a tool utilized within Reichian therapy, Bioenergetics, Yogic practices, and a host of other schools. It can be used in reimprinting a particular circuit, as well as releasing muscular holding patterns. Wilson notes that fear and first circuit imbalances may be at play in fundamental breathing restrictions—that *"people are strangling their inner organs every day because they are afraid."*

Fear plays a significant role in C-1 processing. If the world is perceived or imprinted as fundamentally bad or threatening, then you may end up living in perpetual fear of the harshness that is the world and others.

The tremendous effect that ongoing fear can have on the physical body directly derives from how perceptions are processed by the senses and the body with no conscious linguistic/rational processing. It is a guttural, whole-body response that permeates throughout your being. As such, the sense of fear can feel like, and very well may be, an all-consuming experience. Any attempt at rationalizing through it can seem useless. As the body does not operate through linguistic means, if you try to communicate with the body with messages that are too logically defined, the body may begin resisting. It is for this reason that the body needs to be felt positively and *deeply*; and it needs to be given the space to integrate the kinesthetic, proprioceptive, and interoceptive sensory information coming from the navigation of the physical environment.

Alli called this the *"art of speaking in blanks,"* in which there is enough pause and incompleteness to evoke and evaluate your bodily reaction. The body speaks in reference to its own experience. The use of broad generalizations or language that refers to groups lends itself to becoming muddled or misinterpreted. For this reason, if an individual is working on or wishes to focus on the biosurvival circuit, the most appropriate language would be personalized, embodied terms such as "I feel…" or "my senses are telling me…" rather than "they all" or even "this feels like." Ownership of your experience is important.

Commitment is also a major influential component of the biosurvival circuit. Your integrity and the ability to keep your word—especially to yourself—can negatively or positively reinforce the state of the first circuit. Saying what you mean and meaning what you say reinforces safety and the ability to trust yourself and the world. To break these self-promises can have a crushing effect on the subconscious, and leads to imbalances and negative feedback that resonate throughout the psyche. When questions of integrity are in play, it impacts the inner child still residing inside yourself, and like the infant, speaks of the world's ability to trust signals of safety and survival.

NAÏVE CONSCIOUSNESS

Wade's holonomic model of the evolution of consciousness (1996) describes "naïve consciousness" in which the most rapid rate of new neural connections occurs between the ages of two months through five years old. This is the time during which Circuits 1 and 2 develop and are imprinted. In naïve consciousness, the child forms what is known as the "body-ego" in which they discover and possess their body with the ability to construct a memory image of it. Life revolves around reacting to reduce tensions and discomfort, and developing second order emotions such as anxiety, desires, security, depression, and rudimentary love.

In naïve consciousness, because cognitive memory is not yet accessible, the child finds a need to recreate past experiences in the present, utilizing the body-ego to create a somatic memory. This is done through ritual and routine to reinforce the experience and neural connections.

Naïve consciousness primacy tends to be more commonly found in adults within socially isolated areas of industrial nations, and is more prevalent in "lower class" or "blue-collar" populations. It is important to note that the individual who operates primarily from naïve consciousness is not unintelligent, but their cognitive patterns tend to be unaware of certain degrees of abstraction, and may tend toward more superstitious or animalistic thinking. There may also be an evinced negativism and general resistance to suggestion unless it is bestowed by a source of authority symbolic of power and security. These traits are due to the emphasized functioning of the R-complex over other brain structures.

Wade notes two psychological disorders associated with strong imprints or heavy utilization of this stage. The first is Borderline Personality Disorder (BPD), which is marked by poorly structured self-representation and blurred boundaries between internal and external landscapes. The second is Dependency Personality (clinically called Dependent Personality Disorder in the current version of the Diagnostic & Statistical Manual of Mental Disorders [DSM-5]), which is defined by a significant other becoming the center of their personal meaning rather than themselves. This individual requires the other to protect them from the dangers of life as they maintain an inadequate self-image, pacific temperament, and inability to initiate action. The dependent personality maintains a submissive position in interpersonal interactions without harboring resentment or repressed aggression.

As concepts of causality have yet to fully form, death does not exist as a construct to this individual. For adults primarily operating in this stage of life, the concept of death tends to be met with ideas of continuation beyond death in an afterlife or underworld. Due to this, the fear of death is markedly absent save for (perhaps) some vague concept of unpleasantness.

NEUROCEPTION & POLYVAGAL THEORY

"Neuroception" is a term coined by Dr. Stephen Porges to describe how neural circuits determine whether situations or people are safe, dangerous, or life threatening (Porges, 2011:11). Conkbayir states that this is *"a bit like having safety antennae"* (Conkbayir, 2021:84).

The detection of safety or threat triggers neurobiologically-determined prosocial or defensive behaviors, thereby facilitating adaptive behaviors.

The polyvagal theory describes three stages in the development of the autonomic nervous system (Porges, 2011:16):

- Immobilization ("freeze")
- Mobilization ("fight or flight")
- Social communication/engagement

Mobilization will be explored more in Chapter IV (Circuit 2) as it relates more to activation of the sympathetic nervous system and the peripheral nerves and muscles. Social engagement will be explored more in Chapter VI (Circuit 4).

The immobilization, or "freeze," response in the face of threat is expressed in some mammals as "death feigning" (fainting goats are a great example of this). In humans, there is a behavioral shutdown, often followed by weak muscle tone. Heart rate and breathing slow as blood pressure drops; the pain threshold becomes elevated. Mammals also immobilize in essential prosocial activities such as conception, childbirth, nursing, and in establishing social bonds. Neural circuits in the brain involved in the freezing response have, over time, evolved to serve intimate social needs by growing receptors for the neuropeptide oxytocin which is released during childbirth and nursing. The social bonding component of oxytocin will be discussed further in Chapter VI (Circuit 4).

> *"The polyvagal theory strongly suggests that we focus more on creating a sense of safety and security, rather than the elimination of threat (or the perception of threat)."*
> — Mike Gathers

ATTACHMENT THEORY

"Attachment Theory," developed by Dr. John Bolby (1953), can provide a useful model of early childhood imprinting of biosurvival consciousness. Attachment theory builds from the foundation that infant behavior associated with attachment is primarily driven by proximity to an attachment figure—generally, the primary caregiver—in stressful situations. Infants become securely attached to adults who are sensitive and responsive in social interactions with them, and who remain consistent during the period from about six months to two years of age. In cases of sensitive caregiving, the patterns of communication between caregiver and the infant lead to an attachment relationship that creates an internal working model of security. When patterns of communication are consistent, predictable, and filled with "repairs" in the event of inevitable "ruptures," this working model of security becomes established (Siegel, 2012:202). Four categories of attachment styles have been proposed:

- Secure: ~60% of infants in the US are thought to have secure attachment style/imprint—the infant's caregiver(s) were sufficiently present, attentive, and responsive to the infant's needs; the relationship and environment nurtured feelings of safety and security
- Anxious-avoidant: ~15–20% of infants in the US are unresponsive/indifferent to the parent following insufficient attunement
- Anxious-ambivalent: ~15–20% of infants in the US—clingy behavior at first, then rejects the caregiver's attempts to engage as care cannot be consistently relied upon
- Disorganized: ~5% of infants in the US—both excessive (anxious) approach and excessive avoidance (withdrawal); the infant's maternal figure is considered to be the "good enough mother"

These attachment styles can become solidified within the infant's psyche, which may play into adult relational dynamics (Fraley & Shaver, 2000; Brennan & Shaver, 1995).

NEUROBIOLOGY OF CIRCUIT 1

There are several short, brain-growth stages within the first year of life (Lampl et al., 1983). The first major postnatal brain-growth spurt covers the ages between three and 10 months, which works mostly to mature the cerebellum to facilitate its role in activating and controlling motor actions. If the child does not already have adequate sensory and support inputs (as discussed above), these new cerebellar connections will build on a somewhat less than optimal set of functioning networks so the new controls and their functioning will not themselves be optimal (Epstein, 2001).

At birth, each neuron in the cerebral cortex has approximately 2,500 synapses. By the time the infant is 3 years old, the number is approximately 15,000 synapses per neuron, roughly twice the amount of the average adult brain (Rogers, 2011). Synaptogenesis is prolific in the first five years of life, with synaptic growth depending highly on environmental input—play, exploration, communicating with others, and enjoying secure and responsive relationships. These activities allow for opportunities to strengthen existing synaptic connections through repetition and subsequent mastery of skills (Churches et al., 2017). *"Synaptic connectivity increases as a result of engagement with the environment and the people and experiences within it...synaptic connectivity, brain growth and consequent behavior develop in line with these negative experiences"* (Siegel, 2012:157).

It has been demonstrated that this synaptic connectivity and plasticity may be able to be "sped up" with increased ability to engage with the environment. In a study, infants sat on a parent's lap at a table; in front of them were objects covered in velcro. The child had mittens with the soft side of velcro covering the palms to allow the objects to be "picked up." To be able to "pick up" and interact with the environment showed advanced reaching behavior toward the new objects, even when not wearing sticky mittens, compared to control infants not provided mittens at all (Galvan, 2017:104). In another study, researchers tied a ribbon to an infant's ankle, and tied the other end to an overhead crib mobile. Over time, infants learned the association between their ankle kicks and the ability to elicit the "reward" of moving the mobile (Galvan, 2017:104).

The development of language is associated with multiple brain systems—the cerebrum, cerebellum, brain stem, pituitary gland, and hypothalamus (Kuhl, 2010). By the age of six months to a year, neural circuits have formed to discriminate and create all language sounds and acquire grammar. If the circuitry does not get used, it becomes rearranged or lost (Dowling, 2004). Bilingual children have been shown to outperform monolingual children on tasks measuring executive functioning skills later in development (Poulin-Dubois et al., 2011:1).

Stress has a wide-ranging effect on neurodevelopment. When infants are continually exposed to stressful/threatening situations, or their attachment needs go unmet, they eventually develop a hyper-reactive stress response so that even when there is no danger, the infant's brain and body exist in a perpetually heightened state. There seems little distinction between a real and an ongoing perceived threat. Conscious fear is a product of cognitive systems in the neocortex that operate in parallel with the amygdala circuit (LeDoux, 2016). Social aggression and avoidance have been linked to activity of the ventromedial hypothalamus; it has been proposed that it may encode a general internal state of threat modulated by space and experience (Krzywkowski et al., 2020). Continuously high cortisol levels are linked to high activity in the right frontal brain, which is responsible for producing irritability, fear, and withdrawal from others (Conkbayir, 2021:60).

At birth, the hypothalamic-pituitary-adrenal (HPA) axis is not fully developed. In response to constant stress or perceived threat, the HPA axis continually signals to increase blood pressure and suppress important functions like immunity and digestion (Kinlein et al., 2015). Chronically high basal levels of cortisol (as has been observed in maltreated children) has demonstrated immune suppression, reduced synaptic plasticity, and other deleterious effects that shape the way the brain circuits interpret environmental threat and the magnitude and duration of stress response in the future (Tarullo & Gunnar, 2006:637). Early childhood stress has also shown suppression of oxytocin and dopamine systems in children (Hughes & Baylin, 2012:69).

Childhood trauma seems to directly impact brain development, demonstrating an overall decreased brain size, less efficient processing, an impaired stress response, and changes in gene expression. Cognition can be affected with impaired readiness to learn, difficulty with problem-solving, language delays, poor concentration, and poor academic achievement (Bartlett & Steber, 2019). In a study of childhood maltreatment, a retrospective study of Romanian orphans (who were known to have been exposed to abusive or neglectful conditions) at 10 years following adoption, showed comprehensive neurological abnormalities—PET scans showed decreased metabolic activity in the orbital frontal gyrus, the infralimbic prefrontal cortex (PFC), the amygdalae, the head of the hippocampus, the lateral temporal cortex, and the brainstem. Autism, hyperactivity, impulsivity, language and fine and large motor delays, dysphoria, and disorganized attachment were also commonly noted (Chugani et al., 2001).

CIRCUIT 1 ENERGY

QUALITIES OF BALANCED CIRCUIT 1 ENERGY

- Centered, grounded
- Friendly, affectionate
- Healthy, unlimited physical energy
- Ability to manifest abundance
- Able to express anger without doing harm
- Ability to care for oneself while respecting others' needs
- Sexual: affectionate, able to trust and be vulnerable; body sensuality

QUALITIES OF EXCESSIVE CIRCUIT 1 ENERGY

- Egotistic, critical, aggressive
- Forthright, frank, firm, sarcastic
- Domineering, punitive
- Greedy/hoarding
- Addicted to wealth/accumulation/consumption
- Sexual: indiscriminate, focus entirely genital; nervous; possible sadism

QUALITIES OF DEFICIENT CIRCUIT 1 ENERGY

- Chronic fear and victimization
- Feels at the mercy of the environment; unable to stand on own
- Lacks confidence; weakness
- Overly agreeable/cooperative
- Feels spacey or unfocused
- Unable to achieve goals

- Self-destructive, suicidal
- Sexual: feels unlovable; fears abandonment; low libido, possible masochism/fetishes

CIRCUIT 1 ACTIVATION
CIRCUIT 1 ACTIVATING ACTIVITIES

Activities that allow you to feel the body more fully, or experience sensations or perceptions of safety and having basic needs met. For example:

- Cooking and consciously immersing yourself in a fulfilling meal
- Epsom salt bath while consciously paying attention to the sounds and rhythms of the body including heartbeat, breath, digestive movements, etc.
- Activities that stimulate the vagus nerve, which may include gargling water, humming, "OM"ing, vagal nerve stimulation
- Grounding in nature or gardening (horticulture therapy)
- Cuddling or being securely held
- Massage—particularly foot or abdominal ("hara") massage
- Floatation/isolation tanks
- Resting/Sleeping—adequate rest allows oneself to "recharge" and feel more safe/secure
- Trying to look at the world through the eyes of an infant—constant wonder & receptivity

CIRCUIT 1 ACTIVATING SUBSTANCES

Opioids, sedatives, low dose ketamine, kava kava, magnetite, amber, He Sho Wu (Fo Ti), nutmeg, chickweed, giant redwood, common box, burdock, dragon's bone, St. John's Wort, calendula, kanna, goji.

CIRCUIT 1 CALMING ACTIVITIES

Breathing exercises (e.g., blowing bubbles); having a cozy place to crawl into and relax; big hugs; head and shoulder massages; tapping; picturing a happy place or favorite activity; naming five favorite things; breathing in a favorite or soothing scent (aromatherapy); practicing yoga/mindfulness; identifying emotions with an adult (nurturing figure); being in nature/outside; listening to soothing music; repeating positive affirmations (Conkbayir, 2021:115).

KETAMINE

Ketamine is a Schedule 3 drug (in the USA), meaning it can be prescribed by a physician. It is used as an anaesthetic. At doses 6–10 times less than the anaesthetic dose, it produces a state of altered consciousness with psychoactive effects similar to psychedelics (without being classified as one) (Wolfson, 2016). Also known recreationally as a party drug (i.e., "Special K" or "K"), it has a higher risk of abuse and addiction than classic psychedelics (i.e., psychedelics that work on the 5-HT$_{2a}$ receptors, such as LSD, psilocybin, and DMT). Classification can vary to include it as a dissociative, deliriant, or psychotomimetic (Grob & Grigsby, 2021). Ketamine acts as a partial N-methyl-D-aspartate (NMDA) antagonist, affecting gluta-minergic function and neural-signaling pathways that results in synaptogenesis (the generation of new synaptic connections). This neural plasticity is thought to be the basis for research demonstrating quick-acting, potent, antidepressant effects (Berman et al., 2000; Galvez et al., 2018; Zanos & Gould, 2018). It has also demonstrated promotion of blood flow to the anterior cingulate, orbitofrontal, and dorsal frontal lobes (Holcomb et al., 2001). It has been hypothesized that it increases glutaminergic activity in the prefrontal cortex while strengthening the connection between the PFC and the amygdala, allowing for more executive control over emotional reactivity (Vollenweider & Kometer, 2010).

Ketamine-assisted psychotherapy (KAP) has become increasingly available, ranging from KAP-focused clinics to companies that will mail it to your home. The effects of ketamine on consciousness vary depending on the dose. Four levels have been put forth (Kolp & colleagues, 2016). The first level, with the lowest dose (intravenous 0.25–0.5mg/kg or 25–50 mg intramuscularly), creates a mild, relaxed, dissociative state said to be "empathogenic," and softens the personal ego, but with it remaining intact.

This would correlate to induction of Circuit 1 activation. The second stage (intravenous 0.75–1.5 mg/kg or 75–125 mg intramuscularly) is referred to as an "intermediate dissociative state" characterized by out-of-body experiences with feelings of separation from the body, traveling through space, and transpersonal experiences with intense visions and reports of meeting noncorporeal or archetypal beings. In the 8-Circuit Model, this would correlate to the induction of Circuit 7. The third stage (intravenous 2.0–3.0 mg/kg or 150–250 mg intramuscularly) tends to induce a "severe dissociative state" with reports of near-death experiences (NDE) and total dissolution of the ego. This may involve loss of the sense of identity, feeling as though you are in a state similar to death, and a reviewing your life with a moral inventory. In the 8-Circuit Model, this would correlate to the induction of Circuit 8. The fourth level is said to induce a classic mystical experience of feeling one with the Universe, becoming white light, and with deep senses of sacredness, ineffability, spacetime transcendence, peace, and joy. It has been suggested that ketamine could be used as *a safe and reversible experimental mode for NDE phenomenology, and supports the speculation that endogenous NMDA antagonists with neuroprotective properties may be released in the proximity of death*" (Martial et al., 2019:1).

INTEGRATION INTERVENTION MODEL CONSIDERATIONS
CIRCUIT 5 ACTIVATING ACTIVITIES

Circuits 1 and 5 are vertically connected, with Circuit 1 acting as an anchor to Circuit 5 shock experiences. Circuit 5 activities and exercises may facilitate Circuit 1 imprints becoming malleable and receptive to conscious change/re-imprinting.

CLINICAL APPROACH CONSIDERATIONS
(REFER TO RECOMMENDED READING FOR RESOURCES)

- Somatic Psychotherapies—Reichian, Bioenergetics, Hakomi
- Sensorimotor Psychotherapy
- Trauma Release Exercises
- EMDR

Counter-ACEs (positive influences) ameliorating impact of ACEs (Conkbayir, 2021:109):

- Having a caregiver with whom you feel safe
- A predictable home routine (e.g., regular meals and bedtime)
- Beliefs that provide comfort
- Liking school
- Teachers who care
- Good friends and neighbors
- Feeling comfortable with yourself
- Opportunities to have fun

Five principles of trauma-informed care (Conkbayir, 2021:119):

- Safety
- Trust
- Choice
- Collaboration
- Empowerment

Leary's Bio-Evolutionary Stages 1–3		
Stage 1	Biosurvival Receptivity	The unicellular organism and the newly-born mammal float passively, capable of receiving stimuli. This stage is concerned with intake, approach vs. avoidance, pleasure vs. pain, and security vs. danger, and the basic seed striving toward life. The definition of self as a viscerotonic entity—a greedy, incorporative, endomorphic ego-identity. Stage 1 performs a visceral-cellular function for the human group—health and food. An amoeboid intelligence, very close to its DNA.
Stage 2	Biosurvival Intelligence	This relates to the muscular, bony marine organism, equipped with a multi-neuron nervous system capable of memory, integration, and evaluation of stimuli. A being capable of attack-approach in addition to ingest-approach. This reflects a self-directed, infantile, driving nature. Where Stage 1 organisms can only receive or flee using amoebic flow, the Stage 2 organism is capable of selective, aggressive biting-stinging behavior in addition to sucking, incorporation, digestion, etc. Differentiation into cell types has occurred.

The human infant is the neurological equivalent of a marine organism. The vegetative circuit of the infant imprints the basic reality, the first attachment of the organism to the environment. |

| Stage 3 | Biosurvival Fusion | In species evolution, Stage 3 is the amphibian. In the development of the individual, Stage 3 is the infant linked neurologically with the Mother. This stage introduces the first social inter-organism linkage—maternal-infant. Instead of devouring or fighting each other, for the first time two organisms connect neurologically for mutual survival. The communication is viscerotonic, cellular. Sea-cow, frog, octopus are appropriate totems. Greedy, sensual, unfolding. |

Table 3: *Leary's Bio-Evolutionary Stages 1–3*

Naïve Consciousness	
Primary Motivation	Physical security & safety at the level of sustenance, reproduction, and avoidance of pain and change.
Ultimate Value	Security through ritual.
Attitude Toward Life	None—unaware of life; it is a given inherent in the nature of things.
Perception of Death	None—death is more or less the same as life, maybe a little worse.
Self-Boundaries	Permeable. Includes people, animals, and environment. Some identification with the body, but no true self-image.
Perception of Temporality	Simple present. The past is alive in the present.
Concept of Other	Merged with other, particularly the primary other. People not well differentiated from other animate beings in the environment.
Locus of Control	External—more competent or powerful other.
Level of Abstraction	Object permanence in space and time. Magical thinking. Pre-logical (efficacy and phenomenalism). Syncretic. Early preoperational or concrete reasoning. Concrete, minimal abstraction. Egocentric viewpoint. No societal role.
Options for Actions	One: what the ritual has been or what the more powerful other says.
Correct Opinion	One: what the ritual has been or what the more powerful other says.

Table 4: *Wade's Holonomic Theory: Naïve Consciousness*

Relevant Circuit 1 Assessments

The following questionnaires can be useful tools in self-assessment in dimensions relevant to the associated circuit and/or material covered in relationship to that circuit. Here we look at avoidant and anxious attachment styles and Adverse Childhood Experiences (ACE's).

Experiences in Close Relationship Scale (ECR-S)—Short Form

The ECR-S measures two subscales of attachment: Avoidance and Anxiety. It can be used to learn tendencies about yourself or others relevant to Circuit 1 imprinting and attachment styles. This can help you to understand your relational patterns, particularly in romantic relationships.

Instruction: The following statements concern how you feel in romantic relationships. We are interested in how you generally experience relationships, not just in what is happening in a current relationship. Respond to each statement by indicating how much you agree or disagree with it. Mark your answer using the following rating scale:

1=Strongly Disagree
2=Disagree
3=Slightly Disagree
4=Neutral
5=Slightly Agree
6=Agree
7=Strongly Agree

1. It helps to turn to my romantic partner in times of need.

2. I need a lot of reassurance that I am loved by my partner.

3. I want to get close to my partner, but I keep pulling back.

4. I find that my partner(s) don't want to get as close as I would like.

5. I turn to my partner for many things, including comfort and reassurance.

6. My desire to be very close sometimes scares people away.

7. I try to avoid getting too close to my partner.

8. I do not often worry about being abandoned.

9. I usually discuss my problems and concerns with my partner.

10. I get frustrated if romantic partners are not available when I need them.

11. I am nervous when partners get too close to me.

12. I worry that romantic partners won't care about me as much as I care about them.

Scoring Information:

Anxiety = 2, 4, 6, 8 (reverse), 10, 12

Avoidance = 1 (reverse), 3, 5 (reverse), 7, 9 (reverse), 11

When an item is "reverse" scored, use the following values instead when calculating your total score: 1=7; 2=6; 3=5; 4=4; 5=3; 6=2; 7=1

Items 2, 4, 6, 8, 10, and 12 are scored separately from items 1, 3, 5, 7, 9, and 11. The even-numbered items will give you your score with respect to an anxious attachment style, and odd-numbered items will give you your score with respect to an avoidant attachment style. The lower your score, the more secure you are in your attachment style and relationships, whereas higher scores on either scale suggest ways you may feel insecure in your relationships, and how this may affect your interpersonal behavior and relational patterns.

Wei, M., Russell, D.W., Mallinckrodt, B., & Vogel, D.L. (2007). The experiences in Close Relationship Scale (ECR)-Short Form: Reliability, validity, and factor structure. Journal of Personality Assessment, 88, 187–204.

ADVERSE CHILDHOOD EXPERIENCE (ACE) QUESTIONNAIRE

As the ACE score increases, so does the potential risk for chronic health problems. Identifying ACEs early can help with prevention and early intervention.

While you were growing up, during your first 18 years of life: (For each question, answer 1 for Yes and 0 for No.)

1. Did a parent or other adult in the household often or very often: Swear at you, insult you, put you down, or humiliate you? Or act in a way that made you afraid that you might be physically hurt? _____

2. Did a parent or other adult in the household often or very often: Push, grab, slap, or throw something at you? Or ever hit you so hard that you had marks or were injured? _____

3. Did an adult or person at least 5 years older than you ever: Touch or fondle you or have you touch their body in a sexual way? Or attempt or actually have oral, anal, or vaginal intercourse with you? _____

4. Did you often or very often feel that: No one in your family loved you or thought you were important or special? Or your family didn't look out for each other, feel close to each other, or support each other? _____

5. Did you often or very often feel that: You didn't have enough to eat, had to wear dirty clothes, and had no one to protect you? Or your parents were too drunk or high to take care of you or take you to the doctor if you needed it? _____

6. Were your parents ever separated or divorced? _____

7. Was your mother or stepmother: Often or very often pushed, grabbed, slapped, or had something thrown at her? Or sometimes, often, or very often kicked, bitten, hit with a fist, or hit with something hard? Or ever repeatedly hit for at least a few minutes or threatened with a gun or knife? _____

8. Did you live with anyone who was a problem drinker or alcoholic or who used street drugs? _____

9. Was a household member depressed or mentally ill, or did a household member attempt suicide? _____

10. Did a household member go to prison? _____

Now add up your "Yes" answers: _____ This is your ACE Score.

The higher your ACE score, the more adverse childhood events you reported experiencing as a child (e.g., abuse, neglect, and other trauma or major stressors). These types of experiences can strongly impact the development of personality, your beliefs about yourself and the world (especially with respect to safety, security, or self-worth), defense mechanisms developed to protect yourself from danger or perceived threat, and other long-term consequences on thoughts, feelings, behaviors, and interpersonal relating. Having a positive support person/system, role model(s), or other type of support (e.g., spirituality) through these challenging times can help to buffer the negative impact of these experiences. However, if your ACE score is high, it can be helpful for you to reflect on how these experiences may still affect your life, and consider if/how you might improve your life by addressing these deeply-rooted issues.

CHAPTER IV

CIRCUIT TWO (C-2): BOUNDARIES, EMOTIONS, & POWER DYNAMICS

EMOTIONAL-LOCOMOTION CIRCUIT (LEARY)
ANAL EMOTIONAL-TERRITORIAL CIRCUIT (WILSON)

"People will forget what you say. They will forget what you do. But they will never forget how you made them feel."
— Maya Angelou

Following the development of the biosurvival circuit in early childhood, the young human starts becoming conscious of their existence as a separate entity from the primary caregiver/nurturing figure, and the environment in which they interact. Attention becomes able to focus on what is determined to be part of self, and differentiate it from what is "else" or "other than Self." You become capable of forming concepts of what makes you up, what is yours, and establishing boundaries with what is not—in short, you develop a formal ego and an appropriate ego perspective. With this realization of separateness comes complex personal emotional reactions that you now own and understand to come from within rather than a nebulous pleasure versus pain affinity or aversion as was the instinctual behaviors of the first circuit. Objects or occurrences that impact the newly-developed Self come with feelings or specific reactions to them.

The child's brain continues to develop and create new neural connections with larger regions becoming more available and active. While the autonomic, bioregulatory, lower-brain centers remain active in sustaining key survival functions, the evolutionarily newer limbic system and medial temporal regions (including the thalamus and hypothalamus), now become more active and prominent in directing drives and initiatives. The limbic system (referred to as the paleo-mammalian brain in the triune brain model), is primarily responsible for the functioning and processing of immediate emotional responses, behavior drives, motivation, long term memory, and sense of smell.

Within the limbic system, the structure of the hippocampus plays a key role in memory consolidation and storage. The amygdala processes a number of emotional responses and conditioning, most notably, fear. The interaction of these two structures define which memories carry the most impact on the psyche. The limbic system is also believed to be the source of dualistic thinking patterns (Eldar et al., 2013; Mieda, Taku and Oshio, 2021), exhibiting the ability to only construct polar-opposite conceptualizations. A particular region of the hippocampus, the dentate gyrus, as well as the lateral subventricular zone (associated with the olfactory bulb), seem to be the two key areas where the brain generates new neurons (neurogenesis) throughout one's life (Abdissa, 2020). (Neurogenesis and neuroplasticity are discussed in more detail in Chapter X on metaprogramming in Circuit 6.)

Wilson posits that if we were to consider only the first two circuits of development and the associated brain activity, there appears virtually no difference between humans and the vast majority of domesticated animals. The drives, operations, and reactions are practically identical. Primary life directives are essentially derivatives of the "four F's": feeding, fighting, fleeing, and fornication; these are all driven by the hypothalamus of the brain. The fight-or-flight response is an activation of the sympathetic nervous system that prepares and engages the peripheral nervous system, and shunts blood flow to the extremities to allow for a quick physical response. Other means of activating the peripheral nervous system and the muscles of the extremities (e.g., intense exercise) also work with the second circuit.

Imprinting for this circuit happens in early childhood, generally before the age of three. In Piaget's model of development, this circuit correlates with the "pre-operational" stage (Piaget, 1970). Wade, in her work on the holonomic model of the evolution of consciousness, refers to the egocentric stage, which is prominent between 18 months to six-years-old, with the schema of external objects being concrete by the age of three. There is recent evidence that the actual formation of the ego, and thus "separateness," can begin at, or even before, birth. If this occurs, it is considered premature and rarely formed enough to reach the high level of neural construction associated with imprint vulnerability—which will still generally occur within the 18-month to three-year range.

Studies of prenatal development have pointed to a direct correlation between traumatic events during gestation to either the child or mother, causing a chemical or hormonal disruption to the womb environment. The more frequent these traumas, the greater the likelihood of creating what becomes a reinforced reaction in the child of a premature sense of self and an awareness of external interferences. This early sense of separation from the immersive oneness of the womb experience can act as a detriment to thorough bio-survival imprinting and development, thereby causing a negative imprint or stunted functional neurodevelopment in this realm.

> *"Most people function on a level of 'chronic low-grade emergency'... Too much emotions by the parents or parent surrogates, when imprinting the second circuit, leads to chronic, daily, hour-by-hour emotionalism.... Thus, in most people, reason remains—as all cynics have noted—the slave of emotion, and is generally used only to justify the reflexes (passions, compulsions) of the glandular system. Circuit 2 checkmates Circuit 3."* (Wilson, 2020:139–140)

Once the child realizes that they exist as a sovereign entity, they begin to assess the world around them differently than in the passively receptive manner of the bio-survival circuit. Understanding the world with which they interact as something now external, they start evaluating how to navigate and manipulate their environment and those within it. This is epitomized by the "terrible twos" stage in which the child becomes highly emotional and reactive, as well as coming to the realization that such emotional reactions often result in the "reward" of fulfillment of their needs or demands. As this realization sets in, they learn to leverage this to their advantage, manipulating those in the position to meet such demands.

Tantrums, a common occurrence during this phase, are thought to be a reaction to the limbic system's lack of capacity for ambivalence or conceptual gradients. Dr. Robert Kegan states that this results from a *"system overwhelmed by internal conflict because there is no self yet to serve as context on which competing impulses can play themselves out—impulses ARE the self, are themselves the context"* (1982:88). Developmentalists consider this a time of pain and selfishness involving high anxiety, paranoia, and egocentrism. Also associated are self-centered power struggles, aggression, hedonism, amorality, and little-to-no impulse control. Economic and social theorist Jeremy Rifkin (2009) states that the destructive drive and unnecessary aggression arises from an infant's needs for connection being unmet by their caregiver. In tribal societies, this destructive drive is less likely to appear because of greater opportunities for the child's needs being met by the abundant population of adults taking care of the children.

According to Piaget, the first limitation of the preoperational stage is animism (Santrock, 2011). Animism is defined as the ability to distinguish between animate and inanimate objects (Shaffer et al., 2010).

This circuit correlates to Freud's anal stage of development, hence Wilson's naming it the "anal emotional-territorial circuit." Toilet training and the learned skill of controlling bodily functions demand the ability to consciously own, use, and manipulate one's body. With this stage also comes mastery of gravity, the act of walking, the overcoming of obstacles, as well as the aforementioned manipulation of others. These act as key vulnerable points within this stage where heavy conditioning and imprinting may occur.

This imprint ends up defining your sense of personal freedom, status, and political awareness. The crux of your emotional intelligence is derived from these imprints, which form into personal values, beliefs, and convictions, further becoming self-defining factors for most, throughout most of life.

Also imprinted during this period is the sense of your hierarchical status within the larger family dynamic and social environment. You generally imprint into either an assertive/dominant or passive/submissive role, with this tendency playing out throughout your life, based on the experiences during this time. The sense that you are either the "top dog" or "bottom dog" becomes instilled, and varies little from the classic mammalian pack status. If a child imprints as a dominant type, they tend to express the dynamics of an "authority" reflex" whereby they swell up their muscles and vocalize (yell, growl, howl, etc.) when faced with conflicts and challenges. Those who have been imprinted as primarily submissive tend to shrink their muscles, lower their head, and crawl away from confrontation. Wilson states that *"the ego is merely the mammalian recognition of one's status in the pack; it is a role that one takes on"*.

> *"The Anal Emotional-Territorial Circuit. This is imprinted in the 'Toddling' stage when the infant rises up, walks about and begins to struggle for power within the family structure. This mostly mammalian circuit processes territorial rules, emotional games, or cons, pecking order and rituals of domination or submission." (Wilson, 1983:40)*

Placing this circuit into Dr. Timothy Leary's Interpersonal Grid (see Figure 2, below), the second circuit is imprinted in an up and down direction relating to managerial-autocratic (sections A & P from the center of the grid), and self-effacing-masochistic (sections H & I from the center). These include:

- Trust/Dominant: I'm okay/you're okay (choleric, fire)
- Trust/Submissive: I'm not okay/you're okay (phlegmatic, water)
- Suspicious/Dominant: I'm okay/you're not okay (sanguine, air)
- Suspicious/Submissive: I'm not okay/you're not okay (melancholic, earth)

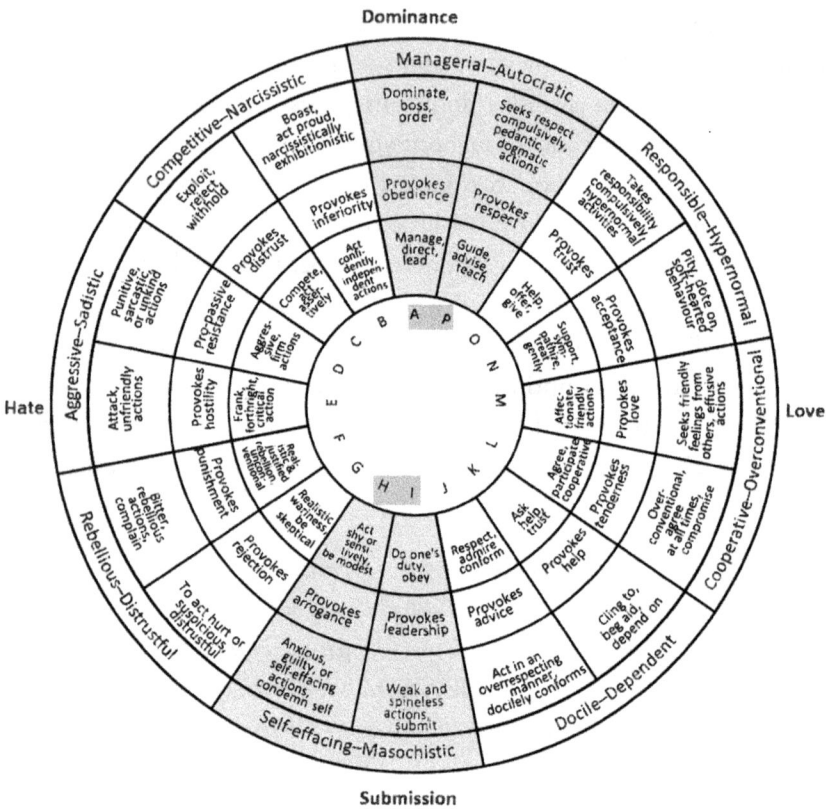

Figure 2: *Dr. Timothy Leary's Interpersonal Grid: Upward-Downward Imprint*

Due to neural imprinting, these roles can become deeply ingrained, and lifelong patterns for reflexive muscular engagement programs can result in a physical appearance reflective of the individual's imprint typology. For example, those who take the heaviest imprint in the emotional-territorial circuit tend to develop a "mesomorphic" body type in which the majority of the body's resources become shunted toward strengthening and emphasizing the large skeletal muscles for purposes of attack and defense. Often the individual will become large and difficult to knock down, but still light and mobile enough to be able to move efficiently and effectively. Body builders have often taken a heavy second circuit imprint.

Whereas the biosurvival circuit is primarily imprinted by the influence of the primary nurturing caregiver, the emotional-territorial circuit tends to more closely relate to the relationship dynamic with the disciplinarian. This person tends to be perceived as the child's invincible protector and image of strength. If this figure has a strong second circuit imprint themselves and tends to be encouraging of the child in their ability to interact with, claim, or have dominion over their space for themselves, it becomes likely that the child will also develop a heavily dominant imprint. If this figure has an excessively dominating presence, the opposite may occur, creating a passive/submissive imprint as the child is quashed in their attempts to assert control over themself or their environment.

The nature of a societal structure can also be defined by the dominant type of imprinting within that culture. Patriarchal societies tend to express qualities more closely aligned with the emotional-territorial circuit and imprints. Matriarchal societies, on the other hand, tend to emphasize the biosurvival circuit.

Wade associates this cutting away from the maternal figure to identify more with the paternal figure as a breaking away from Source, or if you will, the Eastern concept of the Dao. While the mental ego remains aware that Source exists, they do not comprehend exactly "what" is existing. The awareness of this drives the ego into an extroverted projection, creating an inner voice and self-identity. These things, being merely a product of consciousness, are perceived as the source itself, from which the consciousness is derived.

The unfolding of self-awareness, coupled with the dualistic perceptions, creates a sense of your mortality. Suddenly there is an understanding of a beginning, and with that, an understanding that there must also be an end. Some developmental psychologists describe this realization of death as true self-awareness. As the concept of death is comprehended, with it forms a subsequent *fear* of death. While this fear becomes real to the individual, the awareness of it remains only as a *possibility*—things and people die, but you do not yet seem to comprehend the inevitability and certainty of death.

Situations in which there is a greater demand to take control of your environment due to threats (real or perceived), dangers to self, or a need to protect others will take a particularly strong imprint. Those who are taught to "listen and not speak" (e.g., internalizing sayings such as "children should be seen and not heard" or other similar cues from adult figures) tend to become unable to take on challenges without the opportunity to conquer it. They may be unable to claim a space as their own and may subsequently take a passive/submissive imprint. As with a more assertive/dominant imprint, this tends to play out throughout your life if it is not consciously addressed later.

As formal language is still elementary and undeveloped during this time, body language and simplistic vocalizations tend to be preferred as the primary means of communication. Puffing up of the chest or tightening/engaging muscles, fists, or a clenched jaw all convey attempts at reacting to an affront on the emotional-territorial circuit, or to place yourself in a more assertive/dominant role. While there is a general resistance to power exercised by others—sometimes with violent reactions—an individual with an underdeveloped second circuit tends to become obedient when overpowered, and thus loses their personal autonomy. Those possessing physical characteristics denoting power are automatically seen to confer moral authority.

Simple growls and grunts or submissive groans or whines may be used depending on your placement on the dominant-submissive spectrum. In these cases, tone and inflection convey implicit pre-linguistic information, much like the sounds made by other mammals. This system is used by humans in adult life as well. In particular, this has been found to be the case in socio-economic subsets that tend to emphasize emotional-territoriality. In the United States Marine Corp (USMC), for instance, the use of the simplistic vocalization "urr/er" is used to convey a wide range of things depending on the tone and situation in which it is used.

Studies of military and employee populations showed a marked tendency to fixate at this level, maintaining it into adulthood. A prevalence was found in males, particularly those who belong to lower socioeconomic classes, which, according to Wade, suggests *a rather substantial adult population evince egocentric consciousness.* This circuit is highly adaptive for survival in hostile environments, such as inner-city neighborhoods, combat zones, and prisons. The military is a wellspring of second circuit dynamics in which one's status within a structured hierarchy is overt—an appeal to the superior within the hierarchy, with a heavy emphasis on muscular strength and endurance, discipline, and the defense of territory. For this reason, those who have a strong emotional-territorial imprint will often either be drawn to this scenario or have historically been placed or shunted into these positions as they can be very useful here. In other social environments, such as many conventional work settings, these tendencies may act as a hindrance. Despite this, many function primarily at the emotional-territorial level in modern society—often successfully.

Other linguistic preferences may heavily emphasize the bodily functions brought under control during the development of this circuit—particularly, anal retention and excrement. Insults such as "dip shit," "you no good shit," and "asshole" may frequently be used as little more than vocal means of the lower primate tendency to throw feces at offending individuals. Overt genital references such as "dickhead," "pussy," or allusions to taboo sexual acts such as "motherfucker" or "cocksucker" may also be frequent go-to insults.

The establishment of territory, turf, boundaries, and belongings are of key importance to this circuit. The child defines their space, or claims things as their own. To stake this claim, the child may lick or otherwise mark an object. Later in life, this plays out as power politics between people, such as the nature of exchanges between parent and a child, an employer and employee, and leaders and followers. Patriotism and nationalism also stem from this same drive as a pride in what is "theirs" and where they belong. This may be a prominent facet of the personality in those strongly imprinted in this circuit.

Emotions become excited whenever there is an imposition on the sense of self or territory. Anger tends to be the most common emotion to arise. Despite a general cultural stigmatization against expressing anger, it plays an essential function when growth or change becomes oppressed, or when one must muster a force within themselves to get out of a dangerous or detrimental situation. Anger may also arise when a drive to move is not afforded or has stagnated. An appropriate expression of this is within a healthy environment with the ability to let it go when it no longer serves the individual. This is required to maintain a balanced state of body-mind.

Boredom also seems an expression of emotional-territorial stagnation in which frustration derives from an internal drive or need for self-challenge, risk-taking, or achievement that is not being met.

Observing or participating in events that activate any of these emotional engagements, drives or opportunities to "flex one's muscles" may appeal to those with strong C-2 imprints. Some examples of these include:

- the emotional rollercoasters of soap operas
- highly competitive or violent sports including mixed martial arts
- the hybrid of the two aforementioned examples in the billion-dollar industry of scripted professional wrestling
- making oneself known or exerting aural dominance by making the most sound or impact including cars, firearms, fireworks, etc.
- breaking things as in rage rooms, arm wrestling, chopping wood, loud music/concerts, and in associated activities (slam dancing, mosh pits, circle pits, walls of death, etc.)

FEELINGS VERSUS EMOTIONS

"Let's not forget that the little emotions are the great captains of our lives and we obey them without realizing it."
— Vincent van Gogh

Emotions are gut reactions to stimuli, and it is important to distinguish between "emotions" and "feelings." Feelings result after the initial reaction or emotion becomes processed through cognitive engagement. They are thought about, reflected on, or rationally processed, after which one comes to some conclusion as to how to feel about it. Etymologically, the word "emotion," or to "emote," means "to move outward." They are immediate, sometimes seemingly irrational, responses to stimuli. They are actually non-rational or pre-rational, rather than irrational. When one does things for emotional reasons, there is little or no rationalization to it. Something may not make sense, but it will just "feel right."

The emotions at this level lack definition, complexity, or the tone of more mature emotions in later stages of development. Their range of expression remains limited and unmodulated. Between the ages of two and five years old, recognition of emotional expressions improves by as much as 40%, with happiness being the most easily identified. Surprise, fear, and neutral expressions were identified with the least accuracy (Galván, 2017:189). Emotions can often become a melting pot of strong negative forces including shame, rage, hate, disgust, and grief.

Notably absent from this list is a sense of guilt. While the individual now recognizes that other humans exist and are separate from objects, both tend to be seen as only a means of achieving personal gratification. This is the reason manipulation of others can be so prevalent. A person operating in the emotional-territorial circuit may lack general empathy, while being completely oblivious or intentionally non-cognizant of the feelings of others. Dr. Lev Vygotsky says of this stage that one can mentally represent events and objects and engage in symbolic play; however, their thoughts and communications are typically egocentric, and they assume that what other people see, hear, and feel are exactly as their own (Galván, 2017:118). There exists little differentiation between other people and objects other than the level of complexity and engagement necessary to interact with each. In this stage, children believe that everything around them is alive (Bernstein et al., 2008; Babakyr et al., 2019). Objects are also perceived as living and potentially useful, but contain little meaning beyond that. They appear animated only in terms of how they immediately relate to the individual.

In this sense there can be no such thing as a true two-way interpersonal relationship in second-circuit consciousness. The mentality is one of an "eye for an eye and a tooth for a tooth." Wade notes that the primary social motto of this stance is "everyone is out to get a free lunch," and everyone is either "with me or against me." Thoughts remain binary in terms of those being the dominant or strong ("haves") versus the weak or submissive ("have-nots").

THE EMOTIONAL TANK

Acting on these drives to satisfy your desires, knowing and acknowledging what is wanted, and expressing these, maintain what Alli refers to as an individual's "emotional tank." This is essentially the state of your emotional health, and your capacity to maintain an internal balance. When your emotional tank becomes depleted—meaning emotions are deficient, suppressed, or not active—it can lead to apathy, depression, and attitudes that amplify the negative aspects of life. When the second circuit becomes caught in this process, it can produce a number of negative emotions including futility or helplessness. Insecurity, rage, and envy of others perceived as not having such concerns is also commonplace.

The need to have a sense of control over your life and emotions often lies at the root of this. Often it can seem as though these things are occurring *to* them from external forces, rather than from *within*. It can feel as though you have lost all ability to control these reactions. To counteract this, Alli says it can be helpful to explore aspects of your life in which you are able to exert some degree of control—to take charge, and claim it as you own doing. People may, however, start doing this in ways that are detrimental to others. Unfortunately, desperate attempts to feel a degree of control in life may turn into acts of controlling others as a projection of the frustration they feel about their life. These can act as the origin of some abusive relationships or domestic violence situations.

For this reason, it becomes important to emphasize a healthy means of handling these emotions. When the emotional tank becomes full, a person may develop exploitative outlets along with an inflated sense of self-importance, delusional behavior, or immature posturing that others may find emotionally toxic.

Alli goes on to discuss how the state of your emotional tank can have an effect on your subtle/energetic body. He identifies three primary drains to this tank. First is the victim syndrome discussed above. The second is the compulsion for companionship, courtship, and fundamentally, the search for a "soul mate" or "other half" to compliment and complete a sense of something missing. The third scenario is what he calls energy (or emotional) vampires—individuals who seem to drain others of their life force through their interactions with them.

"When we allow for an authentic emotional experience in the presence of another, we can increase our capacity for emotional regulation when we are expressing those emotions while in connection and relationship with that person (I-thou)." (Gathers, 2020)

You can learn to experience emotions and emotional reactions without placing judgments on them. They can be recognized for what they are: pre-rational, physiological reactions to stimuli. You can see the world as "just a game," and playfully express these emotions in a healthy manner. When emotions are rationalized or judged, they become repressed to varying degrees. When this occurs and the emotions are left unprocessed or unfelt fully, they hold the capacity to immobilize self-expression.

PERSONAL POWER

Personal power, and how it is defined, determines the types of power structures that you will bring into your life. Your sense of personal power and dominion over self is a major focal point of this circuit. It can be generated through "following the path of the heart," in which attention is paid to personal needs and preferences. When this is lacking, a victim mentality or a type of paranoia can develop in which the world is perceived to be actively working against you. To develop a victim mentality, however, necessitates two other players—the perpetrator and a savior figure. Being aware of, and knowing your beliefs, makes it more difficult for others to invade the self. If you feel self-fulfilled, there remains little room for others to invade or take up space.

The ability to "win" or to feel special in some sense, also enables self-esteem. As such, goal-setting—and the achievement of these goals—help to support your self-dominion. When these things are recognized as belonging to oneself, it lays the foundation for the ego-strength necessary in upper circuit activation.

It's important to distinguish whether one imprints and develops this self-defined dominion, or if it becomes projected outward as externally manifested dominion over others. After all, there are two types of winning—those that benefit only yourself while others lose; and winning that acts in the interest of the greater whole where everyone wins. Much of this shows through one's personal motives. The depth of these motives is directly correlated to the level of power they convey. If motives are more selfish and negligent of others, or at the expense of others, then it ultimately becomes limiting and shuts off the receptivity to the larger wholeness of existence.

Emotions can define this dynamic. Alli points out that in social environments, unless emotions are shut down, the most emotional person in the room tends to dominate everyone else, and the locus of the dynamic will hinge on this particular individual's emotional state.

Mental health disorders that may fall into categorization of the emotional-territorial circuit include antisocial personality disorder, the paranoid personality, narcissistic personality types, and other Cluster B personality disorders/traits as described in the DSM-5 (Axis II; e.g., borderline, histrionic, and hysterical personality disorders). "Antisocial personality disorder" used to be known as "sociopathy." It stems from a mental construct whereby an objective reality does not exist, and thus socially constructed concepts are meaningless to such an individual. Some of these socially constructed concepts include culturally appropriate behavior, empathy, and honesty. In the paranoid personality an individual has pervasive and unwarranted suspicion, coupled with a restricted affect. The narcissistic personality contains a grandiose but fragile self-image that encompasses a lack of empathy, a willingness to manipulate others, and a prerogative to outrightly either take in or reject information depending on how it fits their world-view or ego preference.

> *"It is Dr. Leary's conclusion that most of the tension, depression, chronic tiredness, persistent anxiety, etc. of 'normal' game-playing consciousness is due to the continuous overuse of the second Circuit. That is, the emotional person is 'a lurching lunatic,' he says, because the emotional-glandular circuits are turned on almost all the time." (Wilson, 2020:136)*

NEUROBIOLOGY OF CIRCUIT 2

Between 10 months to two years of age, there is slow brain growth while the child practices, improves, and perfects already learned skills. As control of movement improves, neural pruning occurs to allow for a sharpening of efficiency and specialization into neural networks. If there has not been enough experience, or if the child is limited in their ability to explore the range of possible movements, these networks may not develop to their full potential.

The next major period of brain growth happens between the ages of 2–4 years, and mostly affects the maturation of the senses. The child can see, hear, taste, touch, and smell virtually on the adult level by the end of this stage (Epstein, 2006). The child has reached the age of the Vygotsky fusion of thought and language development, meaning that the child now speaks in concepts and thinks in words (Vygotsky, 1962). At around age 2, the density of neurons in the dorsolateral prefrontal cortex (dl-PFC) is 55% above the adult mean, but only 10% above adult levels by age 7 years, showing a prolonged pruning process during this time (Galván, p. 127). Given that most children tend to have the same capability to experience sensory input, stunted development may be the result of a lack of association of this input. According to Dr. Herman T. Epstein (2006), *"Association is the key to almost all mental functioning."*

CIRCUIT 2 ENERGY

QUALITIES OF BALANCED CIRCUIT 2 ENERGY

- Able to fully accept & experience feelings
- Able to form relationships free of emotional neediness/sexual enmeshment
- Friendly, optimistic, concerned for others; has a sense of belonging
- Creative, imaginative, intuitive
- Gutsy or bold sense of humor
- Empathetic: can merge with the body/mind of another person and psyche to better understand them
- Sexual: Extremely sensual, radiates a full & healthy sense of sexuality; highest goal is a wonderful orgasm; may desire to have children

QUALITIES OF EXCESSIVE CIRCUIT 2 ENERGY

- Emotionally aggressive, explosive
- Overly ambitious
- Manipulative
- Caught up in delusion
- Over-indulgent, self-serving, egocentric, proud
- Depressed empathy: can't distinguish between oneself and the other person
- Tendency to be prejudiced, manipulative, self-serving
- Sexual: obsessed with thoughts of sex; sees people of the opposite sex exclusively as sex objects; requires frequent sexual gratification

QUALITIES OF DEFICIENT CIRCUIT 2 ENERGY

- Uncontrolled empathy: inability to differentiate one's feelings from others
- Lack of self-worth, self-negating, resentful
- Inner emptiness drives to unhealthy/codependent relationships or situations
- Martyr complex, distrustful
- Extremely shy, timid, docile; buries emotions

- Attachment, insecurity, frustration
- Burdened by guilt
- Unconscious sexual repression leading to overwhelming or disturbing sexual dreams

CIRCUIT 2 ACTIVATION
CIRCUIT 2 ACTIVATING ACTIVITIES

Activities that activate the peripheral nervous system/skeletal muscles, sympathetic nervous system, and adrenals:

- High impact physical activity: hitting, kicking, push-ups, pushing, pulling, or rocking; singing/rapping, dancing
- Chewing crunchy foods
- Shouting/screaming into a cushion; crashing into pillows or a crash pad
- Wheelbarrow walking
- Squeezing a stress ball or making playdough; bouncing a ball
- Ripping up or crumpling a piece of paper
- Outdoor activities: raking, sweeping, chopping wood, etc.
- Playing with children (especially in groups) and observing hierarchy/power dynamics
- Learning to be in assertive/dominant and/or docile/submissive roles
- Admit to being wrong, even if you are not
- If accustomed to losing, creating three small victories
- Watch sophomoric/slapstick comedy
- Uphold one's integrity/accountability

CIRCUIT 2 ACTIVATING SUBSTANCES

Alcohol, depressant drugs, barbiturates, benzodiazepines, cordyceps, *Tribulus terrestris*, yohimbe, epimedium, lu rong, panax ginseng (central circulatory stimulant), cayenne (central circulatory stimulant), prickly ash (Peripheral Nervous System [PNS] stimulant), yarrow (PNS stimulant)

CIRCUIT 2 REGULATING SUBSTANCES

Bupleurum, ashwagandha, black cohosh, marigold, lady's mantle, pennyroyal, licorice, wormwood, senna, raspberry, red clover, shatavari, hibiscus

Wilson (1983) proposes that if someone wants to understand or exercise their second, emotional-territorial circuit, simply go to the nearest pub, get roaring drunk, and begin yelling at people (at your own risk, of course). Alcohol has well-established impairing effects on inhibitory control (Weafer & Fillmore, 2016), which in turn, increases the likelihood of impulsive actions. It is known to modulate behavior such as increased aggression (Graham et al., 1998), impulsivity (Choi et al., 2018; Dick et al., 2010), violence (Menkes & Herxheimer, 2014), and depression (Choi et al., 2018). Disinhibitory behavior from alcohol consumption also affects verbal, attention, sexual, cognitive, and locomotor behaviors (Cooper, 2006; Rose & Duka, 2007; Tobor, 2020; Weafer & Fillmore, 2012).

Alcohol affects specific brain regions including the cerebellum, hippocampal gyrus, superior frontal gyrus, left basal ganglia, and right internal capsule. Functional connectivity of the default mode network (DMN) has also been shown to be affected by alcohol consumption. *"These different brain regions which are related to memory, motor control, cognitive ability, and spatial functions might provide a neural basis for alcohol's effects on behavioral performance"* (Zheng et al., 2015:9). A significant decrease in connectivity between the frontal-temporal-basal ganglia and cerebellar components have been shown with alcohol consumption, which may impair one's higher-order cognitive function and motor planning (Rzepecki-Smith et al., 2010). The direct effects on lessening frontal executive function and inhibition of the limbic system can allow the limbic system to dominate with thought processes and behaviors that are considered Circuit 2 tendencies.

Integration Intervention Model Considerations
Circuit 6 Activating Activities

Circuit 2 and Circuit 6 are vertically connected, with Circuit 2 acting as an anchor to Circuit 6 shock experiences. C-6 shocks expand boundaries beyond the individual self, and allow conscious control of one's nervous systems, belief systems, and worldview. Circuit 2 thought patterns tend to be the dualistic, black-and-white thinking of the limbic system with high emotionality when there is any challenge to autonomy, power structure, ego, or beliefs.

Pranayama

"To turn off this circuit and send energy to higher circuits, the yogin practices pranayama (literally energy control) via breath-control. As Crowley noted, it is physically impossible to remain in an emotional state if you will stop and do 20–30 minutes of pranayama... Magicians and Sufis get the same effect by rhythmic movement and dance." (Wilson, 2020, p. 346)

Clinical Approach Considerations
(Refer to Recommended Reading for Resources)
- Emotion Regulation Therapy
- Play Therapy
- Desensitizing
- Operant Conditioning
- Primal Scream Therapy

Leary's Bio-Evolutionary Stages 4–6		
Stage 4	Emotion-Locomotion Receptivity	The second circuit emerged when living organisms left the water, developed backbones, controlled territory, and established dominance hierarchies. This is the exploratory, self-centered period during which the child begins to master gravity, coordinates mobility muscles, and moves upwards against gravity—but before cooperative emotional distinctions are made. The child defines a new self. Phylogenetically, this stage produces animal forms which operate as "emotional loners," surviving without group cooperation. ["emotional consumerism" — Wilson 2020, p. 331]
Stage 5	Emotional Intelligence	Programmed to avoid helplessness, master territory, and attain autonomy, new neural networks are activated to facilitate the transition from marine to land-life. Complex strategies are developed—muscular power, speed, camouflage, evasion—all designed to master survival. The child begins to walk and sense the complex web of emotional hierarchy which comprises mammalian politics. The selection of the appropriate emotional-political response is determined by the second imprint. There are times to approach, avoid, attack, dominate, submit, give or take. Learning the complex nuances of pecking order, dominance hierarchy, and territorial response is important to survival for the young child. Motor-muscular responses are no longer automatic approach-or-avoid tactics. Incoming signals are scanned, evaluated, and inter-

		preted and the appropriate emotional response selected.
Stage 6	Emotional Fusion	This next stage involves group communication and cooperation among members of the colony, herd, or group. Intricate social networks emerge. The individual's survival depends on discriminating social differences and fitting into the social web. The organism inhibits some autonomy to adjust to the group. The Second Circuit imprint determines the emotional style— the interpersonal ego which persists into maturity. ["Internalizing the rules of the social game" — Wilson 2022, p. 331]

Table 5: *Leary's Bio-Evolutionary Stages 4–6*

Egocentric Consciousness	
Primary Motivation	Survival of the mental ego as self
Ultimate Value	Egoic survival by force and cunning
Attitude Toward Life	Life is equated with the existence of mental ego—identified with self, not understood as abstraction
Perception of Death	Personified as a subjective enemy. Death is competitive, selective, and arbitrary, and can be overcome or outwitted. Alien/Other capable of overwhelming the mental ego
Self-Boundaries	Firm. Located at the skin (I am inside my skin; everything else is outside)
Perception of Temporality	Very short view of past and future—simple present dominates experience. Many memories of causality are tested—not trusted. Little impulse control; future is not "real." Little ability to foresee consequences of actions
Concept of Other	Environment: objects, people, animals, and some rudimentary abstractions viewed as Alien/Other. Other feared as potential threat to the self to be overcome or manipulated for own ends. Subservient to others perceived to be more powerful. Domineering to others perceived less powerful. Peer relationships do not exist. People are not seen as equal or similar to self
Locus of Control	Internal—the self for its survival
Level of Abstraction	Pre-conceptual to concrete operations. Animism less ascribed to objects, now ascribed to abstractions
Options for Actions	Two: one is chthonic: subconscious paranoia source—own way or fear of annihilation if yield to other
Correct Opinion	Own way

Table 6: *Wade's Holonomic Theory: Egocentric Consciousness*

Chapter V

Circuit 3 (C-3):
Map-Making, Logic, & Problem-Solving

Laryngeal-Manual Symbolic Circuit (Leary)
Semantic Time-Binding Circuit (Wilson)

"Man's achievements rest upon the use of symbols... We must consider ourselves as a symbolic, semantic class of life, and those who rule the symbols, rule us."
— Alfred Korzybski

Around the age of seven, the child tends to enter another transitional phase of life in which new neural connections spike, and certain brain regions become more active and accessible. Around this time, the child transitions from the realm of imaginative and superstitious thinking to a more deductive rationale and logic. Formal operations become more commonplace as the activity of the frontal lobes of the brain increase. Within the triune brain model, the frontal lobes are referred to as the "neo-mammalian brain," which developed after and out of the paleo-mammalian brain.

A primary attribute of this stage is the ability of the child to now intellectually separate hard interpretations of their experiences of reality from representations of and information about reality. This comes in the form of symbols or metaphors. Prior to this stage, stories told, television shows or movies seen, or imagined situations would be no less real—with no less impact on their psyche and nervous system—than a direct experience.

In developmental psychology, this phase has been referred to as the "concrete operational stage," wherein:

> *"the individual can apply logical thought or rules to physical objects (hence concrete operations). Children become less egocentric and come to understand properties of transference—that something can stay the same in quantity even if its appearance changes (e.g., transferring water from a tall thin glass to a short wide glass)." (Galván, 2017:118)*

followed by what Dr. Jean Piaget (1970) referred to as the "formal operational stage," which typically develops around age 12, in which children,

> *"gain the ability to think abstractly, combine and classify items in a more sophisticated way, and the capacity for higher-order reasoning. The adolescent can do mathematical calculations, think creatively, use abstract reasoning, and imagine the outcome of particular actions." (Galván, 2017:118)*

Freud referred to this developmental period as the "latency stage" of psychosexual development as the libido seems to be relatively dormant. Wade did not explore a particular stage with the developments of this time. That is not to say it goes without other significant psychospiritual landmarks. Michael Washburn discusses the refinement of inner speech or "inner thinking," and its ability to begin commanding working memory, cognitive flexibility, planning, and self-control during this time. (Alderson-Day & Fernyhough, 2015)

This inner speech also transforms the executive function of the ego that developed in Circuit 2. With this forms the "ego ideal"—the ego's fantasized depiction of its ideal life, and what would fulfill its highest hopes (Washburn, 2023:193). The superego also comes into being here, known as an inner voice of "conscience" which impels action by enforcing discipline and the avoidance of fear or repercussion (Washburn, 2023:194).

> *"Like the ego ideal, which ranks the ego's desires, the superego ranks the ego's fears" (Washburn, 2023: 196)*

This inner speech also allows for a process of removing from conscious-ness those parts of self that the ego cannot acknowledge and insists are not-self. A subsystem containing these parts are constructed because the ego finds them immoral, improper, or otherwise threatening and harmful to the sense of self. This subsystem is what Jung referred to as the "shadow." (Washburn, 2023: 198)

Prior to this stage, the superstitious and fantastical thinking of mystical creatures (e.g., fairies or monsters) are taken literally. The nervous system registers it with the same intensity as any other event. A scary story or movie is processed and experienced within the psyche in the same way as a sincerely frightening or traumatic life event. As the child transitions away from this fantastical thinking, they become able to mentally step aside and recognize it as a story not based on real events, and thus not to be taken with the same intensity or physiological response. Improved cognitive abilities allow men-tation to override physiological activation.

"This is imprinted and conditioned by human artifacts and symbol sys-tems. It 'handles' and 'packages' the environment, classifying everything according to the local reality tunnel. Invention, calculation, prediction and transmitting signals across generations are its functions." (Wilson, 1983:40)

It is this transition that some educational approaches—such as Waldorf education—take into consideration when not emphasizing reading until around this age. While, of course, capable of learning to read earlier, the idea in the Waldorf curriculum is that a premature focus on reading can override the child's natural developmental timeline of moving from the immersive, imaginative experience into a separation of mental constructs and symbolic thought. This may stifle or cut short the full development of the second cir-cuit, potentially causing either deficiency or repression of emotional com-ponents and ego development.

The human race has developed into a symbol-using species with the creation of written language capable of conveying meaning and ideas with-out vocalizations. This was a major evolutionary step, in which what would otherwise be arbitrary combinations of lines and dots can be imbued with significance and meaning. They can convey this meaning, and be used to pass on information, teach, and change the way in which a person thinks and perceives the world. Further, this information can be readily distributed to anyone familiar with that particular set and combination of symbols (language), long beyond the passing of the original source (person) presenting the information. In a bio-evolutionary sense, this truly marks an incredible ability, now often taken for granted.

Also developing from this comes the ability to record and place events within a linear spacetime of causality or order of occurrence. Past events can be bound to the dates and times they occurred, establishing a past, present, and future that exists beyond the immediate experience of Circuit 1 and 2 consciousness. This is what Wilson (1983) refers to as the establishment of the human time-binding function—as derived from the work of Alfred Korzybski (1958). Time is now conceptualized as well as experienced, and society has subsequently become a creature of time.

With the activation of the semantic circuit comes the ability to mentally organize and categorize objects and events, to create connections or associations between multiple units of information, compare and contrast incoming information, and further subdivide or compartmentalize it to more easily store information within memory. Internal dialog begins to form, allowing logic and rationale to be processed more internally without being nearly as reliant on physically acting out, testing, experiencing the results, or verbally processing to reach a conclusion. Thought experiments and philosophical considerations become more available.

In general, the operations of the left cortical hemisphere tend to take place in these more linear fashions that stress deductive logic and the categorization of information. The establishment of schools of thought and models of understanding forms out of this new cognitive agility, using so-called "left-brain" activities such as mathematics, the hard sciences, and most anything found within academia.

In contrast, the right hemisphere tends to stress more holistic, creative, intuitive, and supraverbal patterns. The right hemisphere intuits and creates the nature of the universe, while the left tends to have more of a role in creating the models and maps through which it can be understood and articulated.

Over time—both in the individual's lifetime experience, and in the larger historical scope of society—the understanding of the nature of reality seems to change when the maps and models used to describe it change. As these increase in complexity and become more refined in order to communicate more complete sets of useful information, the nature of things seems to change. In actuality, of course, our mental constructs of this nature are what change. This process has accelerated exponentially over time as our instruments of perception and analysis improve.

The microscope and telescope broadened our models of perception into new unseen worlds, allowing for the development of more refined explorations and understandings of quantum physics and astrophysics. The self-augmenting, exponential growth of technology that we now witness in real-time is happening at a much quicker pace than at any time in human history. That pace continues to accelerate, especially with external digital storage of information. The breadth of information available to humans is now unfathomable. Where early computers filled entire rooms, much of the population now carries a much more powerful device in their pocket, one that is capable of communicating around the world; taking pictures and videos that can be instantly uploaded and shared; and accessing the non-material database known as the internet, which contains the knowledge of nearly the entirety of human existence. All of this derives from the ability to use tools to perform work, and the use of symbols to convey signals and information.

The use of text messaging as a primary means of communication is an example of the semantic circuit in operation. Text messages exchange only symbols (with a consensus meaning) without the ability to extract meaning from other aspects of interpersonal communication such as tone, inflection, or body language—each of which speak to and are registered by the first, and in particular, second circuits. Without these, texting becomes a purely C-3 transference of linguistic information containing no emotional content other than that which the symbols convey. Because of this, much of the subtlety in exchanges can be lost and can easily result in misinterpretation. Emotional states or tone remain absent, and it is left to the receiver to interpret this. Projection can become a problem as the receiver places their own assumptions or emotional state onto the information. This pitfall to C-3 communication has been somewhat curbed by the use of proxy C-2 emotional/body language: emojis. These visually display facial expressions or other imagery so the receiver may have a fuller understanding of the desired message.

On the other hand, the masterful use of words and symbols have the ability to both denote complex intricacies of the sensorial world of the bio-survival circuit, and connotations of emotional tones that can arouse strong reactions in the individual. Novels, poems, music/lyrics, and stories can bring a person to tears. Descriptions of injustices toward others that one has never had direct interaction with can elicit deep and genuine grief or anger. Fear can be elicited through news stories and propaganda. Persuasive, beautiful, or charismatically arranged words can influence decision-making without any direct meaning or reference to actuality (e.g., as in marketing and advertising).

Despite the power inherent in the semantic circuit to strongly impact your state of being, the third circuit often gets overtaken by the lower circuits. If semantic circuit symbolism activates these lower circuits to elicit either survival anxiety or emotional engagement, or if a direct activation becomes prominent, these reactions will override the logical rationalism of the semantic circuit. In neurobiology, this is referred to as limbic hijacking—the activation of older brain structures which override the newer structures in the interest of self-preservation, even when unnecessary. Survival and emotions take precedence in most cases, and demand to be taken care of before resuming logical thinking. In these cases, whatever map/model is presented to alleviate this anxiety or unpleasant emotion will be more easily adopted as correct. In other words, ideas become easier to sell if they can appeal to resolving an activated lower circuit/older brain center, even if that imbalance was temporarily brought on by Circuit 3 symbolic input. As Wilson (1983) puts it: *"Whoever can scare people enough, can sell them quickly on any verbal map that seems to give them relief."*

As mentioned above, the semantic circuit imprints around the ages of 6–8 years old in many, although this may not always be the case, particularly if there has been significant trauma early in life that may hinder neurodevelopment. When imprinting does occur, those who take their strongest imprint in this circuit tend to take on a body shape that is thin and tall. This is the result of the majority of their metabolic energy being shunted upward toward the head to emphasize mental development. This is referred to as the ectomorphic (or cerebrotonic) body type.

Individuals with particularly strong third circuit imprints may ignore, or even become hostile toward functions of the bio-survival and emotional circuits that have not served them well. The drives of these circuits may be seen as illogical or even puzzling as they do not adhere to rational logic. Anything involving playfulness or doing something "just for fun" can seem silly. It doesn't make sense to participate because there is no logical reason to do so. Emotions, and the emotional reactions of others, may seem baffling and nonsensical. For this reason, they may avoid social situations that involve interacting with these elements.

Wilson notes that this imprint site correlates with the left cortical hemisphere, as well as being linked to the delicate muscles of the larynx and fine motor movements of the hands; this allows for verbal diversity and increased dexterity and tool use. According to Wilson, Leary (following the behaviorists) regarded the capacity for thinking as a form of sub-vocal speech with subtle vibrations of the opening and closing of the larynx during speech (Wilson, 2020:132). Dr. John B. Watson (the founder of behaviorism) said thought involved "internal speech" or "subvocal talking," while Dr. Lev Vygotsky conceptualized inner speech as an abbreviated form of external speech (Reese, 2000:10–12). This open-and-close mechanism in the three realms of fine motor movements, speech, and thought is further described by Wilson: *"Open the first to receive, close to grasp being the dawn of manual intelligence; open-and-close the larynx rhythmically being the mechanism of speech; open-and-close also being the digital computer device of frontal lobe thinking"* (Wilson, 2020:346). Recent research has demonstrated that subvocalizations occur in over 80% of trials of internal reading and thought generation (Cho et al., 2014). These traits are found in higher mammals, and seem most developed in humans and cetaceans (whales and dolphins). Fine dexterous movements are associated with the anterior parietal lobe area in the premotor and motor cortices, along with orofacial movements (relating to the jaw, mouth, and tongue) and breathing control (Newmeyer et al., 2007). Dr. Herman T. Epstein (2006) states that during this phase in neurodevelopment, new contacts can be made between concrete functions and sensorimotor functions. There has been evidence in functional MRI (fMRI) brain imaging studies of some correlation between persistent speech disorders and overt or subtle fine motor deficits with an increased activation of the cerebellum in those with such deficits (Redle et al., 2015).

Examples of how this circuit imprints on personality are the strictly rational approach of Spock in *Star Trek,* or Dr. Spencer Cooper from the sitcom *The Big Bang Theory* who continually becomes confused by the emotionally-based reactions of others in favor of his research in physics.

Those who have a strong third circuit and come to recognize how its model-building actually works to define one's reality—given how the experience of "reality" seems to be mentally processed internally—will later be able to redefine their own reality according to their own symbolic and linguistic terms. This will be explored further in Chapter X on Circuit 7, which is anchored to C-3. Wilson relates what society generally considers as "genius" to be someone capable of taking the multidimensional information of the higher circuits—which often defy words or proper description—and are able to successfully integrate this information enough to construct third circuit symbolic models and linguistic means of conveying the information. They are able to construct new maps and models of the nature of Universe that the lower circuits can make some sense of.

If the model is accurate and able to be successfully conveyed to others, then those able to do this define the cultural understanding of the nature of Universe. The language, metaphors, and definitions strongly influence how people think; thus, they contain a lot of influence, not only in the words used, but in *how* they are used and culturally defined. To redefine terms is to redefine perception.

The semantic circuit also relates to your ability to absorb, organize, and communicate information. You are capable of paying attention to the external world while interpreting and deriving concepts and categories of information from it. If you cannot assimilate this information in a timely manner, you may find yourself becoming mentally "constipated" until you can organize or "digest" it effectively.

Confusion results when your ideas, concepts, and thought patterns do not coincide with their true symbolic nature. Alli (1987) states, *"Our thinking is only as flexible as our minds are open to interpreting the Unknown as a value."* When you are unable to differentiate incoming information from internal biases of self-definition or models already in place, a discrepancy develops and mental clarity suffers. This is not to fault the existence of biases—these are normal based on past experiences—but instead cases where an individual remains unaware of, or actively denies having a bias at all. This can cause an inability to update models as new information comes in through a false sense of objectivity.

The swift rate at which information and linguistic communication occurs in the semantic circuit can become excessive. Internal thoughts and ideas can seem to come at a very fast pace. Speech may also become rapid, or one may display wild gesticulations of the hands (i.e., "speaking" with the hands). Humor or sarcasm may be used by those whose mind seems to race regularly as a reaction formation to the wide breadth of content in their head. When the semantic circuit is excessive, they may seem as though they are highly caffeinated—talking rapidly about ideas, concepts, and facts.

This circuit has a negatively entropic nature: information tends to accumulate and create greater degrees of order—rather than chaos—through the use of maps and models. This negatively entropic function acts as a purveyor of technology, curiosity, philosophy, and information-gathering, and continues exponentially. As we will see in the next chapter, evolution and society has a built-in brake for this runaway logic train with Circuit 4.

NEUROBIOLOGY OF CIRCUIT 3

Around 4–5 years of age, synthesis of new brain cells come to a virtual halt (Winick, 1968); it seems there is a cessation of activity of DNA polymerase (the enzyme involved in the replication of DNA), and an asymptote in total DNA per brain. Despite this, the brain increases about 30% in weight after that age, indicating an increased weight per brain cell due to the increased arborization of neurons in sending out longer and more branched axons and dendrites. This allows for the creation of functional connections among more distantly located groups of neurons (Conel, 1939–1963; Rabinowicz, 1979), and thus, more complex mental functioning.

The next stage of rapid brain growth begins around age six. Connections are made between already existing neuronal groups that associate previously separate mental and sensorimotor functions, thereby resulting in *"abstract sensori-motor capacities as well as concrete reasoning"* (Epstein, 2006:4). The thalamus acts as a driving force of cortical development. Another period of consolidation of these new functions seems to occur in the slow brain growth period between ages 8–10 years, overlapping with significant changes in myelination and cell body size in the prefrontal cortex (Galvan, 2017:127). Starting around age ten, the next rapid brain growth stage onsets with significant increases in neuronal arborization. This creates more contacts and associations between the earlier-organized networks with new contacts being possible between neuronal groups/networks subserving concrete reasoning.

This allows for concrete reasoning to expand into generalizations. In other words, it becomes possible to manifest what Piaget called formal (or abstract) reasoning that transcends direct experience to deal with the not-directly-observed groupings of those earlier concrete reasoning functions (Epstein, 2006:5).

At this time in development, there seems a tendency for sex differentiation. While total cerebral volume usually peaks just before puberty, biological females exhibit an earlier peak (at age 10.5) compared to biological males (who exhibit the peak at 14.5 on average (Giedd et al., 2015).

Hormonally, the primarily dormant hypothalamic-pituitary-gonadal (HPG) axis becomes activated around the time of puberty. "Permissive signals" allow (or stop inhibiting) pubertal onset. These signals include changing levels of melatonin, body fat, and leptin, all of which are related to weight and energy balance. Adrenarche is an early stage of sexual maturation during the stage of puberty that typically begins around 6–8 years of age. Here the adrenal glands secrete androgens such as dehydroepiandrosterone (DHEA) and dehydroepiandrosterone sulfate (DHEAS), that lead to androgenic effects of pubic hair and body odor (Dorn et al., 2006). DHEA levels were associated with increases in cortical thickness of prefrontal cortex regions, which are implicated in behavioral regulation between the ages of 4–13 years (Nguyen et al., 2013). Gonadarche typically begins around 8–10 years of age with the maturation of observable sexual characteristics including menarche and spermarche (Galvan, 2017:26).

It is believed that individuals do not go through puberty until they are energetically and metabolically capable of doing so (Sisk & Foster, 2004). The "constitutional delay of puberty" may occur due to factors such as diet and physical activity. Those with eating disorders—such as anorexia or bulimia nervosa—may display elevated levels of DHEA and DHEAS (Monteleone et al., 2001) along with decreased levels of luteinizing hormone, follicle-stimulating hormone (FSH), and estradiol (Devlin et al., 1989). Stress can directly influence these hormonal activations. Elevated release of cortisol (the "stress hormone") activates the HPG axis with evidence that those growing up in homes with an absent parent (Ellis, 2004), or were physically or sexually abused in childhood (Mendle et al., 2011) tend to reach puberty earlier in life. Early pubertal maturation has been linked to a broad range of psychopathological symptoms during adolescence. Biological males have shown higher rates of depression, worry, fear, self-injury, social withdrawal, aggression, angry outbursts, law-breaking, or hyperactivity; biological females have shown higher rates of depressive disorders, substance disorders, eating disorders, and disruptive behavioral disorders under these conditions (Graber, 2013).

CIRCUIT 3 ENERGY

QUALITIES OF BALANCED CIRCUIT 3 ENERGY

- Outgoing, cheerful; respect for self & others
- Strong sense of personal power; abundant physical energy
- Emotional stability; strong metabolism, digestion & constitution
- Dynamism, perseverance, achievement
- Skillful, intelligent, relaxed, spontaneous; takes on new challenges
- Enjoys physical activity & good food
- Sexual: cares about one's partner; sense of responsibility toward mate and children; uninhibited, relaxed; can show emotional warmth

QUALITIES OF EXCESSIVE CIRCUIT 3 ENERGY

- Overly intellectual, judgmental; workaholic, perfectionist
- Jealousy, judgment, criticism
- May need drugs to relax
- As employer: demanding; as employee: resents authority
- Superficial superiority complex with hidden inferiority complex
- Prone to nausea, vomiting; easily startled; hyperactivity to sound
- Sexual: demanding, tests one's partner; complains about relationship a lot; rarely fulfilled

QUALITIES OF DEFICIENT CIRCUIT 3 ENERGY

- Depressed, low energy, apathy; hyperemotionality
- Confused
- Lacks confidence/motivation; inability to follow through
- Worries about what others will think; feels controlled by others
- Poor digestion, overall health
- Afraid of being alone
- General intolerance
- Sexual: insecure, needs constant reassurance; jealous, distrustful

CIRCUIT 3 ACTIVATION
CIRCUIT 3 ACTIVATING ACTIVITIES

Activities that activate higher-order cognitive functions work the third circuit. Some examples include:

- Making lists, schematics, charts, or diagrams
- Studying/research, particularly logical topics such as mathematics or the sciences
- Writing/storytelling
- Poems, fables, proverbs, jokes, essays, books
- Word games and trivia questions
- Philosophize, preferably with as many people with differing views as possible
- Problem-solving and challenging oneself by breaking patterns and finding a solution
- Puzzle/problem-solving, video games—integrates hand-eye coordination

CIRCUIT 3 ACTIVATING SUBSTANCES

CNS stimulants, caffeine, nicotine, sugar, chocolate, ginseng, guarana, ginkgo, bacoba, yerba mate, gotu cola, ginger, fennel (stimulant)

CIRCUIT 3 REGULATING SUBSTANCES

Licorice, lemon balm, yarrow, garden sage, red sage, thyme, purple cone-flower, spilanthes, figwort (scrofularia), Egyptian onion, German chamomile, dandelion, linden, rhodiola, peppermint, green/black tea, rosemary

Caffeine is a central nervous system stimulant that can amplify attributes of the third circuit. Most stimulants tend to activate the semantic circuit. Caffeine has become a nearly ubiquitous substance as one of the world's most consumed drugs in a society that demands mental clarity and heavy, linear, rational thinking. This may, in fact, be the most widespread chemical addiction in our culture, due to high Circuit 3 cultural demands being so entrenched, normalized and even expected. Thus, this dependence on caffeine goes largely unrecognized or ignored unless one experiences withdrawal symptoms, cardiac arrhythmia/heart palpitations, insomnia, or other negative effects.

Caffeine has three notable mechanisms on the nervous system that can impact mood, memory, processing speed, and attentiveness (Fiani et al., 2021):

- Adenosine receptor antagonism: adenosine receptors regulate the release of neurotransmitters that play an important role in the regulation of sleep, arousal, cognition, memory, and learning. The blockage of adenosine receptors indirectly affects the release of neurotransmitters such as norepinephrine, dopamine, acetylcholine, serotonin, glutamate, and gamma-aminobutyric acid (GABA). An influx in these neurotransmitters alters mood, memory, alertness, and cognitive function.

- Intercellular calcium mobilization: Calcium is released via synaptic transmission into the peripheral and central nervous systems. Low concentrations of caffeine show an increase in the uptake and release of calcium through the endoplasmic reticulum. Higher concentrations show an inhibition of calcium uptake by the endoplasmic reticulum.

- Inhibition of phosphodiesterases: Caffeine slows the breakdown of the chemical messenger cyclic adenosine monophosphate (cAMP), which then stimulates the release of hormones such as dopamine, epinephrine, and norepinephrine that can alter mood, memory, alertness, and cognitive function.

INTEGRATION INTERVENTION MODEL CONSIDERATIONS
CIRCUIT 7 ACTIVATING ACTIVITIES

Circuit 3 and Circuit 7 are vertically connected, with C-3 acting as an anchor to C-7 shock experiences. Circuit 7 shocks may broaden symbolic-linguistic mechanization or treadmilling by eliciting experiences that may be ineffable, nonlinear, paradoxical, or multidimensional as well as cross-cultural neurogenetic circuitry. These experiences can demonstrate a deeper reality and may potentially open to the mysteries of Universe that can get shut out by the hard-lined, linear, compartmentalized logic of Circuit 3. According to Wilson *"To turn off circuit III, the yogin stops the mechanism of digital computation cold, by dharana (concentration on one image) or mantra (one sound)."* (2022, p. 346)

CLINICAL APPROACH CONSIDERATIONS
(REFER TO RECOMMENDED READING FOR RESOURCES)

- Cognitive Behavioral Therapy (CBT); "talk therapy"

Leary's Bio-Evolutionary Stages 7–9		
Stage 7	Laryngeal-Manual Symbolic Receptivity	The Third Circuit emerged phylogenetically when the left hemisphere of the cortex developed its specialized function of mediating dexterity, manipulation of artifacts, and management of the nine muscles of the larynx which perform symbolic speech. The paleolithic hominid.
		The first stage of symbolic intelligence is receptive, imitative, self-centered. The adult who uses symbols irrationally, as magical repetitious tokens.
		At the first symbolic stage there is no inventiveness, no conceptual thinking, no engineered manipulation. Repetition is the mode of thought and action. Satisfaction comes from grasping the given symbol. Rote performance. ["Student mind"; the knowledge "consumer" — Wilson, 2020, p. 332]
Stage 8	Laryngeal-Manual Symbolic Intelligence	As the third circuit emerges, the child quickly learns to perceive the world through manipulations of the laryngeal cartilages and the manual muscles.
		In stage 8, the brain integrates symbolic-signals—relates, evaluates, coordinates symbolism. The importance and pervasiveness of the laryngeal-manual, cerebrotonic reality has not been understood by psychologists. Sanity and survival depend on the learned ability to adequately manipulate the vocal chords. All thought, and almost all mental consciousness, is performed by silent laryngeal muscle movement.

		The Eighth Stage of species and individual evolution concerns the executive mastery of these two precise muscle systems—larynx and hand—mediated by the left hemisphere of the brain. ["Rational intelligence; programmed learning" — Wilson, 2020, p. 332]
Stage 9	Symbolic Manipulation	Symbol inventiveness and creativity. The breaking up of routinized symbol sequences and the creating of new symbols and symbol connections. The Bronze-Iron Age hominid is the prototype. Chopping, mining, melting the natural forms. The creative use of fire. Creative craftmanship. At certain epochs of history, social groups and individuals have specialized in the static, routinized symbol sequences and creating new fusions. During the pre-adolescent stage, each individual develops their own style of communication. Some are genetically pre-programmed to play this symbol-rearranger role; however, each individual passes through this stage in the cycle of personal evolution. ["Fusion with the historical mind" — Wilson, 2020, p. 332]

Table 7: *Leary's Bio-Evolutionary Stages 7–9*

Chapter VI

Circuit 4 (C-4):
Sexuality, Morality, & Community

Socio-Sexual Domestication Circuit (Leary)
Sociosexual Circuit (Wilson)

"We human beings are social beings. We come into the world as the result of others' actions. We survive here in dependence on others. Whether we like it or not, there is hardly a moment of our lives when we do not benefit from others' activities. For this reason, it is hardly surprising that most of our happiness arises in the context of our relationships with others."
— Dalai Lama

"There is no morality, no moral decision, without freedom. There is only morality when you can choose, and you cannot choose if you are forced."
— Dr. Carl Gustav Jung

The social-sexual circuit develops, and initially imprints around the time of adolescence, and acts to slow down the negatively entropic nature of Circuit 3. Where curiosity, discovery, and scientific innovation progresses at an exponential rate with third circuit frontal lobe dominance, the fourth circuit turns the individual's focus from these matters to those of interpersonal relationships and social interactions. Peer groups, along with emotional and developing sexual attractions to others, become prominent.

This circuit seems primarily defined by your ability to relate to others. When the foundations of the first three circuits have been established (i.e., safety [C-1], emotionality and sense of self [C-2], and model-building to comprehend the world [C-3]), the next natural step becomes extending beyond self and the internally generated models to emphasize sharing and interacting with others (C-4). There is also a strong urge to seek a feeling of belonging to something other than, or bigger than self. While an individual chooses what type of group or social dynamic suits them, previous life experiences may guide the direction toward which one moves. This allows for further validation of these prior life experiences, and the ability to learn from the shared experiences and reality tunnels of others.

Wade attributes this transition to the dawning realization of death-as-certainty, rather than something that happens, but remains a nebulous possibility. Understanding the concept of death, and "knowing" it as an inevitability, seems to propel the individual into further external interaction with the world—possibly as comfort in shared experience and the avoidance of feeling alone in the face of the possibility of lonely death. Many developmental models of psychology describe this stage in various ways—and go no further. This is likely due to the fact that nearly all models, even those that *do* continue further, maintain that the majority of adults develop and operate at this level most of the time, with higher states being fleeting anomalies or are not recognized at all. As such, the first four circuits have been considered the mainstream consciousness within civilized cultures.

Alli (1987) notes three sub-phases within C-4 that an individual goes through. Although there are distinct, progressive steps, the primary driving force behind their development remains the same. The first is adolescence, or what he refers to as the "Big Kid" stage. This is primarily characterized by self-indulgence, egotism, and narcissism. Motives and goals are mostly self-based, and often result in actions considered "socially irresponsible." Within developmental psychology, it is generally accepted that adolescence acts as a mechanism to establish independence (Schegel, 2000). The brain seems to be built to facilitate the important task of transitioning from a state of dependence on caregivers to one of relative independence (Galván,

2017:175). According to Alli, this social irresponsibility can be a result of two different factors—*genetically*, in which fluctuations in hormones influence behavior; or *consciously*, through analyzing adolescent characteristics to mimic and maintain these traits. This is referred to as "neoteny," and can be defined as the person who strives and consciously acts to remain "young at heart" regardless of physical age.

This "Big Kid" stage tends to entail a high degree of what may be considered social immaturity, particularly in recent history. According to Dr. Jerome Bruner (1972), "re-interpretive behavior" leads to human innovation through extensive exploration of the limits on one's ability to interact with the world. For example, contemporary youth experience a period of extended immaturity in the form of "play" and schooling. This may be the result of the increasing complexity of our world and its technologies, which demand an increasing intricacy of skill, and a more exhaustive set of abilities. It has been argued that this may serve the adaptive purpose of extending the period of plasticity (Steinberg, 2014:9–10)—that is, the more complex technology and society becomes, the more it may demand a longer period of "playfulness" or "immaturity" to prolong proliferation of new neural connections.

Adolescence also seems to mark the period in development in which the onset of psychiatric disorders is most prevalent (Jones, 2013). It has been suggested that brain changes in regions involved in emotional processing and behavioral regulation contribute to this (Paus et al., 2013).

Following the adolescent stage comes the "adulthood" stage, defined as the setting of social responsibilities, maintenance of a regular schedule or routine, and an emphasis on keeping events organized according to linear time and cultural expectations. This includes moving into a parental and family role. It is here that Alli notes the influence of the dawning awareness of predetermined mortality. This is also the stage in which many individuals become socially "domesticated" as their previously irresponsible behavior becomes more tame and regimented in accordance with cultural expectations.

The third progression is into collectivization. Here the individual seeks out and identifies with something larger than the self, and larger than the immediate family dynamic of the adulthood stage. The individual often joins groups or extended "families" which have their own structured moral codes and social rules. These groups may be as diverse as churches, military or veterans' groups, communes, gangs, support groups, or subcultures/gatherings. To belong within the group, one often sacrifices individual differences and their own sense of "right and wrong" in lieu of the socially defined collective moral code.

Wade (1996) refers to this stage as "conformist consciousness" and applies labels such as "institutional," "conventional," and "traditional" to choices in one's actions. All of these terms express the compulsion for an externally established organization or peer group to act as a moral guidepost of choices. With this, one may develop a prejudice or fear toward those outside the group. This may also elicit a feeling of projected anger or even hatred towards these outsiders in an "us" versus. "them" dichotomy.

Approval and acceptance within the group becomes heavily sought after, particularly among figures of authority. Meeting expectations of appearance, behavior, and preferences can become preoccupation. While these motives may not be ideal, the growing awareness of the power of appearance can engender them with a newfound understanding of self-control.

From this stage, within the confines of the social arena, the first signs of true personal authority begin to develop, as does an objective empathy that emerges as the world becomes increasingly viewed beyond the solely individual perspective. One takes in many more intersubjective perspectives, all of which hold some sense of validity. This allows one to step beyond personal experience, while distinguishing that which formed within their own perspective, permitting them to become independent from it. One becomes able to observe their perspective rather than being fully immersed in it.

Due to a heavy focus on external validation, acceptance, and conforming to a group expectation or moral set, feelings of guilt or shame also become a prominent component at this stage. Wilson (1983) states that this is to such a degree that this level could almost be named the "guilt circuit," as people spend an ample amount of time hiding their true selves in lieu of the socially expected and accepted one. The individual may begin doing things because they "should," rather than doing what they want or even what they feel is "right." This may be justified under the rationale of "everyone is doing it," or the fear of judgment by others should they not adhere to the collective expectations.

Guilt and shame become a means of maintaining duties and obligations to groups or authority figures, while deterring non-conformity and maintaining *status quo*. A person's sense of right may become defined by what ultimately contributes to the group and sustains the social order.

> *"Shame corrodes the very part of us that believes we are capable of change."*
> — Brene Brown

Alli distinguishes between two types of guilt: animal guilt and conditioned guilt. Animal guilt describes cases in which there is a direct, intuitive sense that something is felt or known as being "wrong" *before* performing the action. This is self-knowledge of right and wrong—the internal moral compass. On the other hand, conditioned guilt is generally felt *after* the actions are performed due to mental processing and reaction to a particular moral program. This second type of guilt may end up building into resentment over these feelings. It is this latter type of guilt that becomes a major factor of the fourth circuit. If the guilt is unjustified, or seems to occur for no apparent reason, it will develop into self-consciousness with feelings of embarrassment or social ineptitude. If this continues unregulated, passive-aggressive or unconscious manipulative behavior can become commonplace.

Author, therapist, and life coach Mike Gathers places an emphasis on the judgment of others as one of the most notable telltale signs of fourth circuit disintegration that reverberates into even further systemic disintegration:

"We see a top-down relational approach...where Fourth circuit judgements give way to third circuit projections which give way to second circuit shame and first circuit fear. By starting with noticing our judgements, we can begin the process of unpacking deeper disintegrated material." *(2021:11)*

Wilson notes that this circuit becomes activated and imprinted as one reaches puberty and the genetic code awakens hormonal shifts, and further develops the organs of sexual reproduction. Further, bio-evolutionarily, it *"mediates strutting, display, courtship, mating, nest-building, care of the egg, etc."* (2020:135). Significant social transitions—such as a change to a new school—can also imprint social components of the circuit. These imprints can be very acute, and the first sexual symbols or experiences of the individual will, in most cases, go on to define the nervous system's sexual arousal mechanisms in a fixed way that will likely remain throughout life. Any sex role remains possible prior to imprinting, but once imprinting occurs, a particular role often becomes solidified. This includes matters of sexual preference, including physical features such as hair or eye color, body shapes, etc. This imprint, if negative, may result in sexual dysfunctions or unpleasurable attitudes toward sexuality. Sex aversion or repulsion may be examples of this. This matter of sexuality differs greatly from the instinctive reproductive drive of Circuit 2. Here, there is an emphasis on the ability to connect with another human. The ability to connect is patently lacking in the highly self-driven second circuit consciousness drives where the needs or emotions of the other individual(s) involved are not given consideration.

Primitive cultures recognize how positive or negative experiences can influence nervous system development that could impact lifelong tendencies. Thus, they hold initiations (rites of passage) during the critical time of imprint vulnerability so the individual may imprint culturally desired traits. Many cultures do this during other imprint periods; however, the passage into adolescence or adulthood (and, thus, into one's adult role within their society) seems most widespread.

Wilson also states that those who take their largest neurological imprint at the social-sexual circuit tend to take on physical traits that emphasize sexuality, or those that would be cross-culturally seen as beautiful, attractive, or desirable. This strong imprint floods their body with such a large quantity of sexual hormones that they seem to continually give off mating signals.

Within the brain, the prefrontal lobe—which is evolutionarily the most recent to develop in humans—becomes particularly active in creating new neural connections during this period. Wilson and Wade both cite the left neocortex with correlations to sexuality. Reward systems involving dopamine and oxytocin releases from human contact (e.g., hugging, hand-holding, and embracing) are of particular significance. The prefrontal cortices have been correlated with complex cognitive tasks known under the collective umbrella of "executive function." This includes decision-making, planning, expressions of personality, and regulation of social behavior. The primary directive of executive function seems to be the orchestration of thoughts and actions with internally generated goals. An influential integrative theory posits that neural activity of the prefrontal cortex yields bias signals that *"guide the flow of neural activity along pathways that establish the proper mappings between inputs (from the environment), internal states, and outputs (behavior) needed to perform a given task"* (Miller & Cohen, 2001:171). *"A research study has shown the activities and programs that best improve executive function in children and adolescents includes computer-based training and traditional martial arts, with strong evidence for aerobics, yoga, and mindfulness"* (Diamond, 2012).

Rule learning is also a key function of the PFC. Wade argues that at the conformist level of consciousness, many logical inconsistencies exist. Conceptual constructs remain limited to absolute and dualistic thinking as the limbic system's influence remains apparent in the inability to tolerate ambiguity. Both the left frontal hemisphere and the limbic system seem very active within this circuit. This can create internal conflicts between your cognitive imperative and emotional reflex. This would be the ongoing tug-of-war many may feel between head and heart.

Compromising parts of your identity to external social structures, and relying on authority figures to provide guidance can be the result of an internal conflict and lack of clarity at this stage. The Self may become an abstraction capable of external manipulation. Social identities become relied upon and defined by the group dynamic. There tends to be a general appeal to the *position of authority* and whoever happens to hold that position instead the one particular person in that position. If one authority figure becomes replaced by a new individual, it is generally of no consequence to the social-sexual circuit so long as *someone* holds the position of authority to uphold the structure. This reliance on external groupthink can be taken to such a degree that an individual may belong to multiple groups who hold opposing dogmatic views without it seeming to cause any upset or dissonance to their psyche.

MENTALIZING/THEORY OF MIND

Theory of mind (mentalizing), refers to the ability to assign mental states—including beliefs, intents, desires, pretending, knowledge, and sarcasm—to oneself and others; that is, an understanding that others have beliefs, desires, intentions, and perspectives that are different from your own (Carlson et al., p. 213).

Brain regions activated during mentalizing tasks in adult participants during fMRI included the medial prefrontal cortex (mPFC), the anterior cingulate cortices (ACCs), temporoparietal junction (TPJ), and the posterior cingulate cortices (PCCs) (Amodio & Frith, 2006). These regions are also engaged for other cognitive operations not involving mentalizing. Activation of the mPFC, ACC, and PCC become engaged in self-perception and perspective-taking in typically-developing adolescents and adults. Activation of the TPJ during mentalizing has been observed in adulthood, but does not seem present in younger children and adolescents who do not consistently exhibit TPJ recruitment (Gweon et al., 2013).

Mirror neuron systems are regions in the inferior frontal gyrus and inferior parietal lobule that are active during the perception and execution of actions. The mirror neuron system co-activates to the actions, intentions, and emotions of both the self and others (Pfeifer et al., 2008).

Over time, a stronger sense of identity and agency forms as interpersonal relations become more stable, and those proving reliable are more likely to be maintained throughout times of change and life challenges.

Once one has attained the adult sex role, this often coincides with finding a mate and reproducing. As noted earlier, this frequently acts as a type of societal brake for the philosophical musings and curiosities of the third circuit. Cultural demands and the needs of children may consume much of the time and energy previously available for such ponderings and activities. For this reason, some philosophical or spiritual teachings expound a vow of celibacy to deter from what Wilson relates to becoming *"trapped in the wheel of karma."* Interestingly, Alli suggests a vow of celibacy for three months or more as a means of re-imprinting negative sexual imprints, and establishing desired sexual patterns thenceforth.

IMPACTS OF SOCIAL EXCLUSION & REJECTION

Isolation or social exclusion can have drastic effects on the psyche and the nervous system. In situations of social exclusion, the neural response has consistently demonstrated activation of the anterior cingulate cortices, medial prefrontal cortices, and the ventrolateral prefrontal cortices (VLPFC). Youth who experience chronic rejection show heightened activation of the anterior cingulate cortices (ACC) during social inclusion. The ACC has previously been implicated in conflict monitoring, expectation violation, pain, unfairness, and social exclusion in adults (Somerville et al., 2006). Evidence shows that social deprivation may also have a direct impact on the length of telomeres, implying it may have a negative impact on overall lifespan (Drury et al., 2012).

Thoughts of, or rumination on "What do others think of me?" has shown activation of brain regions involved in perspective-taking, such as the temporoparietal junction (TPJ), the posterior superior temporal sulcus (pSTS), and those involved in affective states, including the dorsal ACC (dACC), anterior insula, and amygdala, which have been associated with feelings of fitting in with others (Burklund et al., 2007).

NEUROBIOLOGY OF CIRCUIT 4

Adolescents exhibit an interesting pattern of activation and behavior that is distinct from both children and adults. Experience-dependent neural plasticity appears to peak in adolescence and young adulthood, and shows a gradual but consistent decrease with age (Oberman & Pascual-Leone, 2013). Brain regions implicated in emotional processing, reward processing, and motivation undergo significant change during adolescence. Significant reorganization of cortical-striatal circuitry occurs—in particular, those supporting social behaviors relevant to mate selection and the act of mating (Sisk & Zehr, 2005). While adolescents outperform children related to distractibility, and do just as well as adults, they seem to require a broader magnitude of activation in the dorsolateral prefrontal cortex (dl-PFC) responsible for executive function, cognitive flexibility, inhibition, and abstract reasoning (Olesen et al., 2007).

Total cerebral volume, including the PFC, reaches 95% of its maximum size by kindergarten, increases slightly during middle childhood, and then declines through one's 20s (Giedd & Rapoport, 2010). Generally speaking, there tends to be an increase in white matter volumes and inverted U-shaped trajectories in both cortical and subcortical grey matter volumes in adolescence. That is, there is a marked increase to a peak point after which there seems a marked decrease, with peak numbers occurring at different times in different brain regions. White matter (consisting of glia and myelinated axons) volumes increase about 1–2% per year throughout childhood and adolescence (Giedd et al., 2015). Grey matter peaks the earliest in the primary sensorimotor area, and the latest in higher-order association areas (dl-PFC, inferior parietal cortex, and superior temporal gyrus). As children transition into puberty, subcortical regions—such as the striatum and thalamus—also exhibit an inverted U-shaped developmental trajectory (Raznahan et al., 2014).

While a significant number of new neural connection proliferate during this time, significant neural pruning also occurs simultaneously. By pruning away ineffective or no longer necessary synapses, more metabolic energy is freed up, and can be devoted to the more valuable neurons and synapses.

These become more stabilized and strengthened through increased mye-lination around the neurons (Galván, 2017:129).

Three core systems become reorganized at puberty:

- Processing basic attention and visual orientation. This includes the inferior occipital cortex (occipital face area [OFA]), superior temporal sulcus (STS), auxiliary visuoperceptual regions of the visual cortex, and the posterior fusiform gyrus (fusiform face area)—the latter being inactive before puberty. This reorganization allows for better "read-ing" of faces, emotional expressions, and affect (Golarai et al., 2007; Golarai et al., 2010).

- "Mentalizing" (the ability to understand the mental state of yourself and others). This includes the medial prefrontal cortex (mPFC), tem-poroparietal junction (TPJ), anterior temporal cortex (ATC), and cin-gulate gyrus. During self-reflection, this network has greater activation and is associated with more accurate self-appraisals than adults. This suggests that adolescents have more activation of the mPFC than adults when anticipating the emotional responses of others to social emotions such as embarrassment and guilt (Burnett et al., 2011).

- Emotion processing. Includes: amygdala, insula, striatum, and limbic structures that support emotional discrimination, affect, and threat (Burnett et al., 2011). Communication among these regions was enhanced in biological females with higher levels of estradiol and more advanced pubertal status (Klapwijk et al., 2013).

According to Dr. Adriana Galván,

"Asserting that all children and adolescents struggle with cognitive control or that they lack self-control due to an immature prefrontal cortex is an oversimplification... Cognitive control of behavior is supported by a wide network of brain regions, including prefrontal and parietal cortices, that interact with subcortical areas, including the striatum, thalamus, cerebellum, and brain stem, forming a circuitry that supports top-down control of behavior." (2017:145)

The amygdala also seems to play an important role in shaping adolescent behavioral and neural response to the social world, so much so that it has been called an *"agent of change in adolescent neural networks"* (Scherf et al., 2013). It helps to strengthen other key brain regions of sociality, and recognizes their positions in response to the dynamic needs of each developmental stage. In this sense, the amygdala has been said to have a "hub-like architecture" as it is extensively interconnected with the vast majority of cortical and subcortical regions that support social and emotional processing (Scherf et al., 2013). Interactions between the amygdala and the mPFC are fundamental to emotion processing, regulation (Wager et al., 2008), and extinction (Hartley et al., 2011), with the PFCs possibly helping to regulate (or decrease) the amygdala's reactivity to emotion.

THEORIES OF BEHAVIOR

There are several models of adolescent development and behavior as the brain goes through significant changes at the neuronal level.

- **Dual systems model:** This model postulates that risky decision-making stems from the interaction of the *socio-emotional system* (comprised of the amygdala, ventral striatum, orbitofrontal cortex (OFC), and mPFC) and the *cognitive control system* (comprised of the lateral prefrontal and parietal cortices). A surge of dopaminergic activity in the socioemotional system is said to lead to increases in sensation-seeking and risky decisions as it outpaces the development and engagement of the cognitive control system (Steinberg et al., 2008).

- **Triadic model:** This model postulates that three functional neural systems (the PFC, the striatum, and the amygdala) are primarily involved—the PFC being implicated in the regulation of motivational behavior, the striatum involved in the motivation aspects of the model, and the amygdala involved in the emotional components of behavior (Ernst et al., 2014).

- **Imbalance model:** The imbalance model does not focus on specific brain regions; instead it attributes adolescent behavior to coordinated integration of multiple brain circuits, dynamic neurochemical connectivity, and functional interactions across brain circuit development needed for self-control (Casey et al., 2016).

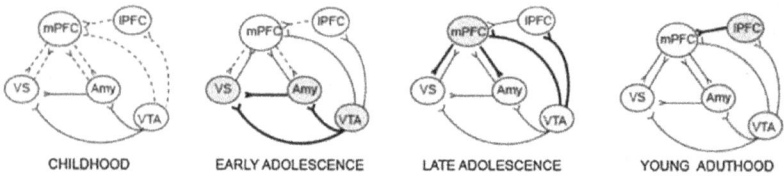

CHILDHOOD   EARLY ADOLESCENCE   LATE ADOLESCENCE   YOUNG ADUTHOOD

Figure 3: *Development of Communication Between Brain Regions from Childhood into Young Adulthood* (Sommerville & Casey, 2010)

THE REWARD SYSTEM: STRIATUM & DOPAMINE

Findings from both performance-based and passive tasks support the hypothesis that disproportionately increased activation of reward systems characterizes adolescent neurodevelopment (Chambers et al., 2003). Animal models suggests that the dopamine system undergoes significant remodeling during puberty.

> *"In a key region called the striatum, dopamine levels increase during adolescence and dopamine receptor expression increases from pre-adolescence to adolescence... Dopamine receptor overproduction [is] followed by pruning during adolescence...about 35–40% greater than seen in adulthood... [with a] longer sustained dopamine release following a social interaction." (Galván, 2017:154)*

Dopamine neurons fire with experiences that include rewards, food or drug consumption, social interactions, and unexpected events or stimuli (surprise!). A neural network called the cortico-ventral basal ganglia circuit lies at the heart of this. This network includes the ventral striatum, ACC, orbitofrontal cortex (OFC), ventral pallidum, and midbrain dopamine neurons with auxiliary structures, including the dl-PFC, amygdala, hippocampus, thalamus, habenula, and parts of the brainstem helping to regulate the reward neurocircuitry (Haber & Knutson, 2010).

During adolescence, risky decision-making activation occurs in the ventral striatum and other mesolimbic circuitry, creating a sense of reward from the behavior. This has been found to elicit an even greater activation in the presence of peers (Chein et al., 2011). Adolescents who reported a decline in risky behavior, showed greater negative coupling between the ventral striatum and mPFC. Adolescents better able to regulate the ventral striatum via the mPFC were shown to exhibit decreases in risky behavior (Qu et al., 2015).

When *actual* outcomes do not match *expected* outcomes in an experience, it is processed by what's called "predictive error signaling," which seems to be coded by dopamine cells. This mismatch provides novel information for the person, who then learns something new. Adolescents have shown to have a higher responsiveness to dopaminergic prediction error. That is, compared to adults, adolescents are more responsive to unpredictable outcomes in terms of modifying behavior in response to the new information (van Duijvenvoorde et al., 2012).

CIRCUIT 4 ENERGY

QUALITIES OF BALANCED CIRCUIT 4 ENERGY

- Friendly, outgoing
- Compassionate, selfless action, humanitarian
- Creativity; spiritual love, spiritual charity
- Sees the good in everyone; desires to nurture others; active in community
- In touch with feelings, empathetic: may feel their aches and pains
- Discriminating
- Sexual: able to surrender/merge in a love relationship; desires oneness of the body, mind, and soul; strong willpower (easier to wait for the right partner)

QUALITIES OF EXCESSIVE CIRCUIT 4 ENERGY

- Demanding, possessive, overly critically
- Tense between the shoulder blades

- Moody, melodramatic
- May use money or sex to control people
- Attitude of a martyr
- Master of conditional love ("I'll love you if...")
- Withholds love to get desired behavior

QUALITIES OF DEFICIENT CIRCUIT 4 ENERGY

- Feels sorry for oneself, or the inability to love self, which leads to insincerity and co-dependence
- Insecure, indecisive; may isolate
- Paranoid
- Feels unworthy of love; terrified of rejection, needs constant reassurance
- Difficulty reaching out
- Afraid of letting go, being free, getting hurt, family members getting hurt, abandonment

CIRCUIT 4 ACTIVATION
CIRCUIT 4 ACTIVATING ACTIVITIES

- Hugging/reaching outward
- Making new friends
- Determines qualities and virtues personally desired in friends/confidants
- Attending social events
- Trying something new
- Breaking previously held taboos
- Couples or group dancing or music making
- Communal storytelling
- Other communal affairs

CIRCUIT 4 ACTIVATING SUBSTANCES

MDMA/empathogens, oxytocin, cayenne, arjuna, hawthorn, chamomile, lavender, rose, lemon verbena, lemongrass, winter savory, balloon flower

MDMA has been referred to as an "empathogen" (Adamson & Metzner, 1988; Metzner, 1983) or "entactogen" (Nichols, 1986), referring to its tendency to increase empathy for self and others, as well as to increase self-awareness or the ability to "touch within," respectively. General effects have been noted to include a lowered defensiveness and fear of emotional injury (Greer, 1985), a general sense of well-being (Downing, 1985), and a *"shift in perspective, a reframing of...belief"* (Adamson & Metzner, 1988). It may also catalyze access to meaningful spiritual and transpersonal experiences, and a sense of healing on the non-verbal level (Grob & Grigsby, 2021).

MDMA stimulates release and inhibits reuptake of the monoamines serotonin, dopamine, and norepinephrine, with its most potent effects on serotonin (de la Torre et al, 2000) with an affinity for the 5-HT$_{2A}$ receptor. This particular receptor is discussed in more detail in Chapter IX (Circuit 6). MDMA also increases serum levels of oxytocin and arginine vasopressin (AVP) (Hysek et al., 2014). Some studies suggest that MDMA increases interpersonal trust, and decreases reactivity to threatening cues (such as angry faces), effects thought to be at least partially mediated by oxytocin release and monoamine activation. MDMA has also been shown to decrease cerebral blood flow in the amygdala and hippocampus while increasing blood flow in the PFC (Carhart-Harris et al., 2015). The same study also showed decreased resting-state functional connectivity between midline cortical regions (ventromedial prefrontal cortex [vm-PFC]) and medial temporal lobe (MTL) regions including the posterior cingulate. There was also increased connectivity between the amygdala and hippocampus, which has been postulated to allow an "unconstrained style of cognition" and "liberation of cognition and imagination" that may account for observations in MDMA-assisted psychotherapy sessions working with post-traumatic stress disorder (PTSD; Carhart-Harris et al., 2015:558).

INTEGRATION INTERVENTION MODEL CONSIDERATIONS
CIRCUIT 8 ACTIVATING ACTIVITIES

Circuit 4 and Circuit 8 are vertically connected, with Circuit 4 acting as an anchor to Circuit 8 shock experiences. Circuit 8 activities and exercises may facilitate Circuit 4 imprints becoming malleable and receptive to conscious change/re-imprinting.

CLINICAL APPROACH CONSIDERATIONS
(REFER TO RECOMMENDED READING FOR RESOURCES)

- Group work/therapies
- Support Groups

Leary's Bio-Evolutionary Stages 10–12		
Stage 10	Sexual-Domestic Receptivity	The Fourth Circuit is activated at puberty with the new neural wiring mediating a more complex level of contelligence, and creates a new reality dominated by reproductive and domesticated sublimation of sexuality.

In the evolution of the species, Stage 10 emerges when Iron Age technology makes possible the mobility of armed bands which initiates the proto-imperial predator state-male-oriented, macho, free-booting, warlike, lawless, rapacious. This Homeric phylogenetic stage is recapitulated in adolescence. The first adolescent stage of neurosexuality is exploratory, receptive, self-centered, self-defined, orgasm-oriented, and narcissistically undomesticated.

Contelligence is obsessed with courting rituals, display, sexual exploration—or, if the genetic template is neuter and/or the sexual imprint is renunciation, the energy is diverted towards intense commitment or non-genital social roles, adolescent idealizations, obsessive anti-sexuality, romantic displacements.

The Fourth Circuit defines social-sex roles which differ as much as the caste types in an insect colony. A large percentage of humans are not designed for procreation and parenthood, but are neurogenetically wired to play other domesticated roles. Phylogenetically, the Fourth Circuit emerged when homo sapiens evolved from the late Bronze-Iron-Age social group in which there was no role differen- |

		tiation among males or among females (except for power-status), and developed the complex social structures of urban civilization.
Stage 11	Sexual Domestication, Parenthood	The Fourth Circuit creates the parent-family-oriented social reality. A complex, genetic pre-programming defines the kind and amount of social-sex types necessary for the preservation of the extended-family. Just as the "DNA brain" of the insect colony activates the appropriate number of workers, drones, and warriors, so does the "species brain" of homo sapiens produce the breeding types of humans.
		Some are sexually neuter, others are designed for parenthood. The variety of genetic and neural human types causes considerable confusion and social conflict. Laws, ethical codes, and educational methods assume a homogeneity which does not exist. The fourth imprint channels and conceals these genetic differences by hooking the nervous system to standard social models. The human is domesticated via imprint to respond in conventional family patterns. At the time of impregnation, powerful bio-chemical and neurological changes occur which produce nesting and child-protective responses. Even those who are not parents are programmed to value and moralize the welfare of children.

Stage 12	Collective Socialization	"Collective socialization is obviously the most effective survival device." In the collective society, individualism, romantic love, and familial loyalty are considered evil and treasonable. The child, whose nervous system develops in socialist-collectives, invests the state with the sublimated sexuality which in pre-socialist societies is fragmented into individual and familial connections. Virtue is not in parental terms, but in the duty to the collective.
		Mating and domestic instincts are co-opted by the state. Nesting behavior, the protective husbandry reflexes, now cherish, feed, support, and defend the state.

Table 8: *Leary's Bio-Evolutionary Stages 10-12*

Conformist Consciousness	
Primary Motivation	Safety and security through predictability
Ultimate Value	Control
Attitude Toward Life	Life is serious because what happens in the past determines security in the future. Life is ultimately fair
Perception of Death	An inevitable, biological process
Self-Boundaries	At the skin
Perception of Temporality	Past, present and future. Future linear extrapolation of the past. Past and future extend in imagination beyond personal experience, but hypothetical futures tend to be bound by experience or history
Concept of Other	People are similar in kind to subject, possessing their own point of view and interior life which may differ from the subject's. Primarily judged by externals, especially group identifications. Authority, by virtue of rules and roles, creates social inequities that are right and just
Locus of Control	External—the referent group
Level of Abstraction	Generalized other (allocentric). Social role. Dualistic; intolerant of ambiguity. Concrete to Formal Operations. Logical, complex, detailed, organized but ruled by emotion
Options for Actions	Two—polar opposites
Correct Opinion	The good or right

Table 9: *Wade's Holonomic Theory: Conformist Consciousness*

Chapter VII

Chapel Perilous: The Bardo

"Only those willing to walk through the dark night will be able to see the beauty of the moon and the brilliance of the stars."
— Archbishop Socrates Villegas

"People have to go out of their mind before they can come to their senses."
— Timothy Leary

The transition between the operation of the fourth circuit and the activation of the fifth or other transpersonal circuits may be tumultuous. This marks a transition out of well-accepted societal structures and organizations, into what appears to be a seemingly chaotic introspective imperative toward self-derived drives and authenticity. To do this entails a leap in perspective that many do not make due to its daunting difficulty and impending cultural scrutiny. For those willing to press forward, there is often a period when the ego-self feels thrown into a whirlwind and displaced, left to wander and try to find its way back.

Wilson (1983) and Alli (1987) called this space "Chapel Perilous"; it has also been called the "dark night of the soul" by St. John of the Cross. It is called *nigredo*—the "black that is blacker than black"—within alchemy. It is the abyss that must be crossed—the same that Nietzsche "stared into" and said stares back at you. It is an existential limbo, full of confusion and disorientation for the ego.

As a result, feelings of anxiety, fear, and loneliness often arise. You may feel lost and outside of yourself. You may feel out of place, both from society and yourself, seeming to lack any "home base" to which you can reliably return. You may feel as though you have lost your footing on self and reality. Life may feel like a movie in which you are merely in a role to be acted out. The whole world may no longer seem to make sense, or may seem to crumble into pieces before you.

> *"The dark night of the soul is when you have lost the flavor of life but have not yet gained the fullness of divinity. So it is that we must weather the dark time, the period of transformation when what is familiar has been taken away and the new richness is not yet ours."*
>
> — Ram Dass

While the movement between the fourth circuit to the more complex circuits is a common stumbling point into this abyss, you can enter this Chapel at any point along your life journey. It exists, not as a particular circuit, but as a state outside of yourself that can occur throughout the process of development. Many of the shocks that activate the later circuits can be exactly that—shocking to the nervous system and the ego-self. These experiences can be very disorienting for some, propelling them into a sort of chaotic, depersonalized state. Some may become trapped within it for years; others may enter and never come out the other side. Further, those who find the exit are not guaranteed any sort of progress or experience of enlightenment. You may go in and out of the Chapel many times before being able to progress in a collected or integrated manner.

> *"I like the image covered by the original meaning of the word pitfall. It is a lightly camouflaged hole in the ground that hunters use to ensnare animals or that the enemy employs to capture members of the opposition. On the spiritual journey, we slip into many pitfalls, and the enemy is usually ourselves." Grof (1993:230)*

Wade (1996:197) discusses this type of experience where, as consciousness broadens with increasing complexity, original repressions may come to conscious light. This results in a triggering of ego-collapse *"creating a peri- lous period of bizarre and painful experiences revisiting the pre-egoic realm."* When this occurs, there is a regression and a return to primary processes of thought. A lack of emotional flexibility and the possible emergence of "sub- selves" as coping mechanisms may develop. Wade associates this neurologi- cally with a support of right hemispheric brain dominance, and a disinhibi- tion of the lower brain centers. The removal of original repression triggers a collapse of the ego which is felt as a downward *"fall into the abyss, the descent into the underworld"* (Washburn, 1988:116). Both Alli and Wade describe processes of "leaving the body" in some manner as this occurs. Alli lists a number of reasons this may occur, including attempts at avoiding "karmic duty" or "destiny"; over-thinking without the experience to ground an egoic shock; or cognitive dissonance that can be created between individual spiritual experiences and religious indoctrination. Also, hesitation to appro- priately let go of the ego or surrender fully to incoming experiences can cre- ate resistance, rigidity, or result in personal dissolution.

Grof's work with psychedelics and the exploration of human conscious- ness (1989:13–14), notes ten key types of "spiritual emergencies that may arise:

- The shamanic crisis
- Episodes of unitive consciousness ("peak experiences")
- The awakening of Kundalini
  Kriyas: *"One can experience intense sensations of energy and heat streaming up the spine, associated with violent shaking, spasms, and twisting movements"* (Grof, 1989:15).
- Psychological renewal through return to center
  "The psyche of people in this kind of crisis appears to be a colossal battle- field where a cosmic combat is being played out between the forces of Good and Evil, or Light and Darkness. They are pre-occupied with the theme of death—ritual killing, sacrifice, martyrdom and after- life. The problem of opposites fascinates them" (Grof, 1989:16).
- The crisis of psychic opening
- Past-life experiences

- Communications with spirit guides and "channeling"
- Near-death experiences
- Experiences of close encounters with UFOs
- Possession states

Several "entrances" into this bardo state have been proposed. As noted above, over-thinking can act as a catalyst for leaving your body. Obsessions of various types can develop out of destabilizing shocks or traumatic events as an attempt to regain control over your life. While this may act as a temporary restorative action, it can also lead to "falling into the abyss." These obsessions can relate to many things—people, drugs, money, sex, ideas, religion, work, health, appearance, charitable causes, or your social status or ego, to name a few. People may become obsessed with the upper circuit shocks or with seeking out novel experiences or new information-seeking— a sort of neophilia. This can reach such levels that you may spin into relatively short-lived sub-manic or manic episodes that end up consuming your limited resources. This results in a crash-and-burn scenario. At other times an obsession can limit the scope of your experiences by accumulating so much force and inertia within your life that it stagnates decision-making. When this occurs, you develop a deep immersion into maintaining day-to-day habits and routines.

> *"Future shamans might lose contact with the environment and have powerful inner experiences that involve journeys into the underworld and attacks by demons who expose them to incredible tortures and ordeals. These often culminate in experiences of death and dismemberment followed by rebirth and ascent to celestial regions." (Grof, 1989:14)*

Wade (1996:197) states that eventually the ego realizes it cannot win in the effort to maintain pre-egoic or dissolutioned states. It begins to divert its struggle against transcendent states toward its own resistances. As this occurs, instincts are tamed, and the ego "re-inhabits the body" to deconstruct fears, defenses, repression, and aspects of the self-complex. Nisagadatta Maharaj says of this process that *"the mind creates the abyss, the heart crosses it."* This exiting is rarely clear, however. Wilson says:

"Chapel perilous, like the mysterious entity called "i", cannot be located in the space-time continuum; it is weightless, odorless, tasteless and undetectable by ordinary instruments. Indeed, like the ego, once you are inside it, there doesn't seem to be any way to ever get out again, until you suddenly discover that it has been brought into existence by thought and does not exist outside thought." (1977:6)

Alli (1987) offers several ritualized methods of working through and exiting Chapel Perilous. Most of these entail introspection and subsequent transference of findings to the conscious or subconscious to reestablish groundwork upon which you may once again stand.

Wilson states:

"If you go into that realm without the sword of reason, you will lose your mind, but at the same time, if you take only the sword of reason without the cup of sympathy, you will lose your heart. Even more remarkably, if you approach without the wand of intuition, you can stand at the door for decades never realizing you have arrived. You might think you are just waiting for a bus, or wandering from room to room looking for your cigarettes, watching a TV show, or reading a cryptic and ambiguous book. Chapel Perilous is tricky that way." (1977:6-7)

and

"When you think you're out of it, you're just in another hall of illusions painted to look like the safe forest outside; and when you think you're inside again, you'll suddenly discover you're actually walking on the road back home. As the traditional Zen saying sums it up:

'First there is a mountain,
Then there is no mountain,
Then there is.'" (1977:10)

CHAPTER VIII

CIRCUIT FIVE (C-5):
PLEASURE SEEKING, GETTING "HIGH,"
& ECO-CONSCIOUSNESS

CYBERSOMATIC CIRCUIT (LEARY)
NEUROSOMATIC CIRCUIT (LEARY, WILSON)

"The most fortunate are those who have a wonderful capacity to appreciate again and again, freshly and naively, the basic goods of life, with awe, pleasure, wonder and even ecstasy."
— Abraham Maslow

"In every real man, a child is hidden that wants to play."
— Friedrich Nietzsche

The fifth circuit marks a major transitional phase in the psychospiritual development of the individual. Whereas the first four stages develop pretty much ubiquitously, and rarely go undeveloped (barring significant trauma, inhibitory situations growing up, or cognitive impairment), this is not the case with the following four stages. Leary (1977) referred to the first four circuits as the "larval" or "terrestrial" circuits, and the last four as the "extra-terrestrial" circuits. This was through his bio-evolutionary lens of the species, under the assumption that humanity would likely have advanced technologically with respect to space exploration as these "higher" circuits became activated. While space exploration can act as a shock or trigger for opening upper circuit awareness (astronauts have often made descriptions of their experiences akin to Circuit 5 consciousness), for our purposes, the higher circuits may be thought of as "post-indoctrinated" or transpersonal. Each circuit going forward entails greater and greater degrees of conscious control over previously culturally indoctrinated imprints and rules.

> *"The second group of four brain circuits is much newer, and each circuit exists at present only in minorities. Where the antique circuits recapitulate evolution-to-the-present, these futuristic circuits precapitulate our future evolution." (Wilson, 1983:41)*

With the fifth circuit, you tend to develop a broader perspective of the world beyond the ego-self. You reach a level of intelligence and self-awareness in which you become more adept at the conscious alteration and control of your body to best suit your needs and desires. For this reason, it has been referred to as the "neurosomatic circuit"—the unlocking of sensory and somatic consciousness. The first circuit relied on the somatic experience limited by external influences, and co-regulation focused around the base requirements for survival. With neurosomatic activation, the emphasis again is placed on the body and the sensory experience; it is, however, now inwardly sought and self-directed toward conscious, pleasurable endeavors beyond just sustaining life. It functions as a striving toward self-embellishment and rapturous experiences that transcend the personal egoic experience.

The body can now become a vehicle of joy and rapturous experience. Survival needs and self-regulation have been tended to, and are generally well-maintained at this point. As such, you can utilize your senses to explore the world for fun and pleasure. Pleasure can now act as its own reward, being sought out for the experience alone.

Being present in the immediate moment of experience is, of course, also a major goal of meditative practices—immersing yourself in your own internal processes, and clearing out cluttered ramblings of the internal monkey-mind to reach the still-point of the moment. With this comes the ability to let life happen around and inside you—without cultural value judgments, or becoming enveloped as part of the unfolding process. You begin to recognize the inherent flow of the universe, and that each entity exists within this flow. As Wilson stated:

> *"The rapturous person is not on [Leary's] Interpersonal Grid at all... The rapturous person is merely here, now, sensing, rejoicing, participating; awareness is usually in the end-organs, not in the strategic computer center of the forebrain." (2020:136–7)*

He further described the neurosomatic circuit as:

> *"Amotivational. There is nothing to do, nothing worth doing...right where you are sitting now" (2020:348).*

Much like the biosurvival circuit—which has an anchoring effect for the fifth circuit—when the somatic, sensory experience is put at the forefront, linguistic processing becomes secondary or of little use. This circuit communicates outside of words, and is fully felt as a sensory intelligence. Movements, gestures, dance, feelings, posture, and attitude are the primary means of communication. For this reason, such experiences and intelligence can become difficult to express in rational, C-3 linguistic terms.

Sounds are one of the most direct means of accessing sensory intelligence. For this reason, music can have a strong impact on you in a way that words cannot. This is because the experience is *felt*; it is not a conclusion drawn from mentation. The act of listening communicates directly to somatic intelligence, and the act of creating aural experiences can lead to altered or ecstatic states, reinforcing and further developing the neurosomatic circuit. This enhanced sensory sensuality can apply to all peripheral sensory receptors with full neurosomatic activation.

Neurosomatic intelligence is not fully experienced, matured, or integrated in everyone, however. Some people will never have a fifth circuit experience. Many develop their C-4 social-sexual intelligence in accordance with cultural expectations, and halt progress at the point of the social responsibilities of maintaining a family or social structure. The responsibilities of raising children and/or establishing and maintaining a career may not allow for explorations in such psychospiritual realms.

For this reason, once some of these responsibilities become less demanding and consuming, many rediscover the desire to move into more rewarding pursuits later in life. Many people in their 40s, 50s, and beyond pursue new, more rewarding careers, go back to school, or take up more creative or spiritually-oriented activities (e.g., yoga, reiki, etc.). As they find that they have more time to reflect on their life, they can discover a desire for more out of it, and a longing may arise for internal growth beyond the societal expectations of Circuit 4 functioning.

Of course, neurosomatic imprinting and growth can develop at a younger age. Those without children, those who are less concerned with career goals, or those who have a significant fifth circuit shock experience or imprint prior to or during these life events, may also develop a strong neurosomatic intelligence earlier in life. Moreover, with dedication, it is possible to balance the aforementioned C-4 life responsibilities with C-5 development simultaneously, although it may need some significant juggling.

Accounts by shamans, medicine men, and spiritual individuals who have activated the neurosomatic experience, report a negative-to-positive sensitization upon its unfolding. Prior to reaching a stage of open receptivity to bliss states, you may feel that you are losing your sense of defined self—your ego. This can be accompanied by the terror of personal annihilation. This has historically been called the "dark night of the soul," "crossing the abyss," or the "chemycalization" process in numerous disciplines such as Gnosticism, Theosophy, Christian Science, and Western alchemy. In the 8-Circuit Model, this is known as "Chapel Perilous," the focus of the previous chapter.

All of these tend to describe an abrupt entering of Chapel Perilous as the self you have known all your life becomes deconstructed or suddenly without any distinct meaning or significance. With any Chapel Perilous experience, nihilism becomes a potential risk. Not all go through this process, however, and there are those lucky enough to bypass it and directly access neurosomatic pleasure.

A positive neurosomatic imprint re-enforces the body as a source of pleasure and grace. One increases the capacity to fully and intentionally utilize, and viscerally experience the body—to be in and rejoice in the present moment, and to become fully enraptured by it. This is akin to what Freud referred to as the "oceanic" experience.

There may also be an expansion of the exploratory movement safety mechanism of Circuit 1; now reaching beyond your individual self into more of a communal perspective in which those around you are seen as part of something greater than self. You may become aware of a global network of individuals all working to keep this shared existence going. As the world becomes a source of pleasure, you may become what Wilson calls "polymorphous"—that every act and interaction can be a source of sensory or sensuous gratification.

Should you take a negative neurosomatic imprint, in the long term you may tend to experience the opposite of gratification—sensory experiences become filtered through a reality tunnel that renders them unpleasant or even painful. These sensory experiences are thus to be avoided rather than sought out.

With a negative Circuit 5 imprint, the body may be rejected—and seen as a source of suffering. Sensuality may be seen as uncomfortable and anxiety-producing. Perceptions can be distorted into a nightmarish reality. Photophobia—where light becomes painful and terrifying— can develop. You may describe interactions with the physical world as a "living hell." In some particularly negative imprints, you may associate the activation with a sort of mind control whereby these experiences are viewed as the workings of an external force.

If you are able to take a positive imprint, the newfound sense of your body as a source of pleasure, joy, and fun can lead to conflicts within the socio-political environment. Self-directed goals may not fall into the expectations of the cultural *status quo* which is heavily based around the first four developmental stages. As such, you may feel inclined to disregard or work counter to the social structure in order to focus on individual fulfillment.

Consider the counterculture movement of the 1960s. Many rebelled against societal systems and "the establishment" which were seen as not looking out for their needs. Instead, focus was put on breaking away from the culturally restrictive morals of the time for more worldly and hedonistic pursuits of love, sex, altered states, spirituality, and larger scale group consciousness through communal gatherings/festivals, music/art, and environmental advocacy. This was a large-scale neurosomatic movement. Drug use also increased during this time; this is not surprising, as such substances can act to catalyze higher circuit activation. Wilson considered cannabis, in particular, to be an external neurosomatic catalyst, with other psychedelic substances found to act more on other circuits.

The neurosomatic circuit is, after all, very much about the ability to get "high" in many different ways, and finding various methods to reach states of bliss. As such, a person may act self-servingly, neglecting others, their jobs, and cultural expectations. To an extent, this behavior may be necessary to form a strong neurosomatic circuit. You must give yourself permission to fully indulge your inner desires, and to know what those desires are—temporarily, at least.

Through these indulgences, you may learn what it feels like to experience self-fulfillment—and what can provide this feeling. You may be able to focus on your inner self, and drive toward personal fulfillment. Forming an inner dependence—rather than one reliant on externals—allows you to continue into higher stages of development that become progressively more subjective and subtle. These demand the ability to look inward with integrity and assurance, knowing that your thoughts and feelings are trustworthy beacons of direction. Intuition becomes clearer the more you become receptive, aware, and attentive to it. This internal dependence is created and honed during periods of solitude. When you are away from others, you are able to better experience and process the internal signals and natural flowing forth of subjective information.

This can be met with criticism as this information may conflict with expectations of how to be a "functioning" or "contributing" member of society. This is particularly true for those who have little-or-no neurosomatic awareness, making such a perspective foreign and not understood. Criticism is likely to also come from those who benefit from maintaining the *status quo* of everyone falling into their designated societal role to the neglect of the individual's inner longings. An internal conflict may be felt over this criticism from others, and the desire for approval, acceptance, and permission to allow you to truly be yourself. You must make a conscious choice, and give yourself permission to be who you are becoming, despite the potential judgment, fears, and opinions of others.

It is important to be aware that this developing state of mind can be seen as a "social threat" as it challenges the established expectations of interpersonal morals and norms. This threatening nature remains even if the outcome is ultimately of benefit. The fear of change (neophobia) or self-awareness can cause a great deal of reactionary anxiety or anger in others. As such, the backlash can be quite harsh, whether being called "self-centered" or "selfish," or even provoking acts of physical violence (most likely by those with a heavy C-2 imprint). It can, after all, be seen by others as a threat to the foundation of their identity or belief system(s).

To an extent, these judgments hold truth. Actions can indeed be self-serving in the interest of growing self-awareness. This becomes a problem, however, when you embellish yourself so much that it becomes a hindrance to your life and progress. This is a case of neurosomatic excess. It can be easy to get caught up in rapturous bliss, and have it become the *goal* instead of a *means* of personal growth. What ultimately develops is personal independence and understanding. When bliss becomes the goal in the long term, it may lead to laziness, personal dispersion, and dissolution of self.

There may indeed be too much of a good thing; and it can lead to pathology and unhealthy psychological states. Unless you approach your experience with enough self-reflection, just as hermits may go to live in the mountains, it becomes necessary to develop the ability to make your own value judgments, and self-regulate your time in bliss to avoid excess/treadmilling. This is the path of the Bodhisattva.

Commonly, you will go through a period in which you may become "blissed out," too spacey, disoriented, or don't feel "all together" as your self-dependence unfolds and personal ego softens. The increase in endorphins and reward neurotransmitters—like dopamine—during this "feeling good" can also provide this sort of spaced-out sensation. It is important not to get stuck in this stage; it can easily happen. At some point, to interact within society, your sense of self must be established again to come down from the cloud of euphoria you have been floating around on.

Your thinking can become more abstract with neurosomatic activation. The inner world of the mind operates more in the language of fuller, more global concepts. Linear progressions of thoughtforms may step aside to make way for less linear, more holistic, or networked concepts. Wilson states that this function is likely located within the right cerebral hemisphere, which functions more in gestalts and abstract concepts (the "creative" hemisphere of the brain) rather than the reductionist, logical processes typically associated with the left hemisphere. He speculates that the activation of this circuit began about 30,000 years ago, based on cave paintings that seem to depict exercises and rituals to activate the right side of the brain. Since that time, shamans and spiritual individuals have utilized a wide variety of methods to open up this capacity.

Sexuality can play a significant role in neurosomatic activation and experiences. Through active prolonging of the sexual experience without achieving orgasm, the senses become increasingly heightened to the point that ecstatic, altered states of consciousness can be achieved.

Such methods have a long history. Tantric and Daoist sexual practices promote the sexual prolonging of, or controlled abstinence from orgasm. Some practices promote the conservation of ejaculate by males *("Jing,"* or essence, in Daoist practices), whereby control of bodily sensations and functions achieve a body-wide sensorial orgasm or appropriate energetic release without ejaculation. By these means you can utilize the pleasure of sexual activity and orgasm to achieve higher spiritual states without the loss of semen. Within Daoist practices, this is said to then be stored internally in the lower *dan tien* where it can be refined into more subtle spiritual energy.

Once you have integrated the hedonic states associated with this circuit and self-awareness becomes more refined, you also become more capable of taking conscious control and regulation of autonomic functions and involuntary reflexes. Control of the breath is one of the easiest places to start this process. Consciously slowing down or deepening the breath, has a systemic effect on everything from blood perfusion, muscle restrictions, and anxious mental states. When you become anxious, the breath tends to become restricted, and the throat and chest constrict further into a feedback loop of what the brain interprets as mild self-strangulation. Willfully deepening the breath can break this pattern, lessening or breaking the pattern of anxiety.

EXPANDING BEYOND YOURSELF

Neurosomatic intelligence also brings about a broader sense of love—one which may expand beyond the individual or the ego-centered forms of love found in the previous circuits. Even the social love of others in Circuit 4 is personal. What develops here extends beyond the singular self, and is no longer limited to those with whom you have direct physical interactions. There develops an expansive, boundary-breaking love of those you have never met—a sense of love for all people, and often, all things. Others are seen as an extension of yourself with the respect and the realization that we are all of one ilk, one family, one species, and one planet, coexisting together. You may experience what Dr. Richard Doyle (2011:20) calls an "ecodelic insight": *"The sudden and absolute conviction that the person is involved in a densely interconnected ecosystem for which contemporary tactics of human identity are insufficient"* (Khamsehzadeh, 2022:260). This is inherent within the "Gaia hypothesis" (Lovelock, 1979) in which the planet Earth can be viewed as a single super-organism upon which we are all relatively recent beings, playing our own transient role.

Irvine et al. (2023) explored psychedelically-induced "transpersonal ecodelia," with findings that suggest *"psychedelics have the capacity to elicit a connection with nature that is passionate and protective, even among those who were not previously nature oriented."* A study by Forstmann et al. (2023) showed evidence that the use of (specifically) psilocybin seemed more predictive of what they termed "nature-relatedness" compared to the use of other psychedelics.

Psychologist Dr. Jesse Bering (2002) discusses the development of "existential theory of mind" as *a way of relating to the world as if reality itself had agency and experience (i.e., a mind). It should be noted that this need not be a belief; it can also be understood as a feeling state.* Yaden and Newberg (2020:179) discuss how spiritual experiences may represent transient, yet intense experiences of existential theory of mind—or "massive mentalization events" in which seemingly dead matter may appear to have a mind of its own, and attachment may be formed to this "seemingly minded world."

This expansion of love for both self and others, strengthens the heart. Fear fades away with the development of self-reliance and the ability to embody who you really feel you are. Activation and regulation of the autonomic nervous system and the immune system can also strengthen the body to where many diseases and problems of the first four circuits can seem to resolve. An increased ability for the body to naturally reregulate itself can be found with this neurosomatic development. The body awakens and balances itself throughout. Wilson states that it can be easy to determine if this circuit has been activated properly by asking how often you go to the doctor. He also notes that, in addition to rarely becoming ill, those with sufficient neurosomatic activation may appear to have a kind of "glow, bounciness, or sparkle" to their appearance or character.

Alli (1987) describes the cultivation of personal charisma within this circuit wherein you may make a *"graceful surrender to stardom,"* along with the ability to be under the influence of your own energies and Will. You may find the ability to act effortlessly, and give total, undivided attention to your unique nature. You may also be able to actively polarize yourself as needed—whether emotionally to effect change externally, or allowing yourself to be affected internally. There may be a polarization of the persona as well, with what is put outward for others to see. There develops an increased awareness of your influence on others, an appreciation of the dynamic, and the newfound role within the grand, universal play in which we all find ourselves.

ACHIEVEMENT VERSUS AFFILIATIVE CONSCIOUSNESS

In Wade's holonomic theory (1996), there is an interesting divergence found nowhere else in the model. Two stages fall into the neurosomatic circuit—"achievement consciousness" and "affiliative consciousness." Unique to these stages are that one is not said to be "higher" or "lower" than another, or preceding or following the other. One or the other instead tends to develop based on hemispheric dominance of the brain and social influence of the individual. A person tending toward left hemispheric dominance is more likely to display achievement consciousness traits, whereas right hemispheric dominance tends to display qualities of affiliative consciousness. Wade states that *"unlike all other stages, affiliative and achievement consciousness share the same level of complexity; neither one is more advanced than the other. Change from either may go to the opposite side of the cortex"* (1996:157). Moreover, William James (1902) used the term "homoduplex" to refer to the duality of human motives, distinguishing the "higher" (altruistic) and "lower" (selfish) aspects of the self. This circuit may act as a pivotal point between these two tendencies.

Common factors are found in both achievement and affiliative consciousness. These stem from two primary processes: an increased de-centering from the external environment, and a simultaneous re-centering on the self. You become able to cognitively separate and disembed yourself from your current social system. This includes an awareness of unspoken or assumed social contracts, and a general relativity of knowledge. Also, awareness of an increased range of possibilities present themselves as cultural confines loosen their hold to critical analysis of subjective experience.

With achievement consciousness, the individual strives to exert control over the environment, generally through manipulative or materialistic means. Here the individual thrives on gamesmanship, competition, politics, and entrepreneurial efforts in the pursuit of status, money, or material possessions. They may attempt to "conquer the world," not by brute force, but by learning the rules and secrets that dictate social dynamics through objective scientific means. For these individuals, truth becomes sought after internally through doubt, reason, and deliberate, systematic analysis while holding oneself apart from what is being analyzed. Life can become a game of discovery—dissecting its inner mechanisms, and finding ways to "bend but not break" the rules.

Achievement consciousness is said to be overly concerned with public image as all rewards being sought are external and socially recognized. As such, the attempts to control remain limited to the socially acceptable. Actions may appear to resemble egocentrism, although much more complex than what is found in C-2 consciousness. Dr. Clare Graves (1970) and Dr. Erich Fromm (1973) both regard many aspects of consciousness as having a "dark side" (a "shadow" in Jungian terms). In this case, it can reveal itself as an exaggerated form of self-oriented pursuits of prestige that may resemble symptoms of narcissism. This may correlate with a profusion of neurosomatic excess. While many of these traits tend to be rewarded, or even admired in some cultures, esoteric or spiritual traditions have often denounced such ego-defined achievements as wrongful attachment, the world of illusion, or "the veil of *maya*." It is considered a common distraction along the path of self-development in which one is striving to ultimately penetrate this veil to reveal the broader, more "enlightened" states on the other side.

Affiliative consciousness—with its greater access to the brain's right hemispheric processes—develops a more holistic perspective that emphasizes connectedness and intimacy on a larger world-wide scale. With the more prominent, connected processing, this hemisphere tends to minimize inharmonious elements and emphasize an intuitive, non-linear, and metaphoric means of thinking and communication. Similarities between events, objects, or people are registered more than differences.

Instead of the "get it while you can" drive of achievement consciousness, "love conquers all" becomes the dictum. Wade also states that the influence of the limbic system remains more intact here than in the more rationalistic achievement consciousness. As such, connected knowledge is developed out of empathic connections and recognized equality through belonging, acceptance, and sharing within a community.

Wade says that this stage generally transitions as the result of some dra-
matic life event that breaks down one's faith in what was previously seen as
an established authority. From a realization that "the rules just don't work,"
there develops a mistrust of anyone but themselves, and a rejection of logic
and abstraction in favor of intuition.

Adoption of a critical view of the social system can be found; yet one
remains only able to do so within the terms and standards of the system.
Because of this limitation, you can begin to choose which rules suit you
without much guilt for breaking others that do not—so long as it does not
hurt others. A general philosophy of pacifism can be seen. There is an avoidance of conflict or confrontation at almost any cost. If another person is
annoying, the tendency will be to ignore it and act like nothing happened,
while still internalizing the event. You may actively deny existing problems
or negative emotions (such as anger), instead developing an inner hostility
toward the offending person in the interest of "keeping the peace" and
maintaining the community.

There may be a rigid opposition to homogenization in mainstream
culture. A tendency to follow new, like-minded peer groups may develop
despite this, creating a subculture with particular sets of norms. Paradoxically, despite the emphasis on inclusion and community, there can be a
strong intolerance toward people who do not share these views on diversity.
This may even be strong enough to elicit a forceful, or passively-resistant
response. There may also be an active denial of differences among individuals, touting that all are the same, and to distinguish any differences of indi-
vidualism is seen to be divisive. This creates what Wade calls a *"pretense of
pseudocommunity."* Dr. Abraham Maslow makes a distinction between this
with the maintenance of the appearance of empathy versus true altruism
(which develops at later stages), and which is untainted by the ego still present in both achievement and affiliative consciousness.

Here the concept of death evolves to be viewed as an event, but not an
end. There tends to be the belief that following death, the individual has not
completely ceased to be, but rather has passed beyond the physical plane

into another plane of existence. The belief may be held that so long as the individual is thought of, they are never truly gone.

AESTHETIC DEVELOPMENT & AWE

Drs. Dacher Keltner and Jonathan Haidt (2003) have defined *awe* as consisting of 1) an appraisal of vastness, and 2) a need to accommodate that perception of vastness into existing mental structures. They further explore five additional factors that account for *"variation in the hedonic tone of awe experiences."* These are:

- Threat
- Beauty
- Exceptional ability
- Virtue
- The supernatural

Yaden and Newberg describe awe as *"a self-transcendent experience...the emotion of self-transcendence"* (2019:253). The most common triggers of awe are nature and art—a well-known, awe-inducing experience in what has been called "the overview effect" by author Frank White (2021). This is the psychological experience of viewing Earth from space, what White describes in an interview as *"a cognitive and emotional shift in a person's awareness, their consciousness and their identity when they see the Earth from space."* (Rivera, 2022, para. 6). There are numerous descriptions of the sense of awe, and an expansion of the sense of being that is felt during such an experience by astronauts—each one reads as an example of a neurological shock activating the fifth circuit. With the private/commercial space race currently underway, such an impactful experience may become accessible to more people, bringing the space migration component of Leary's **SMI²LE** ("**S**pace **M**igration, **I**ntelligence **I**ncrease, **L**ife **E**xtension) equation closer to realization. In the meantime, developers have created virtual reality simulations which try to approximate this sense of awe. William Shatner, the well-known actor who portrayed Captain James T. Kirk in the original *Star Trek* television series, was able to fly into space in 2021. His description of the experience is a great example of the profundity of the overview effect. In his case, awe was coupled with a significant sense of grief:

> "'It was the death that I saw in space and the lifeforce that I saw coming from the planet—the blue, the beige and the white,' he said. 'And I realized one was death and the other was life... It's a little tiny rock with an onion skin air around it. That's how fragile it all is. It's so fragile. We hang by a thread...we're just dangling. We're entangled with each other... We have a war...the stupidity of it all is so obvious.'" (Rivera, 2022, para. 16)

According to Yaden and Newberg (2022:98):

> "One of the traits most predictive of having a spiritual experience is called absorption...an openness to inner experiences as well as the capacity to have one's attention entirely engaged to the point that everything fades away from one's awareness."

While the two psychological traits of "openness to experience" and "absorption" are most associated with spiritual experience, absorption is noted to be the most predictive (Lifshitz et al., 2019).

§ § §

The Awe Experience Scale at the end of this chapter measures six different aspects of awe: perception of vastness, need for accommodation, altered sense of time, self-diminishment, connectedness, and physiological changes. The Tellegen Absorption Scale (Tellegen & Atkinson, 1974), a 34-item questionnaire that measures the capacity to become absorbed, is published by the University of Minnesota Press and is available for research purposes at upress.umn.edu. We have included it for those who may wish to explore the degree to which you may or may not experience these aspects of Circuit 5 in your own life, and perhaps to identify areas in which you may want to cultivate these types of experiences.

FLOW STATES

Psychologist Dr. Mihaly Csikszentmihalyi coined the term "flow state" to refer to *a state in which people are so involved in an activity, that nothing else seems to matter; the experience is so enjoyable that people will continue to do it even at great cost, for the sheer sake of doing it"* (1990:4). He describes eight characteristics of flow:

1) Complete concentration on the task
2) Clarity of goals and reward in mind with immediate feedback
3) Transformation of time (speeding up/slowing down)
4) The experience is intrinsically rewarding
5) Effortlessness and ease
6) There is a balance between challenge and skills
7) Actions and awareness are merged, losing self-conscious rumination
8) There is a feeling of control over the task

It may be characterized by complete absorption in a task where action and consciousness may seem to melt together. It becomes simultaneously demanding of high concentration, while seemingly effortless. There have been reports of people—including some very successful business and tech individuals—seeking "flow states" through the ingestion of subthreshold hallucinogenic doses (microdoses) of psilocybin. A fully immersive flow state of mind may correlate to neurosomatic activation.

NEUROBIOLOGY OF CIRCUIT 5

Brain images of people during meditation have been examined and compared to non-meditators. Findings tend to show that long-time meditators (particularly, Buddhist monks) have thicker frontal lobes (Lazar et al., 2005; Austin, 1998), and that meditation practice produced functional and structural brain changes, especially in areas involved in self-awareness and self-regulation (Boccia, 2015). Meditation and yoga practices have also been associated with reduced amygdala volume (Lazar et al., 2005). The current understanding of the neurobiology of meditative experiences is outlined in the diagram below (Newberg & Newberg, 2005). Drs. David Yaden and

Andrew Newberg (2022:85) also note areas of the attentional network—such as the prefrontal cortex (PFC)—being involved in attention-focused tasks that may elicit non-ordinary or ecstatic states of consciousness, including prayer and ritual practices.

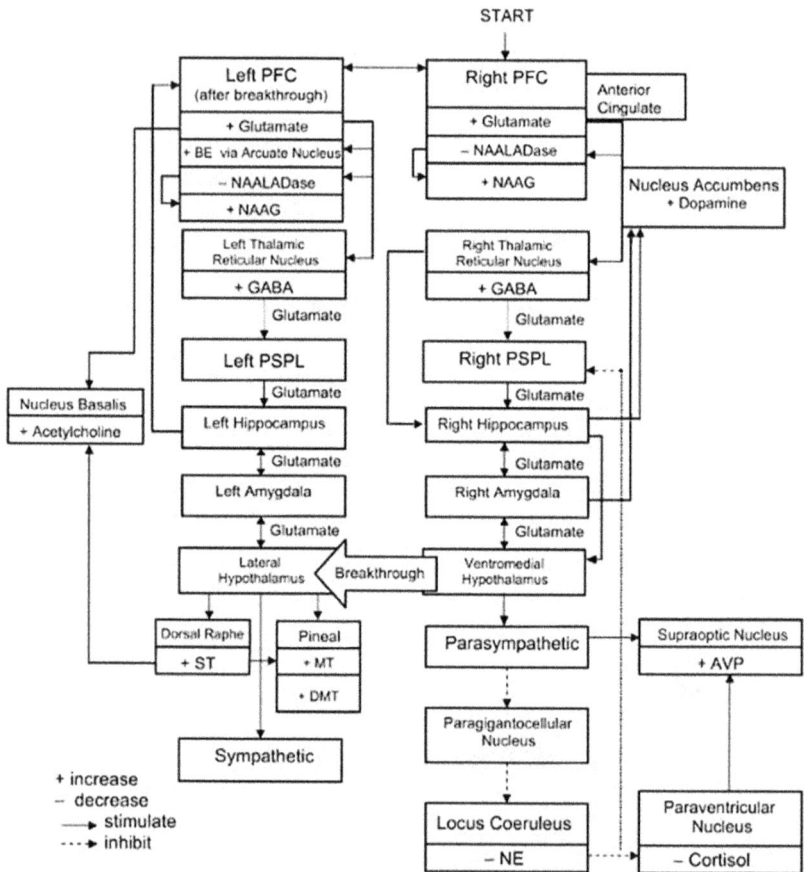

Figure 4: *Neurophysiology of Meditation*

While these practices may demonstrate thicker neural connections, Dr. Arne Dietrich (2003) sought to account for non-ordinary states of consciousness with what he called "transient hypofrontality theory." This developed out of findings that experiences such as *"dreaming, endurance running, meditation, daydreaming, hypnosis, and various drug-induced states"* were correlated with temporary reduction in the activity in the frontal regions of the brain. This temporary downregulation may lead to experiences that feel overwhelming or out of one's control (Yaden & Newberg, 2022:101), as well as accounting for flow states (Dietrich, 2004).

It has been proposed that the dopaminergic system in the PFC relates to the personality trait of "openness/intellect," which reflects characteristics of cognitive exploration, including the tendency to be imaginative, curious, perceptive, artistic, and intellectual (DeYoung et al., 2011). This may be the neural correlate of what Wilson (1983) referred to as "neophilia"—an inclination to seek out new experiences and information, with the dopaminergic reward system providing satisfaction or pleasure from such pursuits.

Relating to awe and absorption experiences, the medial orbitofrontal cortex (mOFC)—known to be involved in the perception of rewarding stimuli—becomes more activated when experiencing "beautiful" (according to the observer's taste) artwork (Yaden, 263).

Experiences of awe have demonstrated neural correlates in the form of reduced activation of the default mode network (DMN; van Elk et al., 2019). (The DMN and its functions and relationship to non-ordinary states of consciousness will be explored in more detail in the following chapters.) Absorption experiences are correlated with increased activation in the following brain areas: superior frontal gyrus (SFG), the bilateral middle temporal gyri (MTG), posterior cingulate cortex (PCC), the lateral occipital cortex, and the temporal pole.

THE ENDOCANNABINOID SYSTEM & CANNABIS

In 1992, Dr. Raphael Mechoulam's laboratory isolated the first endocannabinoid in the human body, a naturally occurring compound that activated the same receptors as cannabis. Since that time, the importance of this endocannabinoid system, and the many functions in which it plays a role, has opened up a new perspective on how the body regulates itself. Cannabinoid receptors have been found in abundance in multiple areas of the brain including major regions of the basal ganglia (such as the substantia nigra, globus pallidus, and putamen which play a role in control of voluntary movement); in the cerebellum (which coordinates movement); the hippocampus (involved in learning and memory); areas of the cerebral cortex, especially the cingulate, frontal, and parietal regions (involved in higher cognitive functioning); the intrabulbar anterior commissure (which links the cerebral hemispheres at the temporal lobes); and the nucleus accumbens (involved in the reward system). *"One of the major effects of endogenous cannabinoids is to regulate the release of dopamine, serotonin, and other neurotransmitters,"* said Dr. Raphael Mechoulam (2019). *"They seem to be major regulators."*

These neurotransmitters have wide-reaching and varying effects. In fact, the endocannabinoid system has been shown to have wide reaching effects in the healing process as well, so much so that Mechoulam goes on to say:

> *"Two eminent scientists at the NIH said that the endocannabinoid system is involved in essentially all human disease. This is a very strong statement, but it seems to be correct. Today we know that the endocannabinoid system—the receptors, the endocannabinoids, the enzymes that form and break down the endocannabinoids—are involved in many physiological reactions, and therefore in many disease states."* (2019)

These two scientists are Drs. Pal Pacher and George Kunos who state:

> *"Modulating the activity of the endocannabinoid system holds therapeutic promise for a broad range of diseases, including neurodegenerative, cardiovascular and inflammatory disorders; obesity/metabolic syndrome; cachexia; chemotherapy-induced nausea and vomiting; and tissue injury and pain, amongst others."* (2013:1)

The endocannabinoid system is a retrograde signaling system, meaning it acts through *post*-synaptic activation via neurotransmitters such as glutamate that signal back across the synaptic cleft causing the release of endogenous cannabinoids. This retrograde action acts to inhibit calcium influx, and suppress neurotransmitter release. This system also guides synaptic plasticity, and has the ability to either potentiate (i.e., long-term potentiation [LTP], which occurs when specific neural pathways and synaptic connections are reinforced over time from repeated activation and association), or depress the connection between neurons. Endocannabinoid signaling influences a multitude of neurodevelopmental processes, including roles in reproduction fertilization and implantation, and developmental neurogenesis and axon guidance. In adulthood they act as regulators of synaptic transmission.

The two major endocannabinoid receptors are CB1 and CB2, which are found in different proportions in different areas of the body:

- **CB1:** Densely found in the central nervous system (CNS) including the spine. Responsible for most associated effects, and become occupied by tetrahydrocannabinol (THC) and cannabidiol (CBD).
- **CB2:** Found more throughout tissues of the body. Receptors have a protective mechanism and complement the immune system.

Cannabis or phytocannabinoids bind to and stimulate these receptors at a significantly greater intensity than endocannabinoids. THC, the major psychoactive component in cannabis, mimics activity of both major endocannabinoid compounds, anandamide and 2-AG. However, THC stays in the body longer, whereas the endogenous cannabinoid compounds are only produced when needed and are quickly broken down. Varying strains can influence brain activity in different ways (e.g., *sativa* tends to activate the PFC, whereas *indica* tends to suppress activity in the PFC). This influence on the PFC is why cannabis use during adolescence and young adulthood— while the prefrontal cortices are still developing—can negatively affect cognitive development. Both *sativa* and *indica* demonstrate a reduction in activity in the hippocampus, contributing to the well-known inhibition of memory. Both also tend to suppress the basal ganglia and cerebellum, influencing action-planning, and the initiation and coordination of voluntary movement. The well-known increase in appetite people experience is due to the high number of CB1 receptors in the hypothalamus, and its connection to the gut.

The heightened pleasure and reward effects of cannabis ingestion result from the influence on the nucleus accumbens of the right hemisphere of the brain and dopamine production therein, as well as influences on oxytocin (the neurotransmitter correlated with bonding and connection). While some utilize cannabis in conjunction with other pleasure-seeking activities, with sex specifically there seems to be some variation in how it affects the nervous system. Some experience an increase in the hormone prolactin with cannabis intake; those who have this increase tend not to experience heightened sexual drive, compared to those whose prolactin levels do not rise. This does not seem to be predicted by baseline prolactin levels—although smoking cannabis (as opposed to ingestion) tends to have a higher chance of elevating prolactin levels (and not increasing libido). Smoking cannabis also seems not to activate dopamine as much as other forms of ingestion.

CIRCUIT 5 ENERGY

QUALITIES OF BALANCED CIRCUIT 5 ENERGY

- Ability to discriminate between truth and untruth
- Content; centered; enthusiasm for life
- Can live in the present; meditate & experience divine energy
- Great sense of timing
- Musically or artistically inspired; may be overwhelmingly prolific
- Sexual: can manifest incredible sexual/sensual energy, or abstain without great effort
- May choose to redirect sexual energy into music, art, or creative endeavors

QUALITIES OF EXCESSIVE CIRCUIT 5 ENERGY

- Arrogant, self-righteous, dogmatic
- Loquaciousness or silence used as a means of control/attention
- Addictive
- Sexual: preoccupied; unconsciously "macho"; may prefer partners who can be dominated or manipulated

QUALITIES OF DEFICIENT CIRCUIT 5 ENERGY

- Timid, quiet, holds back, scared, confused
- Inconsistent, unreliable
- Lack of creativity
- Weak; unable to express thoughts
- Can be devious or manipulative
- Sexual: can't relax; conflict with religious/moral raising or afraid of sex

CIRCUIT 5 ACTIVATION

CIRCUIT 5 ACTIVATING ACTIVITIES

Activities that allow you to feel and take conscious control of the body, or allow for states of awe or rapturous bliss. These include:

- Ecstatic states
- Hatha Yoga, Zen meditation, Pranayama
- Tantra; prolonged sexual play without orgasm
- Endorphin-inducing physical activity (e.g., runner's high)
- Floatation/isolation tanks
- Floating in a boat in calm waters
- Pleasure-seeking activities
- Full body massage for pleasure alone
- Listening to your favorite music with quality headphones, and immersing in the sounds
- Virtual reality experiences that emulate psychedelic or overview effects
- Surround yourself with people who only make you feel good
- Awe-inspiring sights, such as natural wonders
- Allow yourself to get lost in the moment/experience
- Lose track of time or wander aimlessly
- Try to remove "meaning" from life for a time—experience it as qualities & energies

CIRCUIT 5 ACTIVATING SUBSTANCES

Cannabis, blue lotus flower, empathogens, MDMA, low-dose psilocybin, holy basil (tulsi), kava, and anandamide-containing substances (e.g., black and long pepper, black truffles, and cacao)

INTEGRATION INTERVENTION MODEL CONSIDERATIONS
CIRCUIT 1 ACTIVATING ACTIVITIES

Circuit 1 and Circuit 5 are vertically connected, with Circuit 1 acting as an anchor to Circuit 5 shock experiences. See "Circuit 1 Activating Activities" in Chapter 3 for activities to help anchor and counterbalance an overactive Circuit 5 or a shock in this circuit.

CLINICAL APPROACH CONSIDERATIONS
(REFER TO RECOMMENDED READING FOR RESOURCES)

- Dialectical Behavior Therapy (DBT)
- Mindfulness-Based Stress Reduction

Leary's Bio-Evolutionary Stages 13–15		
Stage 13	Neurosomatic Receptivity	The body is temporarily detached from external connections, and becomes a zero-gravity instrument. This is called being "high." The first reaction to new neural signals. Why struggle for external material rewards (emotional, mental, social) which are clumsy, artificial, symbolic triggers for the sensory-somatic-endocrine experience? Einsteinian mobility replaces Newtonian pushing.
		What is it that the user escapes from? The moralistic answer: from social responsibility. The neurological answer: escape from the tunnel-reality of the four artificial imprints.
		Infantile self-indulgence. Establishing a new ego-identity. Moralists complain that the youth culture is infantile. Exactly—as aimless and unproductive as a baby.
Stage 14	Neurosomatic Intelligence	As the endomorphic Biosurvival imprint (Stage 1) is followed by viscerotonic conditioning—discrimination (Stage 2)—so does Stage 14 organize and control the neurosomatic signals of Stage 13.
		At Stage 13 the sensory-somatic signals are received. Sensory consumerism emerges. The body-brain begins to select, remember, relate, and control somatic-sensory function;
		The first post-larval generation believed (naively) that "turning on" was an endpoint. Feel-good consumerism. A small percentage were sophisticated enough to study and master the management of sen-

		suality, to chart and navigate the infinite internal geography of neurophysiology. The vague, theosophical cliché, "look within," now takes on specific anatomical meaning. "Look within" means within the body. Control the autonomic nervous system of somatic reactions which are involuntary and unconscious to the larval.
Stage 15	Neurosomatic Fusion	The fusion of the new energy with others to form the social linkage. Synergy. The linkage—poetically called union or love— is not an accidental development. It is built into the DNA design. Fusion and interchange produce a structure capable of increased contelligence. Our language does not have a scientific term for this communication between two or more persons operating on the neurosomatic channels, free of symbolic-material imprints. It has been called extra-symbolic perception (ESP). Spiritual community.

Table 10: *Leary's Bio-Evolutionary Stages 13–15*

Achievement Consciousness	
Primary Motivation	Personal success that is socially recognized
Ultimate Value	Power to be better than others and have them know it
Attitude Toward Life	Life is a finite game, so "get it while you can." The most successful are the winners
Perception of Death	Inevitable, biological process. End of personal existence
Self-Boundaries	At the skin
Perception of Temporality	Past, compound present, and future. Past and future may be infinite. Past may or may not predict the future. Oriented to the future as a place of setting personal goals, then working forward to meet them
Concept of Other	People are similar in kind to subject, possessing their own point of view and interior life of highly variegated emotions, but not similar in their ability to achieve. Achievers will be rewarded with the good things in life (usually defined materially) over the less capable. More powerful, successful people are admired. People without the measures of success important to the subject are discounted. Others may be exploited within socially acceptable limits
Locus of Control	Internal—the self or self-esteem
Level of Abstraction	Relativism. Dialectical relationships. Vantage point from a dialectic with the system, not entirely outside the system. Empiricism and positivism; materialism. Formal and post-formal operations. Logical, analytical, algorithmic, inferential
Options for Actions	Infinite
Correct Opinion	The one that secures the greatest personal advantage

Table 11: *Wade's Holonomic Theory: Achievement Consciousness*

Affiliative Consciousness	
Primary Motivation	Belonging in close, harmonious relationships
Ultimate Value	Being needed
Attitude Toward Life	Relationships are more important than any outcome
Perception of Death	Not final at some level so long as living people hold the deceased in loving memory
Self-Boundaries	At the skin
Perception of Temporality	Knowledge of past, present and future. Past and future may be infinite. Past may or may not predict the future. Orientation is compound present with indifference to passage of time
Concept of Other	People are similar in kind to subject, but possess their own point of view and interior life of variegated emotions. Sharing information about one's inner life with others will lead to consensus-based community. Differences are superficial; everyone is fundamentally equal. Differences and conflict are threatening. People need to be helped by being in close relationships
Locus of Control	External—Chosen like-minded peer groups
Level of Abstraction	Relativism. Dialectical relationships. Vantage point from a dialectic with the system, not entirely outside the system. Formal and post-formal operations, though not always evident. Holistic, intuitive, spatial, symbolic
Options for Actions	Infinite
Correct Opinion	Consensus of peer group

Table 12: *Wade's Holonomic Theory: Affiliative Consciousness*

RELEVANT ASSESSMENT SCALES
AWE EXPERIENCE SCALE (AWES-S)
SELF-CHECK FOR LEVEL OF AWE

The first step is to complete the following sentence:

I experienced awe when I was _____

_____.

Now that you have chosen a single experience of intense awe, please describe your experience in about a paragraph. While you are writing, please focus as much as possible on the experience itself, rather than what led up to it, what happened afterwards, or your interpretation of the experience. Try to be as descriptive and specific as possible. A description of my awe experience:

_____

_____

_____

_____.

With the memory of that experience that you just wrote about in mind, please answer the following questions about how you felt. While you may have had other experiences that are relevant to the following questions, please answer only about the SINGLE experience that you just described.

1 = Strongly Disagree
2 = Moderately Disagree
3 = Somewhat Disagree
4 = Neutral
5 = Somewhat Agree
6 = Moderately Agree
7 = Strongly Agree

I sensed things momentarily slow down   1 2 3 4 5 6 7

I had chills   1 2 3 4 5 6 7

I experienced a sense of oneness with all   1 2 3 4 5 6 7
 things

I felt that I was in the presence of   1 2 3 4 5 6 7
 something grand

I felt that my sense of self was diminished. 1 2 3 4 5 6 7

I noticed time slowing   1 2 3 4 5 6 7

I had the sense of being connected to   1 2 3 4 5 6 7
 everything

I felt small compared to everything else   1 2 3 4 5 6 7

I perceived vastness   1 2 3 4 5 6 7

I felt challenged to understand the   1 2 3 4 5 6 7
 experience

I felt my sense of self shrink   1 2 3 4 5 6 7

I felt closely connected to humanity   1 2 3 4 5 6 7

I gasped   1 2 3 4 5 6 7

I felt my sense of self become somehow   1 2 3 4 5 6 7
 smaller

I had a sense of complete connectedness   1 2 3 4 5 6 7

I struggled to take in all that I was   1 2 3 4 5 6 7
 experiencing at once

I felt my eyes widen   1 2 3 4 5 6 7

I experienced something greater than   1 2 3 4 5 6 7
 myself

I found it hard to comprehend the   1 2 3 4 5 6 7
 experience in full

I perceived something that was much   1 2 3 4 5 6 7
 larger than me

I felt my sense of time change   1 2 3 4 5 6 7

I felt my jaw drop   1 2 3 4 5 6 7

I felt challenged to mentally process what I   1 2 3 4 5 6 7
was experiencing

I had the sense that moment was lasting   1 2 3 4 5 6 7
longer than usual

I felt in the presence of greatness   1 2 3 4 5 6 7

I felt a sense of communion with all living   1 2 3 4 5 6 7
things

I had goosebumps   1 2 3 4 5 6 7

I experienced the passage of time   1 2 3 4 5 6 7
differently

I tried to understand the magnitude of   1 2 3 4 5 6 7
what I was experiencing

Total Score: _____

According to this measure, the higher your score, the greater your experience of awe may have been for this particular memory. As stated earlier in this chapter, this scale measures the following aspects of awe: perception of vastness, need for accommodation, altered sense of time, self-diminishment, connectedness, and physiological changes. You may wish to reflect on which aspect(s) of awe you may have experienced most greatly, and why. You may use this exercise to reflect on how this experience, and your memory of it, have affected you in small and/or profound ways, both in the moment and over time. Has this experience been enduring over time and has it impacted other ways of thinking/seeing/feeling/being, or was it short-lived and fleeting? Did this experience inspire any insights? If so, how have you (or can you) integrate these insights into your life? Take a moment to reflect on anything else that may be coming up for you that you feel may be significant about this experience.

How often do you experience awe in your life: rarely, sometimes, often, always? You may wish to repeat this exercise with different memories.

CHAPTER IX

CIRCUIT SIX (C-6):
NEUROPLASTICITY, BRAIN CHANGE &
METAPROGRAMMING

NEUROELECTRIC CIRCUIT (LEARY)
METAPROGRAMMING CIRCUIT (WILSON)

"Your brain—every brain—is a work in progress. It is 'plastic.'
From the day we're born to the day we die, it continuously revises
and remodels, improving or slowly declining, as a function of
how we use it."
— Michael Merzenich

"Whatever we plant in our subconscious mind and nourish with
repetition and emotion will one day become a reality."
— Earl Nightengale

The previous chapter discussed the fifth (neurosomatic) circuit in which
you develop an increasing ability to become consciously aware of and in
control of your body's processes and sensory apparatuses. This includes
developing volitional control over, for example, autonomic processes like
breathing and heart rate, with the ability to alter or manipulate how they
can be used to create aesthetically or sensorially pleasurable experiences. A
heightening of pleasure for pleasure's sake from the incoming sensory
signals and somatic sensations is discovered and developed. Leary (1994)

referred to this as "hedonic engineering." As your development and experiences broaden and become more complex, the sixth level of intelligence may become activated. Similar degrees of change and control tend to occur in the realm of your mental processes, belief structures (BS), and neural (internal bioelectrical) signaling. As you become more aware of these internal operations—how incoming information and individual thought patterns are processed—the ability to apply conscious effort into altering or controlling these operations for your benefit becomes more readily accessible.

In computer programming, when a program has the ability to treat other programs as their data and are designed to read, generate, analyze, or transform other programs—even itself—it is referred to as "metaprogramming." The same concept can apply to the human nervous system. Dr. John Lilly (1968, 2014) used this term to describe instances in the human experience where your conscious mind, through an attentive understanding of your psyche, becomes capable of observing, reflecting on, and modifying your socially conditioned mental and cultural "programs." Wilson (1983) subsequently used this term to label the general changes that happen in this stage of development, where the ability to selectively modify the belief systems and prior neural imprints of the first five circuits becomes possible, while potentially facilitating the further development of the higher circuits yet to be explored. As such, our approach to the 8-Circuit Model places an emphasis on this sixth, metaprogramming circuit as a pivotal point within the model with respect to its potential for psychospiritual development and healing—whether for yourself or in guiding others. As the metaprogramming circuit may facilitate the intentional development of the higher circuits (experiences and abilities often sought out through mystery schools, spiritual practices, psychedelic drugs, etc.), we also suggest that circuit six activation or function may lie at the crux of many mystical practices and the exploration or spontaneous experience of many other "non-ordinary states of consciousness" (NOSC). In this respect, it may offer an additional framework within which occult and spiritual practices may be approached.

While the ability to change opinions or behaviors certainly lies within the realm of potential without activating this upper circuit, the range of possibilities available to you often remains limited or rigid. For example, you may give no active consideration to the mechanisms by which choices or decisions are derived, nor may you be aware of internal biases steering your thought processes. Culturally determined constraints on the range of thought patterns and consensus opinions still tend to heavily influence perception, scope of information, and subsequent reactions to it. You will usually stay in line with the instilled cultural biases until the metaprogramming circuit develops, at which time you may come to discover the degree to which many subconscious, internal biases influence your thinking and behavior. You may become increasingly aware of the biases of others in how they navigate and operate within the world.

This recognition leads to a new perspective of others, with a deeper understanding of each having perhaps similar, but completely separate viewpoints, thought patterns, and experiences influencing the way in which they see and operate within the world. With this recognition, you begin accounting for this individualized experience, and an increasing awareness that information and experience seem relative and subjective. While activation of this circuit does not inherently eliminate bias, you tend to develop a more relativistic viewpoint in which multiple thought patterns or models of reality can be simultaneously perceived, evaluated, and held with value. This can make your bias more conscious and less rigid as a result. The concept of self becomes increasingly qualitative, with questions not necessarily having one absolute answer, but a multiplicity of possible correct answers. Accordingly, this circuit is also considered one of neurological relativism and the multidimensional self.

These experiences may correlate to Freud's "oceanic experience" or Maslow's "peak experience" in which you no longer lie "in" socially-defined space, socially-defined time, or the socially-defined ego (Wilson; 2020:145). In occult and esoteric currents, this has been described as the "No-mind" or "no-form" of Zen Buddhism, "omniform" of Platonic idealism, and "Nemo" (no-man) in the language of alchemical Rosicrucianism.

Wade labels this stage of development as "authentic consciousness" (1996), and states that by achieving it you tend to develop greater spontaneity, honesty, creativity, appreciation, and richness of emotion as your self-expression seems to bloom. Thought patterns tend to become more problem-centered and detached rather than ego-centered. Commonly, it allows for a heightened personal independence, possibly with a desire for more privacy or resistance to the elements of culturalization or social pressures. You no longer tend to define yourself by any one particular group dynamic or as belonging to a particular, culturally-defined region, but rather as a human citizen of Earth. Divisiveness and various types of destructive "othering" between in-groups and out-groups have been an ongoing societal issue throughout human history and throughout the world. It may be possible that a widespread development of this more complex intelligence would help in resolving or overcoming this problem. This is further explored and developed in Chapter XII on movement toward what we refer to as the Post-Common Era (PCE).

Wade describes how fear and compulsiveness tend to become less and less, and energies that were bound up in these fear-based processes are freed up and put toward new processes of creativity and self-refinement. The need for external affection and recognition found in the previous stages becomes less sought out as validation becomes derived internally. (Difficulty with acting from an internal locus of control and experiencing/accepting internal validation are common issues encountered in therapy with clients of all ages.)

According to Wade, the complex changes occurring in mentation at this level stem from increasing activity of the right cerebral hemisphere and further coordinated entrainment between the two hemispheres, allowing for the ability to control ego-defense systems of the subconscious. You have a greater understanding of your internal processes, and are able to become more consciously aware of incidences that trigger a response within the earlier circuits and the emotionally driven limbic system. As this occurs, you become better able to separate your emotions from the content of the actual event, and can refrain from acting on them without repression. In other words, you are able to fully feel and recognize the emotional response while maintaining the ability to step aside and not have the reaction consume how you respond. This description seems to rather closely resemble the Buddhist concept of non-attachment.

The human brain, through its early developments, constructs lenses of perception ("reality tunnels") through which every experience is filtered in order to maintain an internal *status quo* that continually reaffirms these constructed models of reality. The vast majority of information that is taken in gets processed through this filter, then molded to fit into and reinforce the reality tunnel. Information that is unable to match or reinforce the established model(s) of the world generally is ignored and remains unprocessed—as though it never happened. These experiences fall into the category of "cognitive dissonance." If the experience is highly enough charged, it may end up being repressed instead—registered, but immediately pushed out of conscious experience, unprocessed.

Prior to activation of the metaprogramming circuit, this filtering tends to be an automatic, unconscious process—neither seen, sensed, nor even taken into consideration. While these programs seem to result from mental processes, the individual tends to remain oblivious to their existence as an internally generated entity. The world we live in tends to be experienced as a mechanical, "objective" reality, existing externally from the individual. With circuit six activation, the nervous system becomes self-aware of its active participation in this process. Its role in creating phenomenological "reality" becomes recognized as a subjective, participatory experience wherein changes in perspective can drastically alter the meaning of an experience.

Cognition now tends to emphasize a more relational understanding, drawing connections between variables with interdependency and open boundaries. Common traits and seemingly disparate information are considered from a systems approach and meta-systemic conceptualization. Relativism, change, and conflict become seen as a more accurate description of the world. An increased tolerance, or even a preference for ambiguity, uncertainty, paradox, and flux can be developed. Despite this, you may still tend to knowingly commit to a particular position, fully accepting responsibility for the choice to do so (rather than being blissfully ignorant of them), and remaining open to new ideas. For example, you might maintain a preference for ideas of a practical nature over abstractions far removed from the physical world you must navigate on a daily basis.

With this more complex understanding of many of the rules of reality and the structure of the self, you might opt to explore or take on pursuits more in line with personal desires without the reins of fear holding you back. You may be driven toward an individual pursuit with less concern for how socially acceptable or even how well-comprehended by society it may be. However, due to an expanded flexibility of neurorelativity—which tends to allow for a deeper understanding and respect for the equal greatness within others—this is unlikely to be done at the expense of others; it is reflective of various occult maxims (e.g., *"Do what thou Wilt shall be the whole of the Law"* [Thelema]; *"An'ye harm none, do what ye will"* [Wicca]). As Wade states: *"Formal laws are redefined by their regulative function and become subordinated to social and self systems as equilibrium systems."* At times, this may result in your being committed to this personal pursuit, while no longer being concerned with placating others who may stand in the way of your progress—so much so that this may come off as rude in your intolerance of others holding you back. You may conclude something akin to Maslow's (1954:179) noted *"dichotomy between selfishness and unselfishness disappears altogether in healthy people because in principle every act is both selfish and unselfish."* To you, your actions may simply be pragmatic to your journey.

Problem-solving may become more internally generated, with choices increasingly being made based on intuition as well as on how rationally optimal it may seem. You may tend to become less attached by ego to a particular choice; this may be interpreted by others as increased ambivalence. You may approach options under the pretense of "whatever happens, happens," trusting that the resulting events will, ultimately, turn out fine regardless of the actual outcome. This is not a case of *pronioa* (in which you think Universe conspires to your benefit), but rather a sense of self-assurance in making the scenario work regardless of the outcome. This may even reach the point in which the chosen choices and paths are seen more as games or playful musings of how the world operates—a gamification of reality with Universe and life being the playing field. It might become entertaining to increasingly pull randomness into decision-making, or even into your life course as a whole. An example of this would be using tools (such as a coin flip or rolling of dice) to make decisions for you, for the whimsy of just seeing what happens.

A tendency toward more flexibility or adaptability brings with it more openness to, and less defense against, dystonic information. Increased awareness of inconsistencies in thought patterns, behavior, or self leads to becoming more likely to put effort into changing these things to coincide with actively chosen beliefs and desires.

The mind and its contents become recognized as functionally identical in terms of neural signaling. Other people (the observed) become understood to exist as a partial subjective interpretation of their full self, as defined by the experience and interpretation of the individual (the observer). By the same token, you come to recognize that you exist only to another person as a filtered form defined by the other person's nervous system. There exists a different version of yourself within the mind of each person who knows you, meaning there exists, in a sense, a multiplicity of various versions of yourself in the heads of others. The observer of the information becomes the one creating and solidifying its definition. This leads to something like the Zen koan Wilson was so fond of asking: *"Who is the master that makes the grass green?"* The answer is, of course, yourself, the perceiver, the definer, and the interpreter of information. Whether this information comes with eyes open or closed, ultimately, what is seen stems from the same thing— derivatives of the brain's signals and internal neural circuitry.

Dr. John Lilly is often quoted as saying, *"In the province of the mind, there are no limits"* (Lilly, 1978). As the mind becomes readily able to reflect upon itself, you may form an idea, then form a new idea about this as a second-level ideation, which may then be followed by a tertiary-level idea about the second-level idea... This process can go on creating meta-ideas to no end. Wilson (1983) relates the mind to a mirror that reflects anything, yet does not hold onto anything. Your mind also can be aware of your ability to consciously reflect something else at any time, simply by altering the angle from which it is perceived.

Activation of this circuit may begin to elicit what are thought of as extrasensory experiences as ego defenses loosen or dissolve. As Alli (2014) states, *"The psychic process kicks into action whenever we are the most creative and alive."* The newly refined sensitivity to internal and external processes via the central nervous system (CNS) and sensory system begins to unfold. With this, a broader range of perceptions may become accessible. Alli describes Circuit 6 as the "psychic intelligence circuit" with a natural sense of clairvoyance forming from this increased CNS sensitivity. He also references states of engaged intuition, telepathy, and what is described as a finer "personal radar" in interactions with others and the external world.

Impediments and psychological blockages can inhibit this ability in many people. A significant portion of brain activity is dedicated to the ongoing inhibition of activity. Recent neuroimaging studies of NOSC and psychedelic states which may elicit circuit six experiences, show a possible transient downregulation of inhibitory function. (For more on this, see "transient hypofrontality theory" in the previous chapter and the section on psychedelics below.) Based on this, it would not be a huge leap to postulate that some of these "extra-sensory experiences" may be experienced or accessible at all times, but our brains filter them out—and that those who claim to experience them may simply have less of a filter. For example, children and animals are thought to possess these extrasensory abilities as they have little in the way of filters and blockages. In these instances, however, the active cognition necessary to understand and utilize it to its full potential as a tool of self-development and conscious change is often lacking. With metaprogramming consciousness, you do.

Alli goes on to discuss this as an innate "animal" sense that can be tapped into and integrated with the conscious mind. When this integration takes place, extrasensory occurrences become available without some of the harsher, more sudden shocks that can trigger this circuit (e.g., intense ritualistic exercises and entheogenic substances). The "inner animal" is said to instinctively know these sensory experiences, while the refined mind processes and integrates them into something available and useful to the individual. During the stages between C-2 and C-6 (C-3 through C-5), this information gets filtered out per cognitive dissonance, as discussed above. As these experiences tend not to be culturally recognized or accepted, there exists little-to-no framework for them to fit into.

This "animal" part of self is the emotional intelligence of the second circuit, which is said to act as an anchor for sixth circuit experiences. Sixth circuit activation can become overwhelming to the nervous system; or the individual may become detached from a firm grounding in cultural consensus reality (e.g., the experiences of "spiritual emergence" or "spiritual emergencies" as described by Grof and discussed in Chapter VII). If this happens, and the experiences or information are unable to be integrated in a healthy way, it can create difficulty for someone trying to navigate within society. This may be a point in development in which you disengage from society altogether to further pursue your spiritual journey. There are many tales of individuals who became hermits to delve deeper into their journey. If you wish to continue functioning within society and feel the need to "ground" yourself from overactive sixth circuit activity in which psychic or extrasensory experiences may become excessive, the use of second circuit exercises may prove a useful tool. A well-known exercise for this is to sit in a chair, bend forward, place your head between your knees, and make grunts, growls, or other animalistic sounds to activate your "inner animal."

Another aspect that can become problematic with sixth circuit activation is the ability to differentiate genuine, expanded perception from psychological projection. As these can seem like subtle differences, it becomes important to take an honest, introspective look at the experiences, and how much of yourself is being put into them. Again, at this level of perception, your neurological biases are considered within the experience; however, differentiating it can be less than straightforward. Carrying too much emotional attachment can often get in the way of genuine perception. It may feel contradictory that you become aware of the processes of your brain circuitry with reality becoming recognized as a subjective interpretation, while simultaneously trying to sort out which newly acquired sensory experiences are based on projections of the psyche. You must learn to question and parse out what may be projection, while at the same time, grasping how all experience stems from the filter of your neurocircuitry—a thin line of differentiation. Many experiences and incoming signals at this stage can seem contradictory, yet each contains a degree of truth. As your awareness of neurological relativism unfolds, you become more capable of holding multiple sets of incoming information simultaneously with a more flexible, undogmatic acceptance of each aspect of truth (a phenomenon Wilson playfully referred to as "catma").

> *"One projects one's expectations of God onto the white noise as if the noise were signals; one bears the voice of God in the Noise. With a bit of proper programming under the right conditions, with the right dose, at the right time, one can program almost anything into the noise within one's cognitive limits; the limits are only one's own conceptual limits, including limits set by one's repressed, inhibited, and forbidden areas of thought."*
> — John C. Lilly

Contradictions and strange loops become more commonplace as your perspective broadens. You become more aware of internal contradictions within the psyche, and better able to discern and integrate these toward a more functional whole. Internal dichotomies may begin to break down— for instance, masculine and feminine parts of self may become more accepted regardless of birth sex. Wilson says that, experientially, *"it is the awareness that I am not male, American, white, middle-aged, or any other category; I am not the previous space-time imprints; I am not the opinion of myself; I am unknown and unknowable"* (Wilson; 2020:140). What may have once been considered the more "unattractive" parts of self may be met with greater acceptance, with an overall increase in self-esteem and decreased ego defenses.

Wilson states,

> *"The sixth-circuit neuro-programmer has no 'personality' in the normal way that men and women have personality...no longer human...they no*

longer possess a 'self' in the way ordinary people possess—and are possessed by—self." (Wilson; 2020:149)

He also quoted one of Leary's favorite metaprogramming metaphors: *"You can be anyone you want this time around"* (Wilson; 2020:149).

Attempts to convey these types of experiences may sound like irrational ramblings of nonsense to those who have never had multidimensional or "peak" experiences themselves. The neuro-programmer will often be fluent with language, yet may become aware of the limitations of verbal language, and opt for more metaphoric language that better encompasses the ineffable symbolism of the right hemisphere of the brain. This revelation may be summed up by a quote Wilson (1983) attributes to Alfred Korzybski: *"When we split verbally that which is never split existentially, we introduce fallacies into our thinking."* In this way, those who have had such an experience sound illogical and fallacious to those without the first-hand experience of holding simultaneously contradictory views. The relative dominance of the limbic system in previous stages, with its inability to process information in anything other than binary, dualistic terms, stands in the way.

L.A. Paul, in his book *Transformative Experience* (2016), says that an experience is considered transformative when it satisfies two subdimensions: "epistemic transformation" and "personal transformation." Epistemic transformation refers to experiences that are impossible to imagine from the standpoint of one who has not actually had such an experience. Personal transformation refers to experiences that change your preferences, perspectives, desires, or values. Activation of the metaprogramming circuit allows for just such a transformative experience.

A.H. Esser notes that this process of individuation often does not happen without its downsides:

"This process of individualization is unavoidably painful. Escapes from the process into self-individualization or mindless other-directness are manifold. They bring about the closed mind that does not want to know itself." (Esser, 1974:307)

As the hold of the ego loosens, you often find yourself intellectually unwilling to let go completely. Total death of the ego remains difficult for virtually everyone. Now develops the dilemma of becoming increasingly drawn toward the breakdown of duality into the unity of Universe/Dao, while the fear of being engulfed or destroyed remains.

During this process, the fear of death may be cast off. Causality becomes viewed as circular. With this, life and death are seen as part of a much larger, universal process. This, says Wade (1996), is the most significant shift to occur, as it has drastic effects on how you look at the world. Maslow (1954:179) also recognized this emerging breakdown of dualism when he described the stage of self-actualization: *"The higher and the lower are not in opposition but in agreement, and a thousand serious philosophical dilemmas are discovered to have more than two horns, or paradoxically, no horns at all."* As Wilson states, these new terms are simply the result of the individual *"merely confronting infinity where we least expected to encounter it—in our own lonely selves."*

C-6 IN RELATION TO MYSTICAL, MAGICKAL, & OTHER SPIRITUAL PRACTICES

"We look for the Secret—the Philosopher's Stone, the Elixir of the Wise, Supreme Enlightenment, 'God' or whatever...and all the time it is carrying us about... It is the human nervous system itself."
— Robert Anton Wilson

There exist many esoteric traditions which have been employed for millennia, and devoted to the search for Self, spiritual development, and understanding, connection with, and exploration of the deeper meanings of existence. Wilson (1983) notes that the vast majority of occult literature carrying validity for self-development, provide activities or tricks to help the mind activate the metaprogramming circuit. This includes the steps of the "Great Work" or "high magick" practices. Leary and Wilson both were influenced by spiritual and metaphysical traditions from both the East and West. Not the least of these were Aleister Crowley's Thelemic practices.

These practices synergistically combine the methods and practices of both the Western Mystery Traditions as developed and practiced by the Hermetic Order of the Golden Dawn (a magickal Order Crowley belonged to, and which is based on an amalgamation of esoteric Egyptian and Greco-Roman traditions, Gnosticism, Qabalah, Rosicrucianism, and Freemasonry), as well as various Eastern traditions, such as Taoism/I-Ching, Theravada Buddhism, Vedantic/Raja yoga, and Hinduism.

These systems are designed to facilitate changes in the consciousness of their practitioners. Such changes can be easily and clearly explained within the framework of the 8-Circuit Model. The lower four circuits correspond to the typical stages of developmental psychology, whereas the higher circuits are more transpersonal in nature (not everyone develops their higher circuits). As previously mentioned, our work emphasizes Circuit 6, the metaprogramming circuit, as a means of initiating intentional, conscious reprogramming of the "human biocomputer."

Many traditions and psychospiritual practices can be utilized to explore, develop, and ultimately transform and balance each circuit—even allowing for a re-imprinting of the circuits. Contemporary mainstream psychotherapy typically focuses on what could be considered the treatment of the lower circuits. It often remains ignorant or dismissive of the existence or importance of the upper circuits and their role in one's well-being, sense of deeper purpose, and overall wholeness as a fully-formed, self-actualized individual. On the other hand, magickal systems tend to be made up of more complex systems of self-exploration and development that may allow for de-programming and re-programming (i.e., metaprogramming) of the individual, spanning all circuits.

Thus, the study and practice of ritual and magick may be used as a tool for the intentional rewiring of your nervous system. As noted in earlier chapters, imprinting occurs at a critical period in the early development of each circuit. It is stage-specific developmental learning, and a period of high neural proliferation which occurs when a particular psychological stage begins. During this time, the person may be exposed to a stimulus (e.g., person, object, event) that becomes heavily associated with that developmental stage, forming the basis of all future behavioral and psychological patterns related to the correlated circuit. This may lie at the root of various personality and mood disorders, compulsive behaviors, and other pervasive effects that unconsciously influence you throughout your life. The alchemical maxim *Solve et Coagula* ("to dissolve and coagulate"; that is, something must be broken down before it can be rebuilt into something new) becomes relevant here. By practicing methods that follow this maxim, you can heal your pasts, transform your identities, and re-program potentially limiting or harmful belief systems, behavioral/emotional/thought patterns, and responses at their core. Moreover, this type of self-exploration and development (which may or may not include the use of psychoactive or psychedelic drugs) can result in an evolving of consciousness into increasingly more complex, expansive, and creative states.

> *"Rebellion is an individual action; it has nothing to do with the crowd. Rebellion has nothing to do with politics, power, violence. Rebellion has something to do with changing your consciousness, your silence, your being. It is a spiritual metamorphosis. Each individual passing through a rebellion is not fighting with anybody else, but is fighting only with his own darkness. Swords are not needed, bombs are not needed; what is needed is more alertness, more meditativeness, more love, more prayerfulness, more gratitude. Surrounded by all of these qualities, you are born anew."*
> — Osho

NEUROPLASTICITY

Neuroplasticity refers to *"the ability of the nervous system to change its activity in response to intrinsic or extrinsic stimuli by reorganizing its structure, functions, or connections"* (Mateos-Aparicio & Rodriguez-Moreno, 2019). It is the brain's ability to adapt. Neuroplasticity seems to be primarily driven at a biochemical level by serotonin (Klöbl, M, et al; 2021) and oxytocin, with oxytocin receptors on serotoninergic terminals impacting serotonin signaling in the nucleus accumbens (Froemke & Young, 2021).

TYPES OF PLASTICITY
(MATEOS-APARICIO & RODRIGUEZ-MORENO, 2019)

- **Evolutionary plasticity:** This may cause both positive and negative effects during neuron proliferation and development. During "critical developmental periods," the organizing process (morphogenetic function) attains the tipping-point threshold of the external and internal environment by triggering or blocking the expression of genetic programs. Not enough stimuli can permanently alter the newly-formed structures. This is generally considered long-term or permanent.

- **Reactive plasticity:** Reaction to environmental changes. An immediate response after a transient exposure to a significant stimulus and limited to the period of stimulation. A single factor can have different effects during different stages of development.

- **Adaptive plasticity:** Functional and/or structural changes from long-term or repeated exposure to stimuli/long-term potentiation at the synaptic and multimodular level. This includes both temporary changes and permanent reorganization.

Functional changes can include:

- Neurotransmitter release
- Receptor action
- Intracellular mechanism of signal transmission

The latter may be the mechanism through which classical psychedelics work via the 5-HT_{2a} receptors as discussed below.

Structural changes involve the transformation of genotype into phenotype and can include:

- Synaptic innervations
- Shape and length of spines and dendrites
- Synaptogenesis
- Reparative plasticity: functional or structural recovery of impaired/damaged neuronal circuits.

LEVELS OF PLASTICITY

- **Synaptic level:** typical of learning and memories as a result of processing information from the internal and external environment.
- **Local neuronal circuit level:** may follow changes in the intensity of incoming signals; e.g., compensation of one region to accommodate for loss or damage in another region.
- **Multimodular level:** supports new relationships among individual regions of the brain.

ACTIVITIES THAT INFLUENCE NEUROPLASTICITY

- **Increases in neuroplasticity:** environmental enrichment, physical activity, hypoxia/ischemia, trauma, SSRI's, Haloperidol, classic psychedelics.

One of the best ways to increase neuroplasticity is through physical activity/exercise (Cassihas et al; 2016, Hötting & Röder; 2013, El-Sayes et al; 2019).

- **Decreases in neuroplasticity:** stress, corticosteroids, depression, aging, irradiation, alcohol, psychostimulants, opiates.

PSYCHEDELICS & NEUROPLASTICITY

Classical psychedelics (e.g., psilocybin and LSD) can act as Circuit 6 activators via the Serotonin 2a (5-HT_{2a}) receptors. As noted in Chapter VI (Circuit 4), the same serotonin 2a pathways act as a key evolutionary driver of the development of the prefrontal cortices (Xing et al, 2020). Research has shown that these classical psychedelics influence neuroplasticity via TrkB, mTOR, and 5-HT_{2A} pathways as well as neurogenesis of new axons, dendrites, dendrite spines, synapses, and increased synaptic functioning (Lukasiewicz et al, 2021; de Vos et al, 2021; Shao et al, 2021), thus qualifying as "psychoplastogens." According to Olsen (2018),

"to be classified as a psychoplastogen, a compound should produce a measurable change in plasticity (e.g., changes in neurite growth, dendritic spine density, synapse number, intrinsic excitability) within a short

period of time (typically 24–72 hours) following a single administration. Because their impact on neural plasticity enables subsequent stimuli to reshape neural circuits, they should produce relatively long-lasting changes in behavior that extend beyond the acute effects of the drug."

Studies have demonstrated *"rapid and enduring improvements—up to 30 days following [a single] administration"* (de Vos et al, 2021) through changes in the expression of plasticity-related genes and proteins, including Brain-Derived Neurotrophic Factor (BDNF).

Other compounds that qualify as psychoplastogens include other tryptamines such as DMT and 5-Meo-DMT, as well as non-classical psychedelic and psychedelic-like drugs such as ketamine, scopolamine, DOI, MDMA, and Iboga. There have been a couple of pharmaceutical substances that also qualify, but are not available. While other antidepressants, notably SSRIs, SNRIs, and tricyclics have also demonstrated a degree of increased neuroplasticity, this effect tends to be significantly slower and through an indirect process, usually relying on neurotrophic factors and other proteins.

One of the areas of the brain that maintains the generation of new nerve components throughout one's lifetime is the hippocampal dentate gyrus. The hippocampus plays a critical role in memory and learning tasks that involve temporal encoding ("time-binding"). Temporal processing is necessary for a form of classical conditioning known as "trace conditioning" in which a conditioned stimulus and unconditioned stimuli are separated by time. Aberrations in the serotonin system can alter trace conditioning, and can break down the ability to separate a past experience (e.g., trauma) from the present, with the 5-HT2A receptors specifically being involved in temporal encoding. Psilocybin has been demonstrated to enhance adaptation to unwanted stimuli in trace fear conditioning tests, seeming to facilitate the extinction of fear conditioning, with potential applications in post-traumatic stress disorder (PTSD; Bangasser et al., 2006).

It has also been proposed that classical psychedelics may influence these $5-HT_{2A}$ receptors by *"removing the brakes on adult neuroplasticity, inducing a state similar to that of neurodevelopment"* (Lepow et al., 2021). According to Terence Mckenna,

"Psilocybin has a unique relationship to the evolution of the human nervous system. In fact, it turns the human nervous system into an antenna for the Gaian mind... If this antenna is not present, then human beings have to think up their own program, and it's usually power crazed, lethal, shortsighted, and grabby." *(Sheldrake, McKenna, and Abraham, 1992:137)*

Animal studies have shown preliminary evidence that sub-hallucinogenic doses of psilocybin (< ~2.5mg psilocybin analyte or 0.25 grams dried fungus) may have a stronger neuroplastic effect (Catlow et al, 2013), whereas larger doses of classical psychedelics activating the $5\text{-}HT_{2A}$ receptors may have a greater effect in increasing global communication and integration between brain regions, including regions that do not commonly communicate (Petri et al, 2014). More research is needed in these areas, but recent research into these classical psychedelics have developed some intriguing new theories about their influence on the brain, and how they may facilitate change in existing neural pathways, patterns, and programs.

For example, Dr. Robin Carhart-Harris has significantly contributed to developments in this area. He has designed modern human brain imaging studies with LSD, psilocybin, MDMA, and DMT. Of particular relevance is his work on "entropic brain theory." In this theory, entropy—defined as *"a dimensionless quantity that is used for measuring uncertainty about the state of a system"*—is applied in the context of states of consciousness and associated neurodynamics. The psychedelic state is considered an exemplar of the primary state of consciousness that preceded the development of normal waking consciousness, and *"a prototypically high-entropy state of consciousness (i.e., higher than normal waking consciousness)...the brain exhibits more characteristics of criticality in the psychedelic state than are apparent during normal waking consciousness"* (Carhart-Harris et al., 2014). These primary states are thought to depend on a collapse of the otherwise highly organized activity within the default-mode network (DMN) of the brain and a decoupling between the DMN and the medial temporal lobes (MTL) wherein the limbic system resides.

Further integrating the components of the entropic brain hypothesis into psychedelic states, the notion of Relaxed Beliefs Under Psychedelics (REBUS) was formulated by Drs. Carhart-Harris and Karl Friston. This postulated something that seems much like metaprogramming via

> "'an entropic effect on spontaneous cortical activity—psychedelics work to relax the precision of high-level priors or beliefs, thereby liberating bottom-up information flow, particularly via intrinsic sources such as the limbic system.' Through this mechanism it is proposed that the potential therapeutic use of psychedelics may work by relaxing 'pathological over-weighted priors that contribute to mental health expressions by sensitizing these priors to intrinsic bottom-up signaling allowing for de-weighting and revision. It is further discussed how psychedelics 'an bring about the revision of other heavily weighted high-level priors, not directly related to mental health, such as those underlying partisan and/or overly-confident political, religious, and/or philosophical perspectives.'" (Carhart-Harris & Friston, 2019)

In addition to dampening the connection within the DMN and its decoupling with the MTL, increased connections and communication between previously unconnected brain regions and systems of the body (e.g., physical, emotional, neuroendocrine, psychological, neurogenetic, spiritual) allow for novel sensory experiences. For example, people under the influence of psychedelics often experience synaesthesia, a cross-wiring of the senses (e.g., you might "taste" color or "see" sound). One of the authors of this book (Turetzky) had a patient who reported an ability to see auras, and who had unique visual and sensory experiences associated with different types of people and their facial features and expressions. In study-ing this case, she described a novel form of synaesthesia that she calls *idiovis-ual-empathic synaesthesia* (Turetzky, 2018). The term *idio* comes from the Greek, meaning "one's own" or "private." So, the name refers to having non-veridical visual experiences (e.g., seeing an aura) in response to reading emotional cues from others, such as facial expressions. The application of NOSC-inducing practices (such as psychedelics, meditation, breathwork, ritual, magickal and other mystical systems) seems able to facilitate the development of such abilities. Based on this case study (along with myriad other reports of extrasensory experiences and abilities), and in consideration of relevant neuroscience research, Dr. Turetzky conjectures that synaesthesia is the basis of the evolution of new senses. Thus, it is proposed that the mechanism underlying the advancement of the upper circuits is the rewiring of your nervous system and other physical/non-physical body systems in ways that create new channels for receiving and representing information. This rewiring impacts both the physical and non-physical dimensions (the "gross" and the "subtle" planes, respectively, as described in alchemy and magick) of self, others, and the world around us.

NEUROBIOLOGY OF CIRCUIT 6

Recent explorations into the field of neurotheology and neuroimaging of non-ordinary states of consciousness (NOSC) have presented some evidence of what may be occurring in such states within the brain and nervous system. Belief in general—whether religious or nonreligious—has been associated with greater activation in the ventromedial prefrontal cortex (vmPFC) of the brain (Yaden & Newberg, 2022:100); while the neural correlates of religious beliefs seem to involve brain regions relating to theory of mind (inferior frontal gyrus and temporal lobes), emotional regulation (middle temporal and middle frontal gyrus), abstract thought and processing, and imagery (inferior and superior temporal regions) (Yaden & Newberg, 2022:101). Theory of mind relates to *"the understanding that others have intentions, desires, beliefs, perceptions, and emotions different from one's own, and that such intentions, desires, and so forth affect people's actions and behaviors"* (American Psychological Association, 2006). Interestingly,

> *"low levels of the neurotransmitter levels, as found in Parkinson's disease, showed a tendency toward decreased religiosity. Additionally, activity in the nucleus accumbens, the primary brain region of dopamine release, was found to precede peak spiritual feelings." (Yaden & Newberg, 2022:101)*

Drs. David Yaden and Andrew Newberg go on to argue that:

"alterations in the thalamus, a central structure that coordinates brain processes between cortical areas and also between the sensory organs and the brain, might be essential for changing a person's belief system and overall approach to life. There is some evidence that supports altered thalamic function associated with intense spiritual experiences." (Yaden & Newberg, 2022:204)

Additionally, they cite research postulating *"a combination of prefrontal lobe and cerebellar function helps people to create various probabilistic models of reality"* (Yaden & Newberg, 2022:220; Blackwood et al, 2004; Demanuele et al, 2015).

CIRCUIT 6 ENERGY

QUALITIES OF BALANCED CIRCUIT 6 ENERGY

- Charismatic; master of oneself
- Access to the "source of all knowledge" (Akashic records/heart resonances)
- Experiences "cosmic consciousness"
- Nonattachment to material things or the fear of death
- Sexual: May experience self as androgynous, no longer needing another person: "distracts one's inner bliss"; Celibacy may be a natural but unnecessary choice

QUALITIES OF EXCESSIVE CIRCUIT 6 ENERGY

- Egomania, pride
- "Psychic arrogance"
- Over-intellectualization
- Authoritarian, manipulative
- Religiously dogmatic
- Static and inaccurate interpretations of events, personal fears
- Recurring nightmares and delusional fantasies

QUALITIES OF DEFICIENT CIRCUIT 6 ENERGY

- Non-assertive
- Undisciplined
- Overly sensitive to feelings of others
- Afraid of success
- Inability to distinguish ego & higher self

CIRCUIT 6 ACTIVATION
CIRCUIT 6 ACTIVATING ACTIVITIES

Activities that allow yourself to become consciously aware of your internal processes, thoughts, and behavioral patterns, and actively manipulate or redefine these processes.

- Sensory deprivation
- Raja Yoga
- Self-hypnosis
- NLP
- Chanting or ecstatic dance/drumming
- Ritual/magickal practices; "sex magick"
- Neidan/Daoist internal alchemy practices

CIRCUIT 6 ACTIVATING SUBSTANCES

Moderate psilocybin dose (~1–3.5 mg analyte), low-to-moderate LSD dose (~100–3500μg), mescaline/peyote, morning glory seeds.

INTEGRATION INTERVENTION MODEL CONSIDERATIONS
CIRCUIT 2 ACTIVATING ACTIVITIES

Circuit 2 and Circuit 6 are vertically connected, with Circuit 2 acting as an anchor to Circuit 6 shock experiences. Experiences of increased perceptual input, greater awareness of your neurocircuitry and internal belief systems/operating programs, and exposure to seemingly contradictory multidimensional perspectives, can be jarring to the rigid dichotomous delineations and boundaries of the second circuit. Activities that activate the second circuit—with its dependency on the definition of boundaries and activation of the "animalistic" emotional dominance of the limbic system's black-and-white thinking—can help integrate experiences of neuroelectric intelligence sufficient to compartmentalize and operate within societal game rules.

CLINICAL APPROACH CONSIDERATIONS
(REFER TO RECOMMENDED READING FOR RESOURCES)

- Motivational Interviewing (MI)

"Motivational Interviewing is a collaborative, goal-oriented style of communication with particular attention to the language of change. It is designed to strengthen personal motivation for, and commitment to a specific goal by eliciting and exploring the person's own reasons for change within an atmosphere of acceptance and compassion." (Miller & Rollnick, 2013:29)

The key quality of MI is a guiding style of communication that sits between following (good listening) and directing (giving advice), designed to empower people to change by drawing out their own meaning, importance, and capacity for change.

- NLP

"The term 'Neuro-linguistic Programming,' coined by [Richard] Bandler and [John] Grinder, refers to purported systematic links between a person's internal experience (neuro), their language (linguistic), and their patterns of behaviour (programming)." (Tothey & Matheson, 2003)

Methods of Neuro-Linguistic Programming may act as a means of behavior and thought pattern modification through programming and re-education of the mind and nervous system.

Leary's Bio-Evolutionary Stages 16–18		
Stage 16	Neuro-Electric Receptivity	The sixth circuit emerges when the nervous system begins to understand and control its own functioning as a bio-electric transceiver. Stage 16 is the passive, exploratory phase of the neuroelectric experience. Self-indulgent reception—in most "psychic" phenomena, the so-called "sensitive" passively receives. There are fewer cases of people becoming transmitters of neurophysical signals.
		At Stage 16 the post-larval human becomes aware of the bio-electric nature of brain activity. It is like removing the panels which protect the computer and exposing the detailed operation of circuitry.
		Sixth Circuit consciousness is crystal-clear, radiant, electric, frictionless, unencumbered by material inertias. It is understandable that a period of self-indulgent playing with raw, direct, smooth humming would occur.
Stage 17	Neuro-Electric Intelligence	Eventually one begins to wonder about the mechanisms and meanings of the new incoming phenomena. The neuro-electric intelligence becomes selective, experimental, recollective. One learns how to control and direct the energies involved.
		The Sixth Circuit is the central bio-computer. It receives signals from Circuits 1–5. These signals, regardless of their original sensory location, reach the brain as electro-chemical signals. The Sixth Circuit brain also receives signals from molecular memory banks within neurons—also in the form of "off-on" signals.
		When the 6th brain is activated, a long, complex & disciplined training is required to establish conscious integrated control.

		The Sixth Brain cannot slow down to the Newtonian rate of emotion-muscular, manual-mental, or domestic-social exchanges in "island realities."
		The Sixth Circuit capacity of the brain operates best in a protective environment which responds at Einsteinian speeds and relativities—or at least where the others present refrain from imposing larval [C1–C4] signals on the transception.
Stage 18	Neuro-Electric Fusion	The synergistic communication between two or more contelligences operating at the sixth circuit. Telepathy.
		The highest, fastest, most complex form of human communication—two or more nervous systems transceiving at electro-magnetic velocities. The ability to transceive at neuro-electric intensities and speeds is designed for post-terrestrial existence.
		It is true that in every generation premature evolutes exhibit Sixth Circuit contelligence. We think of the psychics, the fey, the mediums, the prophets. Great mystic philosophers—as well as the idiot savants and the strange eccentric geniuses who for centuries have been carted off to the insane asylums because they saw too much too soon. Less civilized tribes have often instinctively understood that strange mental perceptions are signs of future endowment, and have defined socially accepted roles for the Sixth Circuit prematures. Such people find no place in "larval society" dominated by C1–C4.

Table 13: *Leary's Bio-Evolutionary Stages 16-18*

Authentic Consciousness	
Primary Motivation	Personal growth for its own sake
Ultimate Value	Fulfilling personal mission, even if not understood
Attitude Toward Life	Calm, insightful acceptance of existential problems and constant flux. Assurance without certainty that life is inherently meaningful
Perception of Death	Physical death is unimportant except as an opportunity for greater unity. Ego death is ardently pursued through persistent practice
Self-Boundaries	At the skin
Perception of Temporality	Knowledge of past, present. Compound present as it shapes desired future. Infinite past and future
Concept of Other	Very little ego-based distortion. True empathy. Respect for personal agency, diversity, and autonomy of others. Relatively free of enculturation and conformity to social expectations. Impatient with people who impede subject's personal progress
Locus of Control	Internal—personal growth
Level of Abstraction	Post-formal Operations. Systems and meta-systemic thinking, perhaps even cross-paradigmatic. Whole brain thinking. Highly original; thinks outside of existing systems. Prefers ambiguity, uncertainty, paradox
Options for Actions	Infinite, including coalescence of all linear and holistic options
Correct Opinion	The one that works best and feels right at the moment; as circumstances change, a new solution

Table 14: *Wade's Holonomic Theory: Authentic Consciousness*

RELEVANT ASSESSMENT SCALES

Dr. Pamela Reed's Self-Transcendence Scale
(doi:10.1097/00012272-199106000-00008)

DIRECTIONS: Please indicate the extent to which each item below describes you. There are no right or wrong answers. As you respond to each item, think of how you see yourself at this time of your life.

Circle the number that is the best response for you.

1 = Not at All
2 = Very Little
3 = Somewhat
4 = Very Much

At this time of my life, I see myself as:

1. Having hobbies or interests I can enjoy	1 2 3 4
2. Accepting myself as I grow older.	1 2 3 4
3. Being involved with other people or my community when possible	1 2 3 4
4. Adjusting well to my present life situation	1 2 3 4
5. Adjusting to changes in my physical abilities	1 2 3 4
6. Sharing my wisdom or experience with others	1 2 3 4
7. Finding meaning in my past experiences	1 2 3 4
8. Helping others in some way	1 2 3 4
9. Having an ongoing interest in learning	1 2 3 4
10. Able to move beyond some things that once seemed so important	1 2 3 4
11. Accepting death as a part of life.	1 2 3 4
12. Finding meaning in my spiritual beliefs	1 2 3 4
13. Letting others help me when I may need it	1 2 3 4
14. Enjoying my pace of life.	1 2 3 4
15. Letting go of past regrets.	1 2 3 4

CHAPTER X

CIRCUIT SEVEN (C-7): GENETICS, GLOBAL CONNECTION, & SYNCHRONICITIES

NEUROGENETIC CIRCUIT (LEARY)
MORPHOGENETIC CIRCUIT (WILSON)

The collective unconscious contains the whole spiritual heritage of mankind's evolution born anew in the brain structure of every individual."
— Dr. Carl Gustav Jung

"Whoever looks into the water sees his own image, but behind it living creatures soon loom up."
— Dr. Carl Gustav Jung

The seventh circuit marks a significant shift within the experience of the individual whereby there seems a movement away from self-generated codes of personal operation and symbols to a source that lies outside the individual nervous system. We now enter the realm of manipulating our own genetics, of synchronicities, strange attractors, numinous experiences, and trans-conscious knowledge.

Throughout the first six circuits, these codes of human functioning progressed through basic survival needs to emotions and boundaries, beliefs, values and ideas, morals, and rapturous pleasure-seeking in perceptions.

These represent the extent to which the ego seems capable of influencing and shaping reality through personal efforts alone.

In the neurosomatic circuit of Circuit 5, you gain the view of "all are one." The metaprogramming of C-6 opens you up to "we are many." In Circuit 7 you find the view that "we are a network."

The seventh circuit acts as a broader recapitulation of the neurological developments of the third semantic circuit that emphasized logic, rationality, and deductive reasoning to build models of the world, while constructing and using symbols to convey them. The symbols now used transcend time and culture. They play a role in making up more than the single individual—but rather that of the entire species. Awareness and dialog form between the central nervous system and signals *located within the individual neurons, unlike the previous circuits which mediate processes between neurons*" (Wilson, 2020:141) coming from within the individual neuron and its makeup—specifically, your DNA and RNA.

DNA (deoxyribonucleic acid) is, of course, the combination of nucleotides—cytosine (C), guanine (G), adenine (A), and thymine (T)—that carry genetic instructions about an organism's growth, development, functioning, and reproduction. RNA (ribonucleic acid) acts in the coding, decoding, regulation, and expression of genes. In the direction of specific proteins, messenger RNA (mRNA) uses guanine, adenine, cytosine and uracil (an unmethylated form of thymine) to convey various genetic commands. This includes phenotypical traits such as hair or eye color, when to grow hair, and developmental progressions such as when an infant begins walking, or an adolescent or adult begins seeking out a suitable partner for reproduction. The ability for the expression of specific genes to be altered and turned on and off is the realm of "epigenetics." It has been demonstrated that a number of factors can alter genetic expression including medications, foods, emotional trauma, or even generational trauma that is passed on to children. If a person's great grandfather experienced a very traumatic event—say war, genocide, or severe food scarcity—this has been shown to activate or deactivate certain genetic expressions that are then passed down through the genetic line (i.e., intergenerational or transgenerational trauma; Švorcová,

2023; Kellerman, 2013; Jablonka, 2009). Tapping into this aspect of self may also open the possibility to make positive change, and directly work with and through some of these deep, generational traumas. Recent studies have shown that external manipulations of genetics can also be performed through the use of light to switch genetic markers on or off in a discipline dubbed "optogenetics." It is within the neurogenetic circuit that the individual becomes conscious of the role of their genetic makeup, and the common lineage of these experiences permeating through the species.

The gene pool becomes seen as a network that connects all humans at a cellular level—a common factor through which all can relate. This genetic component becomes recognized as having a much larger scope of influence and lifespan than the individual, or as Wilson (2020:349) refers to *"the interneuron 'conversation' of DNA and RNA, the templating of individuality out of the collective 3.5 billion-year-old gene pool."* Underlying patterns of creation and form, such as Rupert Sheldrake's work with morphogenetic fields, also falls into this level of intelligent design and awareness.

As such, you may form the perspective of individuals as a transitory node within the much larger existence of the species of which they represent only a small portion. While lineages may die out, the species will continue on even longer with a larger genetic data pool of intelligence. Awareness broadens with recognition of an even more intelligent entity beyond self—Gaia—the concept of the planetary ecosystem acting as one interconnected living organism which will continue on, even if genetic lineages and species pass into oblivion. From these realizations often come an awareness of the temporary nature of physical existence as well as a recognition of the underlying source from which each living thing can be derived. According to Wilson, *"Signals-per-second within the neuron corresponds to miles-per-second outside the body, and time is transformed by the neurogenetic imprint just as it is by the speed-of-light. We enter Eternity"* (2020:141); and you may come to understand what Yeats meant by *"Man has created death"* (Yeats, 1928).

Here you may also consider ideas such as the Eastern concepts of "reincarnation" and "transmigration." It is also here where Isaac Bonewit's "astral switchboard" is found and activated (Wilson, 2020:349). This may also correlate with Eastern tales of "Immortals" and self-refinement into a spiritual immortal, for once awakened to awareness of neurogenetic intelligence, it would become apparent that the broader definition of self or collective DNA/RNA intelligence will carry on forever. For similar reasons you may tap into neurogenetic intelligence and report experiencing a "past life" or "past lives."

> *"A global universal vision. The integrated individual sees and experiences himself and others as part of an ongoing humanity, embedded in the process of creation...feelings of belongingness and feelings of one's separateness and uniqueness as experienced as undue tension...can perceive the concrete, limited and temporal aspects of an entity simultaneously with its eternal and symbolic meaning...can cherish the essence in the seemingly most undifferentiated beings and feel at one with them."*
> *(Miller & Cook-Greuter, 1994)*

Psychologically, this stage of development makes accessible the common elements shared amongst humanity across time and space. This can be called the collective unconscious of Jungian psychologists, the Akashic records by theosophists, or what Stanislav Grof refers to as phylogenetic consciousness. Wade (1996) uses the label "transcendent consciousness." Other cultures and systems use different names for the states obtained therein (e.g., the Greeks called this the vision of Pan, and Hindus refer to it as Atman).

ARCHETYPES

This is the realm of dream imagery and archetypal figures genetically present within the psyche of all of humanity. Archetypes are vague, underlying forms of archaic patterns embedded deep within species-consciousness that universally permeate human existence regardless of culture, place, or time. These underlying themes vary in their specific manifestations as each depiction becomes filtered through perceptions and interpretations of the individual apparatus of the human nervous system, as well as through the individual's culturally ingrained notions of the nature of reality. This is neurorelativity at play—creating one's own unique description of shared universal patterns. A few examples of classic archetypal figures include the Mother, the Wise Old Man (Senex) or the Crone, the Devil, the Trickster or Jester, and the Hero. There are many variations, yet each has commonalities that define them and fit the criteria of the particular archetype.

Personal development shifts toward the transcendence of mundane aspects of existence to more "spiritual" concerns. The inherent limitations within life and individual ego reveal themselves, and a transformation takes place. The ego tries desperately to avoid the concept of impending non-existence by creating new challenges and changes that may temporarily reignite a spark of life in attempts to avoid facing the inevitable head on. After some time, the ego succumbs and comes to accept this "nothingness," causing a radical shift in directed energies. The autonomy that the ego so desperately tries to maintain is set aside, redirecting energy toward reaching outward for guidance and support from the external source of the universal processes that envelops it.

Abraham Maslow (1971) and Michael Washburn (1988) both reiterate the concept that this shift of consciousness can be attained either through the path of joy or the path of suffering as laid out in numerous esoteric traditions. Whether the initial motivation stems from ecstasy or despair does not make a difference in the end—as both lead to transcendence of the ego to grasp "Absolute Reality." According to Wade, this transition begins through a process of detachment from life after having lived it to the fullest. Following this detachment comes an internal quest and a vagueness of anxiety with the awareness of a new state.

As this increases, ordinary awareness becomes destabilized, and nonordinary states of consciousness are cultivated in greater and greater frequency. These states are characterized by feelings of ecstatic unity, the transcendence of time and space, intrinsic authority, paradoxicality in the convergence of opposites, and ineffability. The perception of time can become plastic, seeming to slow down, speed up, stretch out, or not exist at all. Sensory perceptions and the sense of the body fade away as consciousness becomes enraptured in bliss and single-pointedness. Over time, sensations, feelings, sense of self, and space-time become abandoned; you no

longer identify as an independent observer, but rather as an active participant of this process. The only object of awareness that becomes recognized
is that no true individual observer exists—only process and representation,
with all objects no longer considered objective constants.

The collective neurogenetic circuit is imprinted by advanced yogas
(biochemical-electrical stresses). It processes DNA-RNA-brain feedback
systems, and is "collective" in that it contains and has access to the whole
evolutionary "script," past and future. Experience of this circuit is numinous, "mystical," mind-shattering; here dwell the archetypes of Jung's
Collective Unconscious: Gods, Goddesses, Demons, Hairy Dwarfs, and
other personifications of the DNA programs (instincts) that govern us
(Wilson, 1983:41).

> "I think DNA is ultimately trying to create a world where the imagina-
> tion is externalized, where the mind and the external world become syn-
> chronized as one, so that basically whatever we can imagine can become
> a reality. Literally." (Brown, 2013:328)

Holotropic states of consciousness also provide deep insights into the
worldview of cultures that believe that the cosmos is populated by mythological beings, and that it is governed by various blissful and wrathful deities.
In these states, we can gain direct experiential access to the world of gods,
demons, legendary heroes, suprahuman entities, and spirit guides. We can
visit the domain of mythological realities, fantastic landscapes, and abodes
of the Beyond. The imagery of such experiences can be drawn from the
collective unconscious, and can feature mythological figures and themes
from any culture in the history of humanity. Deep personal experiences of
this realm help us realize that the images of the cosmos found in pre-indus-
trial societies are not based on superstition or primitive "magical thinking,"
but on direct experiences of alternate realities (Grof, 1998:19).

SYNCHRONICITY

As C-7 awareness comes about, you may become more aware of increasing synchronicities within your life. The concept of synchronicity was

coined by Carl Jung, who defined it as the co-occurrence of two or more meaningful events that are not causally connected, and which are not likely to occur by chance (1999; 2014; Jung & Main, 1997). As such, it is described as an "acausal connecting principle" (Jung, 2010; Samuels et al., 1986). Moreover, Jung (2010) distinguished synchronicity from merely synchronous events as follows:

> "In all cases, whether it is a question of spatial or of temporal ESP, we find a simultaneity of the normal or ordinary state with another state of experience which is not causally derivable from it, and whose objective existence can only be verified afterwards. This definition must be borne in mind particularly when it is a question of future events. They are evidently not synchronous but are synchronistic, since they are experienced as psychic images in the present, as though the objective event already existed. An unexpected content which is directly or indirectly connected with some objective external event coincides with the ordinary psychic state: this is what I call synchronicity, and I maintain that we are dealing with exactly the same category of events whether their objectivity appears separated from my consciousness in space or time." (p. 3401)

Thus, synchronicity differs from that which is synchronous in that it can also describe a psychic state in the present that corresponds with an event that has not yet happened, and which can later be confirmed upon manifestation (Jacobi, 1959; Jung & Main, 1997). Jung (1973) further specified that the experience of synchronicity involves two factors. For the first factor, an unconscious image enters the psyche either explicitly or in a symbolized form (e.g., dream, premonition). The second is an objective event that later coincides with the first factor (Jung, 1973).

David Hay defined synchronicity experiences as *"an extraordinary coincidence or...a vague sense that somehow one's life has an unfolding pattern to it"* (Yaden & Newman, 2022:209). Dr. Elsa Lau and colleagues described them as "intuitive impressions" (Lau, et al. 2020). In integral theory terms of "holons," a word coined by Arthur Koestler (1967) and summarized by Ken Wilber (1996:17) to refer to *"an entity that is itself a whole and simul-*

taneously a part of some other whole," synchronicity is said to involve the alignment of a smaller holon within a larger one (Khamsehzadeh, 2022:271).

Alli (1987) defined it as two or more events which happen simultaneously or in close proximity that bypass linear cause and effect. They are considered convergences of seemingly unrelated coordinate points, serving to evolve depth and psychological significance. This may include cases of internal imagery such as dreams seeming to correspond to external events, simultaneous feelings/thoughts among two or more people (telepathy), or seemingly incongruous juxtapositions that combine to form new information. Jung defined these as temporarily coincident occurrences of acausal events.

> *"As the individual becomes more aware of these synchronistic experiences, they appear to become more and more frequent to where eventually everything begins to take on meaning in which no accidents exist. As Jung said, 'Synchronicity is an ever present reality for those who have eyes to see.' One's cultural background plays an important consideration here in terms of interpretative lens. Some Native American cultures, for instance, consider all events as being imbued with meaning and the term coincidence seems to lose meaning altogether." (Yaden & Newman, 2022:211)*

There has been some research and speculation on the neurobiology of synchronicities. According to Yaden and Newberg (2022:221),

> *"The neuroscience seems to point to three main findings regarding synchronicity experiences: first, an increased level of dopaminergic activity that motivates one to search for and see more patterns; second, disruptions in areas of the brain responsible for language and abstract thought [Broca's and Wernicke's area] that might be making frames of reference more malleable to change; and third, changes in activity in the limbic system and in particular the amygdala."*

Dopamine has shown linkages to extraversion, positive affect, openness to experience, broad thinking, and mental flexibility (Kaufman, 2012).

There has been some evidence proposing variation in the dopamine D4 receptor gene (DRD4) and the catechol-O-methyltransferase gene (COMT) in the prefrontal dopamine system "predicted Openness/Intellect." The limbic system here has been shown to relate to feelings of existential threat or of supernatural powers. They elaborate on this:

> *"Some people may tend to see coincidences as more important than others due to their disposition to experience surprise at different levels of intensity. If such an emotional response is, in part, responsible for attribution of synchronicity, perhaps it is mediated by dopamine function." (Yaden & Newberg, 2022:219)*

This degree of "surprise" may correlate with the level of "awe," which is explored in more detail in Chapter VIII (Circuit 5).

As such, *"dopamine…might also be involved in whether people see more or fewer patterns"* (Yaden & Newberg, 2022:213). A pathological example of this would be the correlation between elevated baseline dopamine levels and symptoms of schizophrenia or schizotypy in which the ability to effectively distinguish between patterns of reality and delusion becomes difficult. Apophenia is a term referring *"to the perception of connections or meaning in unrelated events"* (Yaden & Newman, 2022:214). Scott Barry Kaufman (2012) referred to apophenia as *"a natural part of human nature"* while noting that in cases where intellect is high (a personality trait related to intellectual interests and critical thinking) and apophenia is also high, creativity can result. However, *"if apophenia is high without an accompanying high degree of intellect, then psychopathology is more likely to result"* (Yaden & Newman, 2022:214). We find it interesting to consider how much of this "intelligence" factor may relate to the ability to integrate experience, and whether facilitated integration training may prove a helpful tool in walking this line between creativity and madness.

NUMINOUS EXPERIENCES & ENTITY ENCOUNTERS

Jung defined a "numinous experience" (Rudolf Otto's term for a unique experience) that is *"inexpressible, mysterious, terrifying, directly experienced, and pertaining only to the divinity"* (Jung, 1963). It may be experienced as *"the feeling of being in touch with divinity or God"* (Yaden & Newman, 2022:165). Yaden and Newman (2022:186) further broaden this definition to include what they refer to as *"revelatory experiences, defined here as voices, visions, or epiphanies that seem to come from a source beyond the self."* These sources may be described or experienced as gods or goddesses, angels or demons, a particular archetype (as touched upon above), an animal guide, or beings such as fairies or the notorious interdimensional machine elves reported by many under the influence of DMT.

Yaden and Newman (2022:177–178) further elaborate on how these experiences with entities may be perceived as separate, while simultaneously a direct extension of oneself:

> *"God is commonly understood as a mind, albeit an ultimate kind of mind. Therefore when people are having numinous experiences, they are perceiving a vast and special kind of mind, but a mind nonetheless... We believe people who have had a spiritual experience may perceive more mind across each of these objects and entities."*

While these experiences become difficult to pin down neurobiologically, there exist some findings into neural correlates of numinous experiences. It appears that, to the brain, experiencing the presence of a higher being may not be that different from experiencing the presence of another person. *"At a neuronal level, feeling the presence of another human being and feeling the presence of God have a great deal of similarity... Brain regions implicated in social interaction include the medial frontal as well as parietal (inferior) areas...[there is a] strong social aspect in numinous experiences"* (Yaden & Newman, 2022:180). Some evidence points to increased activity in the prefrontal cortex associated with the increased focus of attention (Yaden & Newman, 2022:181); however,

> *"One of the common findings in brain scans is a decrease in frontal lobe function. We should expect that a decrease in frontal lobe function would be associated with a sense of losing purposeful control of a person's actions and sense of surrendering one's conscious control (p. 203)... It appears that*

revelatory experiences are more likely to occur when the frontal lobe is less active and may occur through similar brain processes as creativity (p. 205)... The Self-Transcendence Scale...is said to measure the tendency for a person to experience going beyond the self and becoming more intimately connected, or absorbed, with another object, such as God. The gene associated with this scale codes for the VMAT2 receptor in the brain, which regulates serotonin and dopamine neurotransmitters." (Yaden & Newton, 2022:100)

MYSTICAL EXPERIENCES

William James proposed four criteria to qualify as a "mystical experience" (Yaden & Newberg, 2022:227):

- Ineffability: The experience goes beyond your capacity to readily express it in language
- Noetic quality: insight that remains inarticulate
- Transiency: The experience tends to be brief and passing
- Passivity: The experience seems to happen to the experiencer—they often feel as though "along for a ride" and surrendering to it as it unfolds

The noetic quality of an experience has been proposed to have an association with limbic system areas, such as the hippocampus (involved in memory), and the thalamus (involved with general higher-order processing of cognitive data among cortical regions) (Yaden &Newberg, 2022:244). Recent psychedelic research has begun looking at the claustrum region of the brain as contributing a possible "switchboard" role between brain networks that support perception, memory, and attention (Barrett et al., 2020).

It is significant that the language of the mystics seems to fall into two categories: 1) statements of the logically impossible, and 2) statements of the "palpably untrue." We can now see that the first class of mystic utterance relates to the non-dualistic functioning of the later neurological circuits; these statements are illogical because either/or logic is a code relating to the dichotomies of the first four circuits. *"Mysticism is neurogenetics expressed in pre-scientific symbols"* (Wilson, 2020:152).

Desire and serious study alone are not considered enough to attain these states and transitions toward self-transcendence. Though these factors must be in place to do so, it is instead born through an *"arduous psychological and spiritual process and the liberation of a latent stage of consciousness"* (Vaughan, 1989:23). There is a continual struggle, resistance, and applied directed attention in the form of a disciplined practice (such as meditation, qigong, altered breathing, etc.), which makes the perceptual *"realities more pliable and able to be deconstructed"* (Wade, 1996:177). Once these perceptual changes take place, they may be meaningfully integrated into ordinary awareness. Metaphors and imagery are perceived that both hide and reveal The Ultimate. These mystical experiences, like archetypal images, vary in accordance with cultural or subjective filtering or distortions.

You gradually come to recognize that this subjective influence opens up not only to these archetypal figures and images, but also their particular role in the makeup of reality. The world becomes apprehended according to non-Newtonian laws that seem to be acausal, relativistic, holonomic, and interconnected throughout. This perspective seems more than a subjective interpretation, and begins to be experienced as such in ordinary conscious states.

As this occurs more consistently, you experience your relationship with reality as a participatory one, where your attention begins to have an effect on your environment. As such, "paranormal" abilities may be attributed to you. There is a recognition of being inseparable from reality and the world, beyond being merely an observer in the construction of reality. Objects within the world are still understood to be at least semi-permanent, and prone to entropy. Meaning placed on these objects, however, become recognized as artificially created. Improved access to memories, creativity, unhabituated attention, and enhanced sensory acuity seems to come with psychic occurrences. To the individual experiencing them, however, these increased abilities may be seen as having little-to-no value, likely being regarded as more of a distraction from the primary motive of self-development and unity than anything else.

Stanislav Grof reports on these "paranormal phenomena" in his LSD research, saying the following relating to precognition, clairvoyance, clairaudience, and "time travels":

> *"The most characteristic aspect of ESP phenomena in this group is the transcendence of the usual limitations of time and the resulting temporal extension of consciousness. Occasionally, LSD subjects report, particularly in advanced sessions of a psycholytic series, anticipation of events that will happen in the future. Sometimes, they witness complex and detailed scenes of future happenings in the form of vivid clairvoyant visions and can even hear the acoustic concomitants that are part of them; the latter range from ordinary sounds of everyday life, musical sequences, single words, and entire sentences, to noises produced by motor vehicles and various alarming acoustic signals (the sound of fire engines, ambulance sirens, or blowing car horns). Some of these experiences manifest various degrees of similarity with actual events occurring at a later time. Objective verification in this area can be particularly difficult. Unless these instances are reported and clearly documented during the LSD session, there is a great danger of contamination of data. Loose interpretation of events, distortions of memory, and the possibility of déjà vu phenomena during the perception of later occurrences are several of the major pitfalls involved. One general comment should be made in this context concerning the incidence of ESP phenomena in LSD sessions. Objective testing in the laboratory usually fails to demonstrate an increase of extrasensory perception as a standard and constant aspect of the LSD effect. States conducive to various paranormal phenomena and characterized by an unusually high incidence of ESP are, however, among the many alternative mental conditions that can be facilitated by this drug. Another interesting element in this category is the experience of 'time travel.' Here the LSD subject is convinced that he can transcend the limitations of time at will and travel to any particular time period in a way not unlike that of science fiction's time machines. Such an individual can perceive a causal*

connection between his deliberate choice of such time periods and the subsequent subjective experiences. This is usually combined with a similar voluntary manipulation of the location of the events involved. The subject's feeling of making a free decision distinguishes these experiences from spontaneous, elemental, and uncontrollable reliving of episodes from childhood, ancestral experiences, or aspects of the collective and racial unconscious." (1975:177–178)

This indicates a shift in self-guided directives. In the previous circuits, people may tend toward benevolent acts under the guise of altruism with underlying self-interest. With the activation of the neurogenetic circuit, the individual can become enveloped by feelings of gratitude, loving kindness, generosity, and an effortless compassion for the humanity in all others as they are now experienced as inseparable from the self. There is an acceptance of others exactly as they are in every moment, and an acceptance of self and life as it is without a desire to exert control over it. This may be perceived by others as a lack of emotion or of ambivalence, but the opposite may actually be the case—that is, behavior results from the mechanisms of an increased, widely-broadened emotional engagement with the world.

Non-ordinary states of consciousness become increasingly common as there is either decreased sensory input, or its opposite, sensory overload wherein the left hemisphere becomes habituated and the right hemisphere is disinhibited (Wade, 1996). Additionally, communication between the two hemispheres (lateralization) increases with synchronization (entrainment). This gives way to the establishment of hyper-synchronistic brain functioning. In cases of sensory deprivation, the brain is left with only its own internal processes and neural landscapes to encapsulate awareness. This is the basis behind long-duration, sensory-deprivation tanks and dark room retreats where visual input is eliminated. As this occurs, the electrochemical activity in the central nervous system begins to generate visual hallucinations. These begin as variations of four primary geometric forms— spirals, tunnels/funnels, cobwebs, and honeycomb patternings. Over time, these grow in complexity and are eventually followed by idiosyncratic visions of symbols and archetypal figures. The individual may come to recognize these altered states—as well as "normal" waking consciousness—as both illusionary and real in their own ways.

Conventional psychology equates such mystical experiences with a form of regression into pre-egoic states. This is what integral philosophy refers to as the "pre/trans fallacy" (Wilbur, 1980) in which trans-rational mystical experiences become erroneously equated with pre-rational or pre-symbolic states. Washburn views the unfolding states as involving a component of *"regression in the service of transcendence."* This involves lower states becoming accessible to address negative imprints or imbalances within. This clears the field to allow for optimal ego transcendence. To the individual, however, these points become moot as the concrete operations of Newtonian paradigms and hierarchical structures break down where regression and transcendence are experienced as neither opposite nor the same, but an acausal interwoven process.

CIRCUIT 7 ENERGY

QUALITIES OF BALANCED CIRCUIT 7 ENERGY

- Open to the divine
- Feelings of spiritual sanctuary, faith and inner peace
- Able to transcend the laws of nature, "miracle worker"
- Access to the unconscious and subconscious
- Ability to leave and return to the body at will in full consciousness

QUALITIES OF EXCESSIVE CIRCUIT 7 ENERGY

- Constant sense of frustration, hypersensitivity
- Anxiety, confusion, feeling out of control, destructiveness
- Lost in imagination, spaced out, desire to escape reality
- Unrealized power-status
- Mental-emotional imbalances: psychosis, depression, bipolar
- Frequent migraine headaches
- Sexual: sometime passionate, sometimes distant

QUALITIES OF DEFICIENT CIRCUIT 7 ENERGY

- No spark of joy, lack of spiritual connection
- Lack of "vision"
- Feeling of uselessness; no meaningful direction in life
- Confusion, apathy, unable to make decisions
- Alienation, isolation, boredom, depression
- Close-mindedness, negative self-image, introversion
- Catatonic

CIRCUIT 7 ACTIVATION
CIRCUIT 7 ACTIVATING ACTIVITIES

Activities that open your nervous system to a broader spectrum of sensory perception and experience may include:

- Holotropic Breathwork
- Kundalini Yoga
- Meditation
- HemiSync® (i.e., binaural beats that synchronize brain waves)
- Deep brain stimulation
- "The God Machine" (i.e., temporal lobe magnetic stimulation)
- Extra Sensory Perception (ESP) practices
- Attentiveness to synchronicities
- Attempt to eliminate sense of self by covering all mirrors for a week
- Vow of silence—communicating by other means: writing, gestures, eye movements
- Divinatory practices: tarot, *yijing (i ching)*, runes, etc.

CIRCUIT 7 ACTIVATING SUBSTANCES

High dose LSD (200–500µg), high dose peyote, high dose psilocybin (0.35+mg. psilocybin analyte/5g.+ dried mushroom), DMT, datura, ayahuasca, San Pedro, damiana, mugwort, Syrian rue, African dream root, flying ointment.

There has been some experimentation with the non-ordinary states of consciousness that awaken neurogenetic intelligence. Dr. Michael Persinger recorded what he called "temporal lobe transients," or "temporal lobe micro-seizures," in people experiencing highly expansive mystical experiences. He attempted to reproduce these patterns using stimulation with what he called "complex magnetic fields" over the temporal lobes of subjects to create the feeling of a "sensed presence" (Persinger & Healey, 2002; Murphy, 2014).

HemiSync® technology can be used to bring the hemispheres of the brain into an entrained coherence pattern. Declassified CIA documents revealed that the government explored consciousness expansion, astral projection, remote-viewing, and extrasensory perception. After psychedelics were made illegal in 1970, Grof—who as a psychotherapist had administered thousands of legal LSD sessions in his work—developed a form of breathwork based on the rapid breathing pattern many of his patients fell into during their LSD sessions (i.e., holotropic breathwork). One of the authors of this book (Wingate) can personally attest to the powerfully expansive experiences this form of breathwork can elicit, as well as powerful healing that can occur during such an experience. Grof similarly looked at yogic and meditation practices and stated, *"Of all the systems of yoga, Kundalini yoga bears the closest resemblance to LSD psychotherapy"* (Grof, 1975:203). However, as much as these efforts may create transitory C-7 experiences, it would still appear that *"as of now, psychedelic substances are the most reliable means to elicit spiritual experiences in controlled laboratory settings"* (Yaden & Newton, 2022:115). *"These methods do not in fact directly stimulate electric activity as one might expect, but rather dissolve synaptic barriers which prevent large-scale signal throughput, thereby increasing the latent energy level of the nervous system"* (Heffernan, 2017:136). *"The primary tenets of psychedelic information theory dictate that hallucinogens generate information by destabilizing linear perception to promote nonlinear states of consciousness"* (Kent, 2010:170).

AYAHUASCA & *N,N-DIMETHYLTRYPTAMINE (DMT)*

DMT is a fast-acting tryptamine which has peak effects within 2–5 minutes, dissipating by 20–30 minutes (Strassman & Qualls, 1994; Strassman, 1995; Turetzky, 2022). *Ayahuasca* is the combination of two plants, one containing DMT, the other a monoamine oxidase inhibitor (MAOI) which prevents the enzymes of the gut from breaking down the DMT before making it to the circulatory system (Callaway et al., 1999; McKenna et al., 1984). It tends to have peak effects between 1–2 hours after ingestion, and subsides over a period of 4–6 hours. DMT is potentially mediated by multiple neuroreceptors including serotonin, adrenergic receptors, glutamate, and dopamine (Carbonaro & Gatch, 2016). Because it is a naturally produced substance in the human body, DMT has also been theorized to be associated with non-drug NOSC experiences such as dreaming, mystical experiences, encounters with nonhuman intelligence, psychosis, extrasensory perception, and out-of-body and near-death experiences (Luke, 2008, 2011, 2012; Stassman, 2001, 2008; Tillerman et al., 2018). Acute effects of DMT administration have shown many reported encounters with seemingly autonomous entities (Brown & Huntley, 2024; Davis et al., 2020) described as "God," "spirits," "angels," or "aliens," as well as Terence Mckenna's infamous machine elves, and a myriad of others. David Jay Brown has a fascinating book, *The Illustrated Field Guide to the DMT Entities,* that compiles reports of many of these beings. One of the authors of this book (Turetzky) reviewed Dr. Rick Strassman's bedside notes of his early 1990s' DMT studies (the first federally sanctioned psychedelic studies in the United States since psychedelics were criminalized in 1970), exploring a hermeneutic phenomenology of the DMT experience. Fascinating new reports are coming available with recent trials of extended intravenous DMT administration that allows for significantly longer experiences (Luan et al., 2023; Beiner, 2023).

The term *ayahuasca* is derived from the Quechua word composed of *aya,* meaning spirit or ancestor, and *waska,* meaning vine or rope. During an ayahuasca experience, nausea or purging are common experiences, and in many groups considered a fundamental component as a means or representation of catharsis or purification. Other common traits are an awareness of physiological changes in body temperature, feelings of numbness, body lightness, and yawning. Transient tremors and nystagmus can also occur. Vivid, realistic, yet fantastic changes in visual perception are also common, often with eyes closed. These often come soaked in symbolism, and can include visions of people, animal spirits, plants, or hybrids of these things which often offer a significant message to the journeyer. Single-proton computed tomography (SPECT) of acute *ayahuasca* experiences showed increase cerebral blood flow in the anterior insula, right anterior cingulate, medial prefrontal cortex, and the left amygdala/parahippocampal gyrus. All of these areas have been implicated in attention, emotion, and introspection (Riba et al., 2006). Transient anxiety, transient dissociation and depersonalization, distortions in the sense of spacetime, and mystical experiences have all been frequently reported.

INTEGRATION INTERVENTION MODEL CONSIDERATIONS
CIRCUIT 3 ACTIVATING ACTIVITIES

Circuit 3 and Circuit 7 are vertically connected, with Circuit 3 acting as an anchor to Circuit 7 shock experiences. Someone may experience vast interconnectedness, and the structures that have been previously used to create maps and symbolic representations of the individual experience may break down. The symbolology experienced in neurogenetic consciousness becomes nonlinear, multidimensional, and ineffable. Activities that activate the third circuit with its dependency on rationality and rigid linear symbolic structure can help integrate experiences of neurogenetic intelligence—or at least pull the individual out of the clouds enough to be able to navigate the Newtonian world.

CLINICAL APPROACH CONSIDERATIONS
(REFER TO RECOMMENDED READING FOR RESOURCES)
- Jungian Psychology
- Art Therapy

- Internal Family Systems
  The design of internal family systems may lend itself to being particularly helpful in C-7 intelligence integration. As one becomes many, or one becomes all, an individual may experience something very powerful that can leave them feeling fractured in a sense, or needing to figure out how to pull oneself back into the singular human self who goes to work and interacts with their family and community. Exploring different facets of self, recognizing the role each facet plays, and understanding the cohesive ways in which each interplay can be a particularly useful approach as an integrative tool.

- Psychosynthesis
  Psychosynthesis is an approach to psychology that expands the boundaries of the field by identifying a deeper center of identity, which is the postulate of the Self. It considers each individual unique in terms of purpose in life, and places value on the exploration of human potential. The approach combines spiritual development with psychological healing by including the life journey of an individual or their unique path to self-realization.

  The integrative framework of psychosynthesis is based on Sigmund Freud's theory of the unconscious and addresses psychological distress and intra-psychic and interpersonal conflicts.

Leary's Bio-Evolutionary Stages 19–21		
Stage 19	Neurogenetic Receptivity	The nervous system continually receives DNA and RNA signals. Inside the nucleus of every neuron, there "lives" a DNA master plan which contains a record of the chain of bodily reincarnations back to the origin of life on this planet.
		When the seventh circuit of the nervous system is activated, the signals from DNA become conscious. This experience is chaotic and confusing to the unprepared person—thousands of genetic memories flash by, the molecular family-picture-album of species consciousness and evolution. This experience provides glimpses and samples of the broad design of the multi-billion-year-old genetic panorama.
		Neurogenetic consciousness is not restricted to past perspectives. The outlines of the future DNA blueprint are also available.
		Neural entertainment and exploration is the function of this stage.
Stage 20	Neurogenetic Intelligence	Selection, discrimination, organization, evaluation of genetic symbols. The neurogenetic circuit begins to think like DNA and learns the vocabulary of RNA. It begins the identify with the genetic intelligence which deals in the span of species and encompasses the multi-billion-year network of life.
		We can predict the emergence of genetic engineers who understand the alphabet of DNA and can decipher, write, and re-write in amino-script, the book written in the

		vocabulary of guanine, adenine, cytosine, and thymine.
		The function of neurogenetic intelligence is to stop the programmed aging process— as the basic goal of life is immortality. Immortality is attained through control of the DNA.
		To control the genetic code, it is necessary to receive DNA-RNA signals and experientially resonate, identify with them. The genetic engineers use their own brains as their basic instrument.
Stage 21	Neurogenetic Fusion	Here there develops communication with other genetic intelligences. Interspecies symbiosis at the DNA level of energy.
		Interspecies pro-creation—conscious and planful.
		It is obvious that when Stage 20 neurogenetic engineers become proficient in DNA-RNA conversation, they will realize that all organic life is a unified language system.
		Humanity is the DNA engineer—working for all species—past and future. When the Genetic Engineers (Stage 20) begin to merge genes with other species—conscious interspecies symbiosis will occur. The most significant of these genetic fusions will be with species more advanced than ourselves—i.e., ourselves in the future.

Table 15: *Leary's Bio-Evolutionary Stages 19–21*

Transcendent Consciousness	
Primary Motivation	Transcending the egoic self to grasp the absolute
Ultimate Value	Unity with the Ground of All Being
Attitude Toward Life	Reverence and appreciation for life as the manifestation of the absolute. Attachment to life in its manifest forms must be overcome
Perception of Death	Physical death is unimportant except as an opportunity for greater unity. Ego death is ardently pursued through persistent practice
Self-Boundaries	The ego with all its psychic structures. The self is constructed
Perception of Temporality	Simultaneously infinite and historical, i.e., holonomic. Time is constructed. Plastic, fluid, timeless
Concept of Other	Appreciated for their participation in the Ground of All Being regardless of outward form. Great compassion for and identification with all life forms
Locus of Control	External regarding grace and power of the absolute. Being at one with reality leads to participation in creating it
Level of Abstraction	Holonomic, paradoxical epistemology. Spatial boundaries are open. All variables are interdependent. Reality is constructed. Reality is shaped by certain participants
Options for Actions	Infinite and unbounded by Newtonian laws
Correct Opinion	One that will enhance unity with the Ground of All Being

Table 16: *Wade's Holonomic Theory: Transcendent Consciousness*

RELEVANT ASSESSMENT SCALES

You may find these useful as they touch on experiences related to Circuit 7. Most are designed for research studies to collect data about someone's experience, but they can also be a tool for self-reflection to get a better understanding of an experience. They may also be helpful if facilitating a psychedelic session to gather more information on the experience that may be helpful in integration work.

INDEX OF CORE SPIRITUAL EXPERIENCES (INSPIRIT-R):
Questionnaire on Spiritual Attitudes and Experiences

The following questions concern your spiritual or religious beliefs and experiences. There are no right or wrong answers. For each question, circle the number of the answer that is most true for you.

1. How strongly religious (or spiritually-oriented) do you consider yourself to be?
   a. Not at all
   b. Not very strong
   c. Somewhat strong
   d. Strong

2. About how often do you spend time on religious or spiritual practices?
   a. Once per year or less
   b. Once per month to several times per year
   c. Once per week to several times per month
   d. Several times per day to several times per week

3. How often have you felt as though you were very close to a powerful spiritual force?
   a. Never
   b. Once or twice
   c. Several times
   d. Often

People have many different images and definitions of the higher power that we often call "God". Use your image and your definition of God when answering the following questions.

4. How close do you feel to God?
   a. I don't believe in God
   b. Not very close
   c. Somewhat close
   d. Extremely close

5. Have you ever had an experience that has convinced you that God exists?
   a. No
   b. I don't know
   c. Maybe
   d. Yes

6. Indicate whether you agree or disagree with this statement: "God dwells within you."
   a. Definitely disagree
   b. Tend to disagree
   c. Tend to agree
   d. Definitely agree

7. The following list describes spiritual experiences that some people have had. Indicate if you have had any of these experiences and the extent to which each of them has affected your belief in God.
   1 = Never had this experience
   2 = Had this experience and it did not strengthen my belief in God
   3 = Had this experience and it strengthened my belief in God
   4 = Had this experience and it convinced me of God's existence

SPIRITUAL EXPERIENCES

A. An experience of profound inner peace   1 2 3 4

B. An overwhelming experience of love   1 2 3 4

C. A feeling of unity with the earth and all living beings 1 2 3 4

D. An experience of complete joy and ecstasy   1 2 3 4

E. Meeting or listening to a spiritual teacher or master   1 2 3 4

F. An experience of God's energy or presence   1 2 3 4

G. An experience of a great spiritual figure (e.g., Jesus, Buddha) 1 2 3 4

H. A healing of your body or mind (or witnessed such a healing) 1 2 3 4

I. A miraculous (or not normally occurring) event   1 2 3 4

J. An experience of angels or guiding spirits   1 2 3 4

K. An experience of communication with someone who has   1 2 3 4
died

L. An experience with near death, or life-after-death   1 2 3 4

M. Other (specify)   1 2 3 4

_____

_____

_____

(Spiritual Foundations for a Resilient Worldview 5
2000, 1996, 1990. 1989 Jared D. Kass)

DAILY SPIRITUAL EXPERIENCE SCALE (DSES)

		Many times a day	Every day	Most days	Some days	Once in a while	Never or almost never
1	I feel God's presence.						
2	I experience a connection to all of life.						
3	During worship, or at other times when connecting with God, I feel joy which lifts me out of my daily concerns.						
4	I find strength in my religion or spirituality.						
5	I find comfort in my religion or spirituality.						
6	I feel deep inner peace or harmony.						
7	I ask for God's help in the midst of daily activities.						
8	I feel guided by God in the midst of daily activities.						
9	I feel God's love for me directly.						
10	I feel God's love for me through others.						
11	I am spiritually touched by the beauty of creation.						
12	I feel thankful for my blessings.						
13	I feel a selfless caring for others.						
14	I accept others even when they do things I think are wrong.						
15	I desire to be closer to God or in union with the divine.						

Chapter XI

Circuit Eight (C-8):
Non-Local Consciousness, Dissolution, & the Death Experience

Neuro-Atomic Metaphysiological Circuit (Leary)
Non-Local Quantum Circuit (Wilson)

"So the lively force of his mind
Has broken down all barriers,
And he has passed far beyond,
The fiery walls of the world,
And in mind and spirit
Has traversed the boundless universe."
— Lucretius, *De rerum natura*

The most expansive and complex circuit of consciousness may unfold with continued self-work, or with some of the most intense shocks to the nervous system—primarily those tied to death and self-dissolution. As this occurs, the universe may seem to open up or come apart at the seams. As it is happening, you may feel a sense of eschatothesia—that is, it may feel as if you are experiencing the end of the world itself (Khamsehzadeh, 2022:285). Universe breaks wide open, and becomes fully accessible as you seem to cease to exist as an isolated entity from everything else around you. Rather than the world being seen as innumerable separate objects, these become recognized as constructs of your nervous system, and at their root, ultimately existing as a single, continuous ebbing and flowing of interconnection and interaction.

This sounds markedly similar to the concept of Indras's net found in the *Avatamsaka Sutra* (Cleary, 1993). This stage has also been called Nirvana in Buddhism, Samadhi in yoga, the Satori of Zen, and the kingdom of heaven in Christianity. Chinese descriptions tend to use terminology of negative structuring: "no-mind," "not-doing," and "not-existence." This makes sense semantically as a means of describing the perceptual breaking apart of the material world in which the individual, until this circuit became activated, had always been considered as solid, real, and unshakable.

The sense of self deteriorates into oneness with everything. No separation remains; to influence any part of it is to influence the entire system. It is important to note that in some indigenous knowledge systems, the very idea of self-loss has no significance because the "self" is seen as inherently connected to all things at all times, thus leaving nothing to lose (Yaden & Newman, 2022:235).

With this, concepts of death may become seen as irrelevant as you experience firsthand a grasping of the law of conservation of energy in which nothing ("no-thing") ever gets destroyed or created, only converted from one form to another. The perception becomes that we, at our essence, are already immortal, and physical death (as it tends to be thought of), marks nothing more than a transition from one form to another. With this, you shed the fear or anxiety surrounding the concept of death. The deterioration and transition out of the physical body becomes seen as merely another transitory state of being into dissolution and dispersion amongst the vast sea of universal fluctuations. No differentiation remains between living and dying as a localized consciousness, except that death acts as a liberation from the confines of the nervous system and the constructs of space and time.

Desires and attachments similarly may dissolve as these things no longer seem to hold any significance beyond the temporary. As the ego becomes transcended completely, so too does self-driven interest and motives of further becoming; there may seem nowhere to go, and that there never was. All existed prior to awareness of it, and had been present and available the entire time. There develops a pure, non-objective awareness that exists without form, perception, conceptualization, or sensory input—it simply "is." This is not to say that objects do not exist, but rather they are a product of your means of perception. The universe is not empty; rather it is a boundless sea of potential waiting to be interpreted by tools, such as the human nervous system. Objects and physiological structures have been broken down, and no longer dictate your reality.

Consciousness and information become perceived as a coherent co-intelligence which expands outward in all directions into infinity. The self lies beyond the boundaries of space and time. This transcendence occurs through dis-identifying with all forms of mental, emotional, and physical structures. The act of perceiving and interacting entails, and indeed, *demands* a duality as the act of perception creates boundaries between the perceiver and the perceived, but when consciousness reaches a certain level of expansiveness, any sense of self ceases to exist (i.e., Kant's concept of *noumena*). The perceiver, perceived, and the act of perception all cease to exist, leaving no dichotomous subjective/objective universe remaining.

Yaden and Newberg (2022:229) distinguish two forms of mysticism that may relate to the distinction between Circuit 8 and Circuit 7 experiences. First, they describe "introvertive mysticism" as a sense of unity with ulti-mate reality, wherein everything becomes one abstract whole. On the other hand, what they call "extrovertive mysticism" refers to *"feelings of connec-tion with the various people and objects in one's environment, while retaining some degree of differentiation from one another."*

§ § §

The activation of this circuit typically becomes accessible to only a small percentage of humans. Wilson notes reports of only a few individuals—typ-ically, shamans, yogis, and poets—in almost every century who seemed to have activated this capacity. He also refers to this as the "metaphysiological circuit" on account of the transcendence of the mundane material plane. Wade's (1996) holonomic model describes this stage as "unity conscious-ness," possibly derived from the work of Dr. Herb Koplowitz who described "the unitary approach" which is said *"knows and acts on the world as a unit. In the unitary approach, one understands that while it is possible and often useful to draw boundaries which break the world into separate entities and events, the world itself is undifferentiated"* (1984).

Psychological coping mechanisms or restorative actions become cleared away as repression no longer holds any necessity. Feeling and perception are immediate and non-conflictive as a total psychic integration exists—that is, experience becomes immediately processed and integrated. Wade states that this full, unmediated participation with the world contains similarities with the direct participatory reality of early developmental stages and conscious states of animals. There is a stark, distinguishing difference, however, in that the unitive understanding of the quantum non-local circuit exhibits an active awareness of the source and underlying principles of reality absent in such early developmental stages.

Many attributes of these principles were once simply an intuitive "knowing" by the enlightened individual that can now be found in descriptions in the realm of quantum physics, its implications on our understanding of Universe, and its portrayal of the nature of "reality." We will briefly convey some of these tenets of quantum physics, and the breadth of their implications. Although this is no easy task to distill down, such material holds much relevance to at least touch upon, but any deeper descriptions would be beyond the scope of this text. For those wishing to dig deeper into these realms, refer to the Recommended Reading section later in this book.

BELL'S THEOREM

In essence, Bell's theorem states that no isolated systems, objects, or particles seem to exist throughout the universe. Any time a particle interacts with any other particle, the two create a bond through a process known as *quantum entanglement.* This bond will never be broken, remaining from that point on, regardless of space or time between them. As these particles continue to interact with even more particles, a complex network of communication and interaction becomes created. And beyond this, the communication established between them seems to occur instantaneously.

Verbal or auditory communication happens at the speed of sound, around 760 mph (1,236 km/hr), a speed attainable by some aircraft. Visual information is taken in at the speed of light, approximately 671 million mph (1,080 million km/hr). Communication between particles that have become entangled at the quantum level seem to transfer information faster than the speed of light, with the other particles responding instantaneously—whether five feet away, 100 miles away, or on the other side of the planet. This ability is referred to as a "non-local" effect.

It relates to this circuit with the realization that all aspects of the universe become intimately interconnected, and any action will subsequently get responded to throughout the entire system simultaneously. How this occurs is reconciled by this non-local connection, involving no form of energy (in a classical sense). Energy transfer inherently requires time. Rather, the communication is proposed to result from either 1) pure consciousness itself, which implies an inherent intelligence to all particles in the universe, or 2) information in the strictest, non-physical sense. Information alone neither contains nor utilizes energy, rather being the component that places order to energy. Unlike energy systems, which have an inherently entropic nature—meaning they tend toward degradation or greater degrees of chaos over time—information seems negatively entropic; that is, it tends toward higher degrees of order and accumulation through interaction.

WAVE/PARTICLE DUAL NATURE

Experiments have shown that the nature of reality seems to depend on the methods in which it is measured or perceived. Your sensory organs act as the instruments through which the world is experienced. Every particle throughout the universe can be thought of as a "wavicle" (as it simultaneously has the properties of a particle and a wave). Experiments have shown that under certain conditions, using certain instruments, these "wavicles" can be measured as a solid object, inhabiting a particular place in space, with quantifiable dimensions. Under other conditions, however, using other methods of measurement, this same "wavicle" does not seem to act as a particle at all. Instead, it may act as a wave or vibratory function (a "process" rather than a "thing"), lacking physical form, akin to a sound or light wave. Because the same "thing" varies drastically in nature based on its method of perception, and the universe is made up of these "things," the makeup of the entire Universe seems to simultaneously have *both* particle and wave-like forms, undetermined until measured or experienced. This implies that reality and its underlying qualities, including the materiality of physical objects, become the responsibility of the individual who interacts with and interprets it. Each individual literally manifests the reality around them. This is discussed further later in this chapter.

HEISENBERG UNCERTAINTY PRINCIPLE

Extending from the wave/particle dualistic nature, the "Heisenberg uncertainty principle" stems from the basis that the observer of any particular object, event, or reality acts as an active participant in the process of determining its attributes. As such, no firm boundary can be placed between them; they seem mutually dependent on each other, and inseparable. Psychologically, this means that the "self" or ego remains inseparable from, and merely an extension of the world around them. Concepts of a separate Self become recognized as an illusion of their own making through the mechanisms of perception (i.e., the human nervous system). Further components of this principle demonstrate that when making an observation, the precision and methods of the tools used further define the nature of that being perceived. A ruler alone cannot measure how heavy a boulder is or how fast a cheetah can run. The human sensory system is unable to perceive components of the universe available to other animals (e.g., the ability of bees to see ultraviolet light).

Dr. Werner Heisenberg showed that it is possible to measure either the location of an object *or* its velocity; it remains, however, impossible to simultaneously measure *both* exactly—where it is (which demands a solid nature at a determined time), *and* how fast it is going (a measurement over time). This was further established as a principle: that the universe operates in terms of probabilities of occurrence until the measurement is taken. This was the finding of the Schrödinger's cat experiment. The psychological implications of this becomes that your reality forms out of a vast expanse of probability and uncertainty within which you play a key role in how the unfolding of the universe occurs.

THE IMPLICATE ORDER

Physicist Dr. David Bohm postulated that Universe contains multiple layers of reality with varying degrees of complexity and organization (or lack thereof). Bohm refers to the familiar material world (which is perceived and contains physical objects that adhere to standard Newtonian physics), as the "explicate order." He puts forth that behind all of this material "stuff" is what he calls the "implicate order" of "deep reality," made up of yet-to-be observed probability waveforms. The implicate order exists as an undifferentiated ocean of energy that acts as a non-local hidden variable transcending space, time, and causality. This implicate order permeates all space, yet cannot be directly perceived. Only its effects and manifestations can be observed, akin to trying to see wind. Out of the implicate order, physical properties and events are said to "unfold" to make up the explicate order, then enfolding back into the implicate order of probability. When dealing with quantum particles, this process can happen rather quickly with them seeming to blink into existence, and just as suddenly, blink back out of existence, as though it was never there—except for any effect it may have had on the environment around them.

As such, Universe becomes understood as a vast expanse, full of information and potential. This non-zero state of existence is an extension of Heisenberg's work that demonstrates that any probabilistic oscillating system cannot at any time rest. It must always vibrate somewhat in imperceptibly fast fluctuations, hence lacking a precise, determined location or momentum. As this underlying order acts in a wave-like nature, it can also be seen as a set of harmonic sine wave oscillations interacting either coherently or discordantly in a similar manner to two or more musical notes playing upon each other to sound either pleasant or discordant together.

"Space is not empty. It is full, a plenum as opposed to a vacuum, and is the ground for the existence of everything, including ourselves. The universe is not separate from this cosmic sea of energy."
— David Bohm

Wilson used a computer as a metaphor to describe this. Your body and brain can be seen as the hardware through which things are done or experienced. Mind, consciousness, information, and the implicate order represents the software; or in more modern terms, the application or "app" that can be utilized by the brain/body to carry out actions. The information exists in a non-physical form, accessible anywhere at any time, but unless it is "downloaded" onto the hardware and "run," it remains inaccessible. By the same token, without software to run, the hardware remains a useless shell of physical matter. Perhaps an even more apt metaphor for the implicate order may be the internet, an invisible source of seemingly limitless information that is always fluctuating—similar to what some esoteric traditions have referred to as the Akashic Records.

With the implicate order, the dynamic flux and spectrum of order becomes dictated by the context in which it is approached. Because of this, it necessitates being an open system that is ever-changing and infused with varying degrees of chaos or randomness. According to Bohm, *"no closed systems exist."* The greater the randomness, the greater the inability to guess an outcome, or the information it contains. Shapes, processes, and events define themselves based on the use of comparison. The establishment of similarities and differences become matters of relativity to other "things." Bohm takes this further to describe multiple planes or layers of order and chaos at play with other orders behind the implicate order. Within this is contained yet another far more subtle and complex "super implicate order" that acts as the source of organization and creative energy for the implicate order applied to the quantum field rather than the particle. These levels seem to have no limits to the degrees of order and chaos. Their arrangement and interaction make up what is described as the "holomovement."

THE HOLOMOVEMENT

The "Holomovement" is described as an infinite spectrum of implicate orders, unbroken and undivided totality. It does not move from place to place, as location exists only relative to observation, but it acts as a movement by way of fluctuation as a continually enfolding and unfolding process. According to Bohm, all existence acts as a portion of this holomovement *"which manifests in relatively stable form"* (Bohm & Weber, 1983). Characteristics of the holomovement are:

1) The universe of matter floats in a vast ocean of energy known as the implicate order.
2) This implicate order in some sense seems to be conscious or alive. As a result, all matter may also be considered alive/conscious.
3) The holomovement is a spectrum and continuum of consciousness with matter composing the densest rung of this spectrum.

This structuring should not be seen in a hierarchical fashion, however, as it does not inhabit any physical space—space being a construct within the explicate order. Instead, it may be viewed as every point and level interpenetrating every other point. It has been described as an unending sea of light. Physical matter, according to Bohm, is essentially frozen light. This coincides with Einstein's famous $E = mc^2$ equation, essentially viewing matter as a very slowed down form of energy. Interestingly, Dr. J.J. Hurtak and Bruce Curtis, MA, M.Div (2004) explore the acupuncture meridian system as light conducting channels; and biophotonics remains a nascently developing field of study of light as a foundational component of bodily processes and health implications. For Bohm, the element that binds and constructs the bridge between the mental and somatic realms is that of "significance" or "meaning." Significance can be seen as a form of being which contains *concreteness,* whether material or non-material. Meaning (or intent) is that which breaks the symmetry of the timeless order. This imbued meaningfulness acts as the essential feature of consciousness, with matter and everything else being infused with significance. While an elementary particle may not contain self-awareness, it would still be seen as containing significance.

PARADOX

As you come to intuitively access awareness of these cosmic dynamics—whether you are familiar with quantum physics or not—inherent paradoxes become increasingly more apparent. Indeed, they may seem ubiquitous. Recognition and ultimate reconciliation of these paradoxes presents a primary quality of activating the quantum circuit. Dualistic perspectives give way to a unitive awareness. What were previously perceived to be opposites become recognized as mere conditions of relationships between dynamics. The subtle, underlying dynamic of consciousness or information simultaneously permeates both everywhere and nowhere at all. You become able to entertain and process multiple models of reality without their causing conflict (much like the increased ability to juggle multiple tasks in the fourth circuit)—each being accessible to use as interchangeable lenses of observation with which to view the world. You may come to experience a multitude of mutually dependent, interpenetrating, eminent transcendent realities.

Each model acts as a different filter through which things can be seen—under different conditions, different filters, or different methods of measurement—and by which the nature of things is determined. The transitory illusion of Self dissolving to "no-thing" can be quite jarring. At the same moment, this realization can also act as liberation—a freeing sense that you are not only made up of, interpenetrated by, and interconnected with every particle and part of the ever-moving flow of the universe, but that ultimately they are everything at once.

There exists both the realm of form and that of void, and they are not mutually exclusive. To quote Buddhist Master Ch'an Yuan (1987), *"The void is form, and the form is void."* Universe exists both ever-moving and completely still at the same time. In the three-dimensional world of form, paradoxes exist as a result of attempts to describe reality with limited metaphors and linguistic descriptions. When your view has expanded to include multiple orders of complexity and existence, many of these paradoxes resolve or no longer remain relevant. As Garma Chang notes:

Where ordinary sentient beings see an object, they see only its existence, not its void aspect. But an enlightened being sees both aspects at the same time.... Voidness is simply a term denoting the unsubstantial and non-self nature of being, and a pointer indicating the state of absolute non-attachment and freedom. (1959:45)

The path to this stage of consciousness may itself be considered a paradox. Upon searching for it, you reach an inherent conflict: the search itself is never able to obtain its goal. The search for transcendence is ultimately revealed to be the search for the perceiver (Wade, 1996:205). This is a problem: the perceiver, being pure consciousness/information and having no form, cannot be known as an object. The advice stands that *"if one seeks, he will never find; if one fails to seek he will never find; he must seek without seeking"* (Wade, 1996:207). There is nothing to find and nowhere to look for it because "it" has been ever-present and within all things at all times. As long as you seek a destination, you will never realize there was nowhere to go the entire time.

This circuit, unlike previous levels that have a gradient of experiences and operations within them, is said to be binary (ironically, as it shatters many preconceived dichotomies) in the sense that it has either been experienced fully or not at all. These experiences often tend to be fleeting. Longer periods of unitive consciousness become available with practice until it eventually becomes fully integrated into waking consciousness. To those who have not experienced it, an individual expressing or discussing these matters can sound nonsensical, absurd, or even heretical to existing social and cultural systems and norms. As such, a lot of miscommunication can occur. As Lao Tzu states in the *Tao Te Ching*: *"The bright way looks dim. The progressive way looks retrograde."* Wade notes this as the primary reason many mystical teachings have been kept secret except to those considered qualified initiates.

As this circuit becomes accessed more frequently, you may feel filled with an inexhaustible compassion for others, as well as with an effortless altruism. All anxieties and fears around death and suffering vanish, allowing you to accelerate your intellect and physical energy unrestrained without being buffered by psychological hindrances. You may be deeply moved by the suffering of others, but do so without attachment or partiality; rather, every circumstance is approached on equal grounds. This may relate to what Franklin Merrell-Wolff (1973) referred to as "high Indifference" or what Dr. John Lilly (1975) called "neutral reinforcement," which he described as beyond bliss—and according to him, the most rewarding state we can achieve. This can, however, appear unemotional to others.

You may become self-aware even during sleep, with increased occurrences of lucid dreaming. Interestingly, this may be experienced either internally or externally as a felt perception from the perspective of an outside observer; that is, an Out-of-Body Experience (OBE). This perspective often seems to be from just above your physical body, or from a corner of the room, or behind the body. Out-of-body, near-death, past-life, and trans-time experiences have all been reported to correlate to the activation of the metaphysiological circuit.

Many of the heightened activities and abilities attributed to this level of consciousness, and those mentioned in previous stages, still persist. In particular, precognition in both waking and sleeping states is noted. Seeing "halos" or "auras" of the enlightened have been noted throughout accounts of these individuals. Laurent Huguelit, author of *The Shamanic Path to Quantum Consciousness,* dubbed the eighth circuit the "creator circuit" to convey the increased ability to directly influence reality through interaction with the void and the vast expanse of potential within the implicate order. He cites that the "law of attraction" operates here, in which your creative power proceeds directly from "source," which is then nourished by thoughts, beliefs and intentions of desired results. Bohm noted a similar process—that thought patterns determine the course of events and physical form—in much more technical and mathematical terms in his book *Thought as a System.*

Huguelit (2014) goes on to say that the individual has access to and the ability to utilize the subtle field to create personal reality, so that rather than being a passive observer or bound within a fated course, you become an active participant and creator of the structure of the universe. He draws a vertical connection between the first and eighth circuits as a manifestation of the *"infinite, subtle potential transformed into dense physicality."* Wade mirrors this sentiment as the direction of volition dictates the form of manifestation, saying the Heisenberg principle and other effects noted in field, quantum, and chaos theory suggest that the engagement of mind influences the activities of potentials.

> *"I had come to suspect, and now felt compelled to acknowledge, that science and the physical world were products of human imaging. That we were not the cool observers of that world, but its passionate creators. We were all poets and the world was our metaphor."*
>
> — Dr. Roger S. Jones, physicist

Following are varying degrees of subjective experiences recorded by Grof (1975) relevant to Circuit 8 consciousness. These follow his clinical LSD research in which he oversaw thousands of LSD sessions, generating a wealth of insight into these non-ordinary states of consciousness.

GROF'S EXTRAPLANETARY CONSCIOUSNESS

According to Grof, during an LSD session the individual is said to directly experience phenomena related to celestial bodies outside of our planet, and to astronomical events including conditions on other planets, the sun, supernovas, etc. Related are consciousness experiences of interstellar space, *"characterized by feelings of infinity and eternity, tranquility, serenity, purity, and unity of all opposites"* with a seemingly spiritual counterpart in the experience described below. Additionally, there may be insights involving, or even direct subjective experience of, complex theoretical systems such as non-Euclidean geometry, Riemann's geometry of an n-dimensional space, Minkowski's space-time, and Einstein's special and general theories of relativity.

GROF'S CONSCIOUSNESS OF THE UNIVERSAL MIND

Grof described this as one of the most profound experiences observed in LSD sessions. Here, the individual is said to sense being encompassed within the totality of existence, and the underlying supreme principles of being. He describes it as *"boundless, unfathomable, and ineffable; it is existence itself... his principle is totally and clearly beyond rational comprehension and yet even a short experiential exposure to it satisfies the subject's intellectual, philosophical, and spiritual craving."* From this experience often comes intuitive insights into the process of creation of the phenomenal world as we know it, resulting in a temporary but enduring feeling of having achieved a global, nonrational, and transrational understanding of the basic ontological and cosmological problems of existence.

GROF'S SUPRACOSMIC & METACOSMIC VOID

This is what Grof considered the last and most paradoxical transpersonal phenomenon. It entails accessing the *"primordial emptiness, nothingness, and silence,"* which is seen as the *"ultimate source and cradle of all existence"*—the *"uncreated and ineffable Supreme."* It is said to be *"beyond time and space, beyond form or any experiential differentiation, and beyond polarities such as good and evil, light and darkness, stability and motion, and agony and ecstasy."* Causality itself is said to be transcended in such experiences. Grof goes on to say that,

> *"No matter how paradoxical it might seem, the Void and the Universal Mind are perceived as identical and freely interchangeable; they are two different aspects of the same phenomenon. The Void appears to be emptiness pregnant with form, and the subtle forms of the Universal Mind are experienced as absolutely empty."* (Grof, 1975:203–205)

and

> *"In its furthest reaches, the psyche of each of us is essentially commensurate with all of existence and ultimately identical with the cosmic creative principle itself."*

NEUROBIOLOGY

Research into the neurophysiological basis of this stage remains sparse. This may be largely due to the small subject pool available to study, and/or the difficulty in consistently eliciting these experiences in a research setting. However, several pertinent aspects of experiences that relate to unity consciousness have been explored by neuroscience to the degree our technology currently allows.

Wade notes that the transcendent consciousness of the neurogenetic circuit showed a harmonization and synchrony of alpha and theta activity, with advanced practitioners demonstrating increased theta activity. The posterior superior parietal lobe seems to be partly responsible for the representation of boundaries between the body and its surroundings (Yaden & Newberg, 2022:73), which breaks down during circuit eight states. It has been proposed that the broadened sense of connection and feelings of unity are likely associated with inhibition of these regions (Yaden & Newberg, 2022:85). The inferior parietal area may also have associations with mystical experiences. More specifically, in neuropsychological studies, participants with lesions of the angular gyrus reported increased experiences of unity (Yaden & Newberg, 2022:242). Neuroscientist Olaf Blanke has targeted the right angular gyrus using brain stimulation, and has been able to produce reports of out-of-body experiences (Blanke et al., 2002). Selective stimulation of the temporoparietal junction using transcranial magnetic stimulation (TMS) has also elicited experiences similar to out-of-body experiences (Blanke et al., 2005).

A study of non-dual (unitive) awareness in meditators showed increased functional connectivity patterns between habitually anticorrelated brain regions such as the central precuneus and the dorsolateral prefrontal cortex. These findings may correspond to a state of unity of awareness in which extrinsic and intrinsic experiences are increasingly synergistic rather than competing (Grob & Grigsby, 2022:402; Josipovic, 2014). It has also been suggested that one possible construct of non-dual awareness has to do with a breakdown between internally-generated and externally-perceived stimuli leading to a temporary loss of experiential boundary between self and the world (Millière et al., 2018).

Research has been also done in an attempt to account for the neurological foundations of near-death experiences (Nelson, 2012). The following is a breakdown of the characteristics of the near-death experience and their proposed neurological correlates:

- Experiencing a "Tunnel": Reduced blood flow to the retina of the eyes
- Seeing light at the end of the tunnel: A combination of ambient light and REM visual activation
- Appearing "dead": REM state paralysis
- Out-of-body experience: Temporoparietal REM deactivation
- Life review: Memory retrieval via the hippocampus from sympathetic fight-or-flight activation
- Bliss: Reward network activation (dopamine)
- Narrative quality: REM state dreaming and limbic activation

According to Drs. Andrew Newberg and Eugene d'Aquili (2018),

"Near death states are likely associated with intense autonomic nervous system activity. It may be, as in other spiritual experiences, that there is unusual activity in the temporal and parietal lobes that are involved in helping establish the spatial representation of the self."

Dreaming and REM states seem to be completely separate activities; that is, you can dream without being in a REM state, and a REM state can be activated without dream activity (Solms, 2000). Dreams are suspected of deriving from a dopamine mechanism in the forebrain. REM states seem to be controlled by a brainstem oscillator, the pontine tegmentum, via cholinergic stimulation. Specifically, it seems related to muscarinic acetylcholine receptor genes Chrm1 and Chrm3 (Yamada & Ueda, 2020), and the ventral part of the oral pontine reticular nucleus (Reinoso-Suarez et al., 2001). There has also been shown a degree of desynchronization, and according to EEG, theta rhythm in the hippocampus and pontogeniculooccipital areas alongside the well-known muscle atonia (immobility) and rapid eye movements found in REM states. Muscarinic receptor agonists and acetylcholin-esterase inhibitors have been shown to increase REM states and decrease REM latency.

Yaden and Newberg have also noted the possibility of differences in hemispheric dominance in the nature of non-ordinary states of conscious-ness wherein the left hemisphere may be more involved with the sense of self, while the right hemisphere is more involved with the general sense of space. They postulate that this may explain experiences of annihilation—the loss of Self related to the left parietal lobe, and experiences of relational aspects such as connectedness or unity related to the right parietal lobe—although they admit this is *"highly speculative at this point"* (Yaden & New-berg, 2022:243).

INTEGRATION INTERVENTION MODEL CONSIDERATIONS
CIRCUIT 8 ACTIVATING ACTIVITIES

Activities that expand experience beyond the limitations of the physical body. Some examples may include:

- Near-death experiences (NDE)
- Out-of-body experiences (OBE)
- Lucid dreams/REM/dream-state consciousness
- Astral projection
- "Stimulated by visualizing the white light a foot above the head" (Wilson, 2020:349)

CIRCUIT 8 ACTIVATING SUBSTANCES

5-MeO-DMT (toad venom), DMT, High doses of ketamine, ibogaine, high doses of nitrous oxide (NO_2), Haitian zombie powder (puffer fish), Amanita muscaria, Jimson Weed, Belladonna, Flying Ointments

IBOGAINE

As noted in Chapter III (Circuit 1), high doses of ketamine can induce transpersonal unity states that may emulate near-death experiences akin to descriptions of Circuit 8 consciousness. Another substance garnering attention in psychedelic communities that seems to bring about NOSC akin to Circuit 8 states is ibogaine. Ibogaine is derived from the root bark of the West Central African iboga plant. It has been used as a religious sacrament for centuries by regional peoples aimed at "binding" across time through "the work of the ancestors," and across space, socially, by common experiences through the plant.

Ibogaine seems to be an N-methyl-D-aspartate (NMDA) receptor antagonist with a muscarinic cholinergic effect on the body. It has shown marked application in the treatment of opioid abuse, tolerance, and withdrawal. However, its use may remain less widespread due to acute cardiotoxicity and neurotoxicity risk—fatalities have been noted—making pre-screening and monitoring of individuals under its influence prudent (Koenig & Hilber, 2015). Subjective effects of the substance are said to produce an "oneiric" state—that is, one likened to a "waking dream" and having functional aspects shared by brain states of rapid eye movement (REM). Verbal exchanges with ancestral and archetypal beings are reported, as well as the phenomena of "panoramic memory" (a recall of rapid, dense succession of vivid autobiographical visual memories, or a type of "life review" similar to those described in near-death experiences). It has been noted that as these memories arise, those that have previously been activated or were associated with strong emotional responses (such as fear, shame, or anger) in the past are then experienced with equanimity or "tranquilheartedness" (Fernandez, 1982) that allows for a reevaluation and reprocessing of their content (Heink et al., 2017).

CIRCUIT 4 ACTIVITIES

Circuit 4 acts as an anchor to Circuit 8. See Circuit 4 Activities in Chapter VI for activities that can help to ground Circuit 8 shocks or to counterbalance overactivity in this circuit.

CLINICAL APPROACH CONSIDERATIONS
(REFER TO RECOMMENDED READING FOR RESOURCES)

- **Intersubjectivity Theory** is a field or systems theory of psychotherapy, primarily concerned with the mutual reciprocity of the psychotherapeutic relationship. It *"seeks to comprehend psychological phenomena not as products of isolated intrapsychic mechanisms, but as forming at the interface of reciprocally interacting subjectivities."* (Stoloros & Atwood, 1992:1)

- **Gestalt Therapy** is a form of psychotherapy that emphasizes personal responsibility and focuses on the individual's experience in the present moment, the therapist-client relationship, the environmental and social contexts of a person's life, and the self-regulating adjustments people make as a result of their overall situation.

- **Process-Oriented Psychology ("Process Work").** The theory of process-oriented psychology centers around the idea of "process": a meaningful, connected pattern over time that can be observed and tracked through non-intentional signals (e.g., non-verbal communication, body symptoms, dreams, accidents, conflicts). It is claimed that becoming consciously aware of the "dreaming process" may help deal with disturbances, including mental and physical distress, relationship troubles, and social issues. The theory of a "dreaming process" began with Arnold Mindell's concept of the "dreambody", developed from Jungian dream analysis and the observation that dreams and body symptoms are meaningfully connected. Mindell asserted that a therapist could work with body experiences to reveal the unconscious, just as they could work with dreams.

Leary's Bio-Evolutionary Stages 22–24		
Stage 22	Meta-physiological Receptivity	The eighth period of evolution begins when neurogenetic consciousness contacts, and is imprinted by sub-atomic quantum mechanical contelligence. The paradox is consistent. The wider the scope of energy in space/time, the more miniaturized the brain center. The body is controlled and directed by the brain.
		The brain is designed/constructed and controlled by genetic intelligence which contains, within the nucleus of the cell, the blueprint for billions of years of evolution... The basic energies, the meta-physiological contelligence, is probably located within the nucleus of the atom.
		The stages of neuro-atomic contelligence (22, 23, 24) are presented here in personalized form to encourage research and thinking about the future periods of human evolution. Each cell of our body is composed of atoms. Sub-nuclear events inside each atom determine the elemental processes. Thus, we can say that our bodies and our nervous systems are based on sub-nuclear events. The eighth period of evolution involves the transception by the neurogenetic intelligence of nuclear symbols.
Stage 23	Neuroatomic Contelligence	Metaphysiological contelligence integrates, engineers, and organizes nuclear particles. Creates atoms.
		At this stage the basic energies which comprise as structure in the universe are available for management. The metaphysiological contelligence constructs atoms, DNA chains, molecules, neurons; sculpts, de-

		signs, and architects all forms of matter by manipulating nuclear particles and gravitational fields.
		At this point in evolution, contelligence no longer needs bodies, neurons, or DNA designs. It may be that the universe is a nervous system—a contelligent network—in which sub-nuclear structures act as basic neural signals. The space/time coordinates of the unified forcefield is probably of a different order from that of the bio-neural system—billionths-of-a-second time spans simultaneous with billions of light years.
		Instead of forcing nature to fit into the three-dimensional model of our symbolic mind, we must allow our nervous systems to be imprinted by the raw data—learn to think-experience like DNA, like electrons, like subatomic particles. Randomness.
Stage 24	Meta-physiological Fusion	Neuro-atomic fusion (star-light) involves force fields of interstellar magnitude and implies a unified galactic consciousness.
		The assumption is made that the gravitational, electro-magnetic and subatomic forcefields that comprise the universe are part of a coherent and conscious network.
		Any eschatological discussion of galactic fusion must include the phenomenon of Black Holes. Whirlpools of anti-matter.
		Many astronomers believe that there are millions of black holes in our galaxy—indeed, that the center of our galaxy may be a black hole.
		The intense gravitational attraction of black holes sucks in surrounding matter. Black holes, it is thought, may be the anti-

| | | matter, anti-energy counterparts of the positive universe. |
| | | Interestingly enough, many physicists are now coming to the conclusion that the elementary particles within the nucleus are black holes—that the "strong force" which holds the atomic nucleus together is super-gravitational. If this theory is correct, black holes provide the final fusions, the final vortex, the linkage of the universe of everything with the void of everything. |

Table 17: *Leary's Bio-Evolutionary Stages 22–24*

Unity Consciousness	
Primary Motivation	None—living in the Ground of All Being
Ultimate Value	None
Attitude Toward Life	Non-attachment
Perception of Death	There is no death except cessation of the body. Everything is immortal and constantly transmuting; therefore, there is no attachment to life or death because each contains the other
Self-Boundaries	None; the self is the same as cosmic consciousness. Recognition of the body-limited self that exists in historical time, but it and the Absolute Self interpenetrate in this material plane
Perception of Temporality	Holonomic. Grounded in the eternal now, but also existing in historical time
Concept of Other	There are no "others" in the absolute sense. Recognition of the bounded selves that exist in the material plane as multiplicities of the One. Non-attached appreciation and compassion for, and identification with, others who are perfect as they are, but are also suffering from attachment
Locus of Control	Internal—as free will expresses the Ground of All Being and emanates from it
Level of Abstraction	Holonomic. Direct, unmediated apperception of all phenomena. Fully integrated Newtonian and non-Newtonian realities
Options for Actions	Infinite and unbounded by the physical plane, except for eventual physical death
Correct Opinion	Only correct option exists

Table 18: *Wade's Holonomic Theory: Unity Consciousness*

RELEVANT ASSESSMENT SCALES
MYSTICAL EXPERIENCE QUESTIONNAIRE (MEQ)

Although the following questionnaire is typically used after some sort of therapy, experimental healing, or guided meditation/breathwork session or ceremony that may employ the use of psychedelics or other means of inducing non-ordinary states of consciousness, this scale can be useful for both guides or solo practitioners/psychonauts who want to reflect on mystical experience as pertaining to some specific experience, or more broadly, throughout their life. This scale can be a useful tool for gauging some aspects of Circuit 8 consciousness.

Instructions: Looking back on your experience, rate the degree to which at any time during that session you experienced the following phenomena. Use this scale:

0 = none; not at all

1 = so slight cannot decide

2 = slight

3 = moderate

4 = strong (equivalent in degree to any other strong experience)

5 = extreme (more than any other time in my life; stronger than 4)

Factor 1: Mystical	
Freedom from the limitations of your personal self and feeling a unity or bond with what was felt to be greater than your personal self.	0 1 2 3 4 5
Experience of pure being and pure awareness (beyond the world of sense impressions).	0 1 2 3 4 5
Experience of oneness in relation to an "inner world" within.	0 1 2 3 4 5
Experience of the fusion of your personal self into a larger whole.	0 1 2 3 4 5
Experience of unity with ultimate reality.	0 1 2 3 4 5
Feeling that you experienced eternity or infinity.	0 1 2 3 4 5

Experience of oneness or unity with objects and/or persons perceived in your surroundings.	0 1 2 3 4 5
Experience of the insight that "all is One."	0 1 2 3 4 5
Awareness of the life or living presence in all things.	0 1 2 3 4 5
Gain of insightful knowledge experienced at an intuitive level.	0 1 2 3 4 5
Certainty of encounter with ultimate reality (in the sense of being able to "know" and "see" what is really real at some point during your experience.	0 1 2 3 4 5
You are convinced now, as you look back on your experience, that in it you encountered ultimate reality (i.e., that you "knew" and "saw" what was really real).	0 1 2 3 4 5
Sense of being at a spiritual height.	0 1 2 3 4 5
Sense of reverence.	0 1 2 3 4 5
Feeling that you experienced something profoundly sacred and holy.	0 1 2 3 4 5

Factor 2: Positive Mood	
Experience of amazement	0 1 2 3 4 5
Feelings of tenderness and gentleness	0 1 2 3 4 5
Feelings of peace and tranquility	0 1 2 3 4 5
Experience of ecstasy	0 1 2 3 4 5
Sense of awe or awesomeness	0 1 2 3 4 5
Feelings of joy	0 1 2 3 4 5

Factor 3: Transcendence of Time & Space	
Loss of your usual sense of time	0 1 2 3 4 5
Loss of your usual sense of space	0 1 2 3 4 5
Loss of usual awareness of where you were	0 1 2 3 4 5
Sense of being "outside of" time, beyond past and future	0 1 2 3 4 5
Being in a realm with no space boundaries	0 1 2 3 4 5
Experience of timelessness	0 1 2 3 4 5

Factor 4: Ineffability	
Sense that the experience cannot be described adequately in words	0 1 2 3 4 5
Feeling that you could not do justice to your experience by describing it in words	0 1 2 3 4 5
Feeling that it would be difficult to communicate your own experience to others who have not had similar experiences	0 1 2 3 4 5

BOOK II:
INTEGRATE

CHAPTER XII

NAVIGATIONS & APPLICATIONS

*"Wholeness is not achieved by cutting off a portion of one's being,
but by integration of the contraries."*
— Dr. Carl Gustav Jung

There seems to be a myopia of psychedelics-as-panacea as they become increasingly popularized in mainstream popular culture. While we recognize the immense value and potential of psychedelics in psychospiritual healing and development, the 8-Circuit Model offers a broader vision that both deepens our understanding of psychedelic experiences of non-ordinary states of consciousness (NOSC), but also encompasses other psychospiritual and parapsychological phenomena. In this chapter, we discuss the application of the 8-Circuit Model for psychedelic-assisted therapy and other NOSCs. This section offers practical guidance for guides, journeyers, and psychonauts.

NAVIGATING NON-ORDINARY STATES OF CONSCIOUSNESS, PSYCHEDELIC-ASSISTED HEALING PRACTICES, & TRANSPERSONAL DEVELOPMENT

Before discussing our guidelines for applying the 8-Circuit Model (8-CM) to NOSC and psychedelic-assisted journeying, we feel it is important to consider some of the circumstances that have contributed to making psychedelics more socially acceptable in recent years. After psychedelics were classified as a Schedule I substance in the United States under the

Controlled Substances Act of 1970, research and clinical use of psychedelic medicines had been severely curtailed, both nationally and internationally. Fortunately, the collective milieu toward psychedelics in contemporary Western civilization has been shifting favorably over the past few years. Although research and anecdotal advocacy supporting the healing properties of psychedelics had been amassing on the fringes for decades, this markedly profound paradigm shift in the mainstream psyche can be traced to late August 2017. First, the Multidisciplinary Association for Psychedelic Studies (MAPS; Santa Cruz, CA) were granted "breakthrough status" by the FDA for their study of MDMA for treating post-traumatic stress disorder (PTSD). This designation is intended to expedite research for treatments that show significant promise of efficacy, so the treatment can be made available to patients sooner. Mainstream media took notice of this press release, and suddenly the miraculous benefits of psychedelic-assisted psychotherapy began gracing the headlines all over major news sources in print, on TV, and on social media. The following year, psilocybin was granted the same breakthrough designation for treatment-resistant depression, and again in 2019 for major depressive disorder (MDD) to Compass Pathways and Usona Institute, respectively. Shortly after this initial media explosion primed the palates of millions, Michael Pollan published his book, *How to Change Your Mind: What the New Science of Psychedelics Teaches Us About Consciousness, Dying, Addiction, Depression, and Transcendence* (2019). In this book, the author details his experiences trying various psychedelic drugs (LSD, psilocybin, and 5-MeO-DMT) for the first time. This book became a #1 *New York Times* bestseller, which further propelled psychedelics into the mainstream spotlight.

With the narrative around psychedelics changing dramatically, Denver became the first US city to successfully decriminalize psychedelic mushrooms in May 2019. Oakland followed shortly after in June 2019, extending the measure to include all mushroom and plant-based psychedelics. Santa Cruz followed suit in January 2020, further extending the category to include all-natural psychedelics, which also granted legal immunity for the possession and use of 5-MeO-DMT. Ann Arbor, MI and Washington DC have also decriminalized mushroom and plant-based psychedelics (in September 2020 and November 2020, respectively). In 2020, Oregon became the first state to legalize the use of psilocybin in a state-approved setting with a licensed facilitator; Colorado passed similar legalization shortly thereafter. Activist organizations, such as Decriminalize Nature, are helping to get decriminalization measures on the ballot in over a hundred US cities by educating the public about the potential benefits of decriminalizing/legalizing psychedelic drugs, and the harmful impact of the War on Drugs.

It is beyond the scope of this book to discuss all of the countries in which psychedelic drugs are legal, decriminalized, or moving in that direction, but it should be noted that the United States is not alone in this movement. Research and clinical treatments are growing in popularity internationally; and many countries have never impeded indigenous ceremonial use (e.g., in Central and South American countries such as Costa Rica and Peru; and the use of psychedelic medicines such as peyote, San Pedro, psilocybin mushrooms are permitted on Indian Reservations in the United States).

Despite this trend toward decriminalization and improved public opinion, at the time of writing this book, psychedelic drugs are still illegal federally in the United States and in many countries throughout the world. It is important for guides and journeyers to know the legal status where one resides. Although these guidelines are intended for all people working with psychedelic medicines, we are not advocating or promoting the use of psychedelic drugs among unlicensed mental health practitioners, coaches, spiritual healers/guides, or other untrained/unlicensed guides or users. However, there are many people who will choose to use psychedelic drugs for various reasons, and many people who will "sit" for others. ("Sitters" are individuals who act as guides or safe support persons for someone using a psychedelic or psychedelic-like drug.) Whether you are already a seasoned psychedelic guide/user, or a minimally experienced novice, we offer these guidelines as a means of harm reduction and benefit enhancement.

While much of this chapter is derived from the world of psychedelics, it may offer insight and benefit for those exploring states of consciousness in solo or assisted work that may be novel, vulnerable, or potentially uncomfortable to the individual. The material should be considered in this broader sense of harm reduction and support. It is important to consider that, regardless of experience level, unintended adverse experiences can occur which could have been prevented or minimized with proper preparation. Moreover, sometimes a user may have a difficult experience, but if the guide is properly trained in techniques to help that journeyer work through it, that "bad trip" can become a profoundly healing or transformational experience. Conversely, learning various benefit-enhancement techniques, starting in a preparatory phase, can optimize an experience and outcome. Although this chapter largely focuses on utilizing this model to guide the experience (which can inherently foster harm reduction and benefit enhancement just by having a map to help navigate), we have also synthesized this model with a structure based on current protocols for psychedelic-assisted therapy and research. We strongly encourage guides to further research harm reduction techniques as best practices for providing safety and support.

PHILOSOPHY FOR USING THE 8-CIRCUIT MODEL FOR HEALING & TRANSPERSONAL DEVELOPMENT

The application of the 8-CM can be highly effective with or without psychedelic drugs. As discussed in *Book I,* the model maps the different developmental stages of life, including transpersonal stages. It allows for re-imprinting and reprogramming of the human nervous system and belief systems. Psychedelics also have this capacity in their ability to alter perceptions and allow for new ways of experiencing. Scientific studies and anecdotal stories suggest that psychedelic experiences can lead to mystical experiences resulting in long-term positive changes in personality, such as increased creativity, open-mindedness, and aesthetic appreciation. Combining psychedelic drugs with the intentional use of this model can yield profoundly transformational results, both in healing the past and in the development and facilitation of transpersonal faculties and experiences; these include kundalini-awakening/samadhi, extrasensory perception (ESP), out-of-body experiences (OBE)/astral projection, lucid dreaming, telekinesis, non-local/non-duality experiences, etc. However, before proceeding with the potential benefits of NOSC and psychedelic drugs, it would be wise to consider their potential dangers.

NOSCs and/or the use of psychedelic drugs can induce a suggestible state. Although this effect can be a useful adjunct during therapy, this suggestible state is a double-edged sword as it can also be used to manipulate people. The best-known examples include the use of LSD by the United States' Central Intelligence Agency (CIA; Lee & Shlain, 1992; MK-ULTRA/Mind Control Experiments, 2005; Stevens, 1987) and by Charles Manson (Bugliosi & Gentry, 1994). The CIA ran secret mind-control experiments under the code name MK-ULTRA between 1953 and 1964 in which they drugged prisoners, patients, prostitution johns, and students with LSD without informing them or obtaining consent (MK-ULTRA/Mind Control Experiments, 2005). Manson used LSD to influence followers of his cult to commit murders for him (Bugliosi & Gentry, 1994). While the "set" (i.e., internal states such as emotions, belief systems, reality tunnels, etc.) of these individuals may have been predisposed to commit horrific acts, one's *setting* (i.e., the external environment, which includes the *set* of others who are present) can greatly influence psychedelic experiences. Thus, the impressionable state of the user can be positively or negatively taken advantage of by others (Hartogsohn, 2015; 2017).

Persons under the influence of psychedelic drugs or in NOSC may also regress to an earlier developmental stage or encounter previously repressed psychic material (e.g., traumatic memories, unresolved guilt, or other unconscious memories, feelings, and internal conflicts). The activation of such material can result in a seemingly "bad trip" or other adverse reactions (Richards, 2017). Difficult experiences can be extremely overwhelming and emotionally distressing (Bogenschutz, 2016; Hofmann, 2009; Richards, 2017; Strassman, 1984; Ungerleider, Fisher, & Fuller, 1966). If not properly responded to, at best, this might be a missed opportunity for healing; and at worst, it can have a long-term negative impact on the user. Ideally, the guide is a trained mental healthcare professional or indigenous healer. When such an experience is met in a supportive and non-judgmental space, this sort of abreaction can be profound. The experience of unconscious material in a safe space allows for it to be processed and reprogrammed into conscious, meaningful experiences (Ogden, 2004). These can result in the healing and integration of previously unknown or unaccepted aspects of oneself.

In *Prometheus Rising,* Wilson (1983) cites a statement by Mary Baker Eddy (founder of Christian Science) that most illness is manifested fear. Our relationship to, and expression of fear becomes coded into our nervous system. While resulting from a combination of nature and nurture, it is not beyond our abilities to willfully transform this programming in healthier ways that better serve us. The re-activation of imprint vulnerability in the 8-CM is a key factor that allows for the intentional reprogramming of the nervous system. As discussed in *Book I,* each of the lower four circuits has a critical period during which certain environmental and relational experiences influence your beliefs about yourself and your place in the world, and thus how you live in and experience the world. These critical experiences, along with your genetic predisposition and various external indoctrinating stimuli (e.g., family and cultural traditions and values; education; media and social media; politics; the accepted "common sense" and other prevailing belief systems of the times; etc.) all work together to shape your reality tunnel. Deeper explorations of imprint vulnerability applications follow later in this chapter.

You have more power and influence over the world around you than most people realize due to various limitations in your reality tunnel—whether self or other-imposed. As Wilson often quoted, *"What the thinker thinks, the prover proves."* The Thinker includes our beliefs, expectations, dogmas, ideologies, ideas, hypotheses, theories, things that have been suggested to us, our observations and assumptions, perceptions, etc. These things may or may not be true, but it is the job of the Prover to find evidence of these projections.

Apophenia is a phenomenon in which you find meaningful connections among seemingly unrelated things or events. (Pareidolia is a type of apophenia in which you perceive patterns or images in unrelated visual objects; e.g., seeing images in clouds or a face on your toast.) *Gestalts* are incomplete images of shapes that the mind completes by imaginarily imposing what it would expect to see to make the image whole. *Confabulation* is a brain mechanism in which you unconsciously fabricate information when there are gaps or distortions in your memory; it is not lying, as you believe it to be true (in extreme cases, this happens in Alzheimer's disease; Attali et al, 2009). Unconscious stimuli bombard our nervous system and affect us (our behavior, personality, feelings, thoughts, desires) in ways we don't always realize. Such unconscious materials include our own individual associations and linguistic connotations, priming (i.e., an initial exposure to something that can affect later exposures or other behaviors related to the stimulus), archetypal symbols, marketing/advertising, NLP and other hypnotic language techniques, memes, propaganda, and innumerable other stimuli— intentional or not. The brain interacts with the world via projection. Literally everything we experience is a projection of what the mind pieces together from myriad information from the past, present, alleged precognition or other psi and quantum phenomena, as well as potential future and non-local/non-dual influences. All of this illustrates that there are multitudinous factors that influence us and how we experience and relate to the world around us. The more we can understand and experiment with this concept in our own lives, the more conscious we can become of our own reality tunnels, other people's reality tunnels, and how others may be influencing us.

How the Thinker/Prover mechanism works may be akin to a self-fulfilling prophecy, and perhaps even more encompassing in that Wilson's reference extends to more relativistic and transpersonal dimensions. Keep in mind Korzybski's adage, *"The map is not the territory."* It is easy to get stuck in patterns of being and experiencing because it's what we expect, and in turn, we perceive what we project! As Lewis Carroll wrote in *Alice in Wonderland,* *"Why, sometimes I believe as many as six impossible things before breakfast."* It is good advice to explore ideas beyond our belief systems, even if they seem fantastic or impossible. Audrey Hepburn offered another inspiring quote challenging apparent limitations stating, *"Nothing is impossible, the word itself says, 'I'm possible'!"*

Thus, each of us interacts with the world based on our unique bio-psycho-socio-spiritual lens. This lens—our reality tunnel—includes our personalities, belief systems, and how we interact with the world. It is determined by our genetic blueprints, and how it is altered by external stimuli. This complex interaction of nature and nurture determines how we feel, think, and act in the world (insecure versus secure, dominant versus submissive, flexible versus rigid, creative versus fixed, etc.). Wilson often cited the Copenhagen Interpretation of quantum mechanics to support his relativist view that each person makes an individual and unique map of the world based on imprints and other experiences, learning, conditioning, assumptions, and belief systems. However, we become increasingly empowered the more we understand that our psyche generates this map, and because this map is not the actual territory, we have the ability to change and improve this model we've made by understanding and consciously hacking into these feedback loops. Unfortunately, many people become prisoners of their own maps. Wilson referred to this religious belief in and adherence to your own model—and aversion to the models of others—as "model-theism" (Wilson, 2001). For example, you might see this type of staunch fixedness to your own model when you have fears about the world, and use your beliefs and model to create a sense of safety and order in your perception of the world—as in using religion to assuage your fear of death. Alli refers to the degree to which a person can tolerate ambiguity, uncertainty, and change as one's "uncertainty threshold" (Alli, 2009:63).

It was once believed that personality and patterns of behavior tend to be fixed by around the age of 30. However, regardless of how fixed a person might be in their reality tunnel, Leary believed that each person can undergo a re-imprinting process at any age by means of cybernetics and metaprogramming. He defined "cyber" to derive from the Greek *kubernetes,* meaning pilot, and a *"cyber-person as one who sufficiently understood the Heisenberg uncertainty principle and accepts responsibility for one's own realities they define and inhabit"* (Leary, 1994:vi).

This has been demonstrated in a number of ways, for better or worse. On the one hand, cults, kidnappers, and the military use various metaprogramming techniques to brainwash and reprogram members, victims, and soldiers, respectively, and restructure their psyches according to their desired effects. On the other hand, studies have shown that mystical experiences and psychedelic and psychedelic-like compounds can result in significant personality changes, such as an increase in the personality domain of openness (MacLean et al., 2011). Moreover, studies show that psychedelic and psychedelic-like compounds can significantly ameliorate clinical symptoms in various pervasive psychological disorders (Turetzky, 2021). For example, using ayahuasca to treat PTSD and drug addiction (Bouso & Riba, 2014; Liester & Prickett, 2012); LSD and psilocybin for end-of-life anxiety in terminally ill patients (Gasser, Holstein, Michel, Doblin, Yazar-Klosinski, Passie, & Brenneisen, 2014); and ibogaine, which can drastically reduce opiate withdrawal symptoms and cravings (Alper, Lotsof, Frenken, Luciano, & Bastiaans, 1999). It is with a firsthand working knowledge of these studies and clinical practices that this syncretization of psychedelic-assisted healing and transformation with the 8-CM has been based.

The guidelines for working with the 8-CM during a psychedelic journey for healing and transformation (as set forth later in this chapter) are strongly influenced by: the principles and protocols from the MAPS study using MDMA to treat PTSD; the ketamine-assisted therapy training program at Sage Institute (Oakland, CA); the Integrative Psychiatry Institute's (IPI) psychedelic-assisted therapy program; the Yale Manual for Psilocybin-Assisted Therapy of Depression; Integrative Wellness Academy's holistic life-coaching training program; and Oregon's psilocybin facilitator-training certification program. We've syncretized various types of formatting, styles, approaches, and principles from these sources that we feel best align with the 8-Circuit Model. These underlying foundational philosophies and techniques help guide the process and optimize the benefits of the experience.

The MAPS protocol breaks up their sessions into three stages: Preparatory (Prep), Experimental/Experiential, and Integrative. In the early stages of their research, there were three sessions in each stage; this is more variable in the later stages of their clinical trials, offering additional Integrative sessions between Experiential sessions. The Sage Institute model requires two integration sessions between Experiential sessions. The current Oregon psilocybin regulations require at least one preparatory session, a separate administration session, and require that integration sessions be offered but may be declined. How guides/journeyers choose to format their sessions can be discussed, but having at least one integration session within a week after a journey is highly recommended. This is so the material that emerged from the journey can be properly reflected on and integrated before going further and deeper into the process, which the journeyer may find over-whelming. The guidelines provided later in this chapter are based on this three-stage formatting style. However, we've renamed the sessions to better reflect the philosophy of the 8-Circuit Model in each meeting type. That is, the sessions are divided into the Preprogramming Phase, the Metaprogram-ming Phase, and the Integration & Reinforcement Phase (IRP). Addition-ally, we've added the Hermit Phase (HP). (Although the practices suggested in this novel phase are suggested and encouraged in the MAPS model as part of the Integration phase, we're outlining it as a separate phase of personal work to emphasize its importance.) The importance of this phase cannot be understated; it is a time for the seeds that emerged from the journey to be nurtured. Ideally, the journeyer should spend several days in gentle solitude, reflecting on internal experiences, and allowing for a release of old patterns and the emergence of new ways of experiencing oneself and the world. However, if the journeyer is having a difficult time in this phase, it is im-portant to have a support system, either the guide or a trusted friend or fam-ily member who is non-judgmental, respectful, and supportive towards the journeyer's healing and transformational experiences.

The concept of an inner healing intelligence or an inner healer may be described as a Circuit 6/Circuit 7 entity whom one may call forth to access innate healing potential. The reference to an inner healer was coined by Grof (Tarnas & Kelly, 2023), and is used in various psychedelic-assisted therapy models, including those used by MAPS. Moreover, a person under-going a journey (with or without psychedelics medicines, but especially with) may have a transpersonal experience or may speak of their experiences from what seems like a fragmented sense of self (e.g., one might refer to themselves as "we" or talk about different "parts" of oneself). This is normalized and validated from a Family Systems Theory (IFS) perspective which does not pathologize transpersonal experience or multiplicity (Schwartz, 1995). Although beyond the scope of this book, an understanding of this approach can be extremely useful. (See the recommended reading list at the end of this book for additional resources.)

The duration of the journey depends on the method or substance used, and whether a supplemental dose is offered. One guide can suffice for shorter psychedelic journeys (under 3 hours); however, for longer journeys, it is generally recommended that two guides are present so each can take a break as needed without leaving the journeyer unattended. Moreover, each guide can take on a particular role. For example, one guide might take notes while the other offers optional, consensual, non-sexual physical touch if requested. A journeyer might prefer one guide over the other for some reason (gender, commonalities, or other unconscious projections). It is important that both guides work cooperatively as a team, respecting the journeyer's preferences without taking offense.

ETHICS

If you are seeking a guide, it is advised you find someone reputable and trustworthy. Although we do not advocate underground journeying, we have witnessed a significant rise in the underground use of psychedelics by users and so-called guides with little-to-no experience or training. It is important that anyone intending to act as a guide for others should be familiar with ethical guidelines, such as those delineated through HIPAA. With that in mind, this section advocates for a foundational study of ethics when working with others. The Collaborative Institutional Training Initiative (CITI) offers an invaluable human-subjects training program that is highly recommended for anyone considering working with others professionally [about.citiprogram.org/en/homepage]. You should be fully committed to honoring and respecting the journeyer's privacy, confidentiality, safety, overall rights, and well-being. Informed consent regarding the role and responsibilities of the guide should always be discussed and agreed upon prior to undertaking any journeys. Because there is a risk of causing harm to another person under these circumstances, even unintentionally, guides should have professional liability insurance in case a journeyer should have an adverse reaction and decide to file a lawsuit.

As discussed previously, non-ordinary states can put you in a highly suggestible and vulnerable state that can be easily taken advantage of, especially by someone who might be perceived to be in a position of power or authority. Moreover, if any conflicts of interest exist or other personal issues arise in the relationship during or after the work, this should be considered and addressed in advance. It is unethical for mental healthcare professionals to take advantage of their clients, sexually or emotionally; even if you are not a mental healthcare professional, we strongly encourage that this power differential be addressed between guide and journeyer, and unless there was already romantic or sexual involvement, engaging in such a relationship during or after the journey is strongly discouraged.

§§§

"Set and setting" refers to much more than just the external environment. It also includes the mental state of others in the journeyer's presence. Thus, if the guide is unable to recognize and inhibit their emotional reactions and projections, this can have lasting adverse effects on the journeyer. The guide should at least have a basic understanding of transference and countertransference.

Transference is the unconscious projections of a client onto a therapist, and countertransference is the unconscious projections of the therapist toward the client (Eagle, 2000). Transference and countertransference are especially important considerations when working with the 8-Circuit Model and seeking to re-imprint a circuit (especially circuits 1, 2, 4, 5, and 6). Circuit 1 relates to caregiver attachment; Circuit 2 pertains to emotions and power dynamics; Circuit 4 is about interpersonal relationships and sexuality; Circuit 5 is about ecstatic experience; and Circuit 6 is involved with intentionally reprogramming the nervous system and belief systems. Thus, these particular circuits are high-risk for intentional or unintentional projections and/or unwanted advances by either party, especially with respect to imprint vulnerability that may become activated during the journey. The journeyer should be upfront with the guide should they suspect that any strong emotional or adverse reactions might occur, such as personal or family history of mental illness, or intention to work through trauma. Conversely, the role and readiness of the guide are important factors that can affect the journey and outcome. If a guide has little-to-no experience working with mental health issues, or has not done personal psychotherapy work on themselves, it may be overwhelming for an untrained person to "hold space" (i.e., to sit for a person in a way that is fully present, non-judgmental, supportive, and safe—both physically and emotionally) for someone having an extreme emotional reaction during a journey. The guide should be prepared to maintain a safe and supportive "container" (a safe space nurtured by a therapist or guide in which the journeyer can freely, openly, and fully explore and process their experiences without shame or fear of judgment) while asserting strong boundaries, which should be discussed and agreed upon prior to journeying. Again, we are not encouraging untrained professionals to sit with any journeyers; however, we do encourage journeyers seeking psychedelic/NOSC experiences, especially novices, to seek a trusted guide or sitter for safety reasons. We approach this topic from a harm reduction perspective.

Further, if you are not a trained mental health professional, we strongly advise that you not sit for anyone who has severe mental health problems that you are not trained to work with. Always assess if a person you are considering sitting for is a potential harm to themselves or to others. These are the two exceptions to honoring client confidentiality, and where reporting such threats to authority is mandated. If a person expresses that they want to harm themselves (e.g., cutting), or that they want to die, it is strongly advised that you do *NOT* work with this person, and instead help them find the professional help that they need. Also, if a person expresses that they want to harm someone else, they know how to find them, and they make an explicit threat, this person should also be reported to the authorities. Moreover, if someone is generally of a hostile, intimidating demeanor, strongly consider your own safety. The word *psychedelic* is of Greek etymology and means "mind-manifesting"; if a person expresses a desire to harm themselves or others even before taking a psychedelic drug, or if you have suspicions and feel uncomfortable in any way, working with such a person would be taking a huge gamble that you might not be prepared should the journey go terribly awry. We can't stress enough that you consider these factors before taking unnecessary risks that may result in you or others being harmed.

Lastly, the legality of psychedelic drugs where you intend to journey/sit should be considered. Laws—and legal ramifications—for possession and use should be fully understood and considered by all parties involved. Penalties may be particularly severe if you engage in work with a minor. If psychedelic drugs are not legal or decriminalized at this location, all parties should be fully aware of and discuss potential legal consequences.

PREPROGRAMMING PHASE (PP)

While situations may arise where you find yourself unexpectedly sitting for someone else (e.g., at a festival such as Burning Man), it is often most beneficial to meet prior to the journey(s). Ideally, several preparatory sessions should be offered before a metaprogramming journey. The initial meetings are about:

- Building rapport
- Establishing a sense of safety and trust between guide and journeyer
- Addressing safety issues, concerns, and expectations
- Setting intentions
- Assessing background information about the journeyer including their prior knowledge about, and experience with, psychedelics and therapy/coaching
- Introducing and developing a safe and secure set and setting through connection and environment
- Providing psychoeducation as necessary
- Mapping the circuits and identifying any imbalances to be worked with

- Identifying belief systems and reality tunnels (including mental health history)
- Setting a plan for metaprogramming and integration

Although these guidelines are formatted for guides, they can be beneficial for experienced users journeying solo to consider and reflect upon before embarking on their psychedelic work. Moreover, this approach can be effectively utilized in methods that do not include psychedelic drugs.

Assess for any physical or mental health issues or use of medications that could potentially result in complications or contraindications during the journey. If a person has a serious mental illness or health complication, these factors need to be strongly considered before proceeding with this work. It is also important that users/guides take the time to research any psychoactive substances the journeyer may be taking for potential contraindications and other safety concerns. For example, ketamine should not be used if a person has high blood pressure or bladder issues, or if they are taking medications such as NSAID pain relievers, Benadryl, opioids, benzodiazepines, sedative hypnotics (used for sleep disorders), muscle relaxants, or stimulants (alcohol and cannabis are also discouraged). These drugs should be discontinued for at least 72 hours before the journey (always consult with a healthcare professional before making any changes in medications), food should not be consumed within 6 hours, and liquids should not be imbibed for at least 2 hours before the journey. A fast or a cleanse for a week or so before the journey can be a meaningful preparation for the journey—as is done when working with ayahuasca. Other psychedelic and psychoactive medicines should also be avoided for a week before the journey to allow for the purity of the journey experience. With psilocybin, an individual should not have taken lithium within 30 days of journeying as this may carry an increased risk of seizure (Nayak et al., 2021). Journeyers should discuss any dietary suggestions and potential interactions of all medications they are taking with their healthcare provider.

It is helpful to suggest to the journeyer that integration starts from the moment the journeyer sets an intention to heal or transform in some way, even during these first meetings, regardless of how long before the first psychedelic journey commences.

The use of music, eye shades, and appropriate touch can be supportive at various points throughout the journey. If you intend to offer any of these options, this should be discussed and agreed upon before the first session. The playlists Johns Hopkins and MAPS use for their psychedelic-assisted therapy sessions are available on music streaming services, or you can create a playlist of your own, or suggest the journeyer create one. Keep in mind, however, that the playlists used during the Johns Hopkins and MAPS studies were thoughtfully created with a particular vibe and flow in mind, so they can be especially supportive as ambient sound while the journeyer is talking with the guide and for going within; however, the direction should always be entirely guided by the journeyer. This non-directive approach should be clearly communicated and reinforced to the journeyer so they feel fully in control of the direction of the experience; the guide(s) are there for safety, support, note-taking, and to provide a container and assistance in whatever way the journeyer needs. Regarding the potential use of *optional*, non-sexual, supportive touch: this option should always be discussed and agreed upon beforehand. It is essential that the interaction be entirely non-sexual and respectful of the journeyer's boundaries, including the journeyer's desire to discontinue the touch at any time. Examples of supportive touch might be holding their hand or feet. It can be helpful to agree upon non-verbal signals (such as a hand sign) for the journeyer to let you know they want you to offer touch or to stop—should they find that speaking is too difficult. Inform the journeyer that they can change their mind about anything agreed upon in advance, with the exception of guidelines related to safety issues (e.g., agreeing to stay under the guide's supervision until the end of the session, after the substance has completely worn off).

Explain that difficult experiences may arise, but challenging experiences can be the most healing and beneficial if they are able to stay present through them. Ask the journeyer about their preferred stress inoculation techniques, such as pranayama (breathing exercises), muscle relaxation visualizations, meditation, punching or pushing against a pillow, vocalizations, drawing, dance/movement, etc. If they are unfamiliar with working with such techniques, use this opportunity to discuss various methods, and explain that you will encourage them to notice what is happening in their body should such an experience arise. In general, it is important to check in with the journeyer at various points throughout the session to inquire about their somatic experience, and help them to move blocked energy or release tension. This is especially important when an experience seems meaningfully significant. Alli (2014), describes a moving Zazen meditation—called No-Form—which can be a profoundly healing experience that allows for somatic expression and the release of pent-up, blocked, or repressed energy. Information about this meditation and how to perform it can be found on his website: paratheatrical.com/noform.html

Since set and setting are of paramount importance to the journey, use these initial meetings to discuss any paraphernalia, ceremonies, or other adjunctive accessories or rituals that you or the journeyer might find helpful. An altar might be set up. The space might be smudged. A candle and/or other talismans (power objects) might be charged with an intention, or used for protection. Encourage the journeyer to wear loose-fitting, comfortable clothes on the day of the journey, and to bring layers in case their body temperature fluctuates. They should bring water and a light snack to the session. The guide should also be prepared with offerings just in case (be sure to inquire about any allergies or dietary restrictions; additional water and electrolyte-containing fluids should be available and encouraged throughout the session to prevent dehydration—which can be dangerous and potentially fatal). The guide should offer to take notes or photos at the journeyer's request. Again, remind the journeyer that any permissions agreed upon, with the exception of those related to safety, can be changed during the journey; the journeyer should always feel they are in full control of the experience.

Finally, decide in advance with the journeyer about their post-journey plans. Will you be providing a safe space for them to stay overnight? If they are leaving your supervision, how will they get to their destination? The journeyer should not operate a vehicle, so be sure to make definite travel arrangements beforehand—ideally, someone they trust should pick them up. Taking public transportation while in a vulnerable state is not ideal, and should be avoided if possible. Moreover, the journeyer should remain in an uninterrupted state of calm and quietude for as long as possible after the journey, and taking public transportation can be a jarring experience.

METAPROGRAMMING PHASE (MP)
IMPRINT VULNERABILITY

The metaprogramming phase allows for a period of vulnerability and rapid brain change; Wilson (1983:155) referred to it as a state of "consciousness dilation." He further states that *"from the viewpoint of neuro-sociology, how I perceive 'myself' and 'my world' depends on how each circuit has been wired in my brain"* (Wilson, 1983:155). Leary (1988:55) claimed that we are all neurogenetic robots of cultural and evolutionary conditioning, and there can be no escape from such robothood until you learn to take control of your nervous system to reprogram your individual programs. Through this healing and growth, we may become self-defined and flourish.

> *"Most agonizing and intractable social problems are caused solely by our ignorance of the brain's capacity for rote repetition and abrupt change."* (Leary 1988:62)

As discussed earlier, certain neurological imprints tend to occur during critical periods of neurodevelopment, and may remain fairly rigid throughout your life unless some form of re-imprinting or significant self-work occurs. This phase allows for an acute period of what has been referred to as "imprint vulnerability" in which these rigid imprints soften or loosen, allowing for more plasticity in their nature, whereby they can be consciously altered or re-imprinted. States of imprint vulnerability can be achieved in multiple ways as outlined in the previous chapters. According to Leary (1988:58), the human nervous system—despite its tight hold on imprints— ironically holds a pretty fragile concept of reality, and will collapse within a matter of days if signals of one's sense of self and reality are not continually reinforced. The removal of these reinforcing inputs has been noted as particularly effective in allowing for imprint vulnerability because of this.

From his research with isolation tanks, Dr. John Lilly (1975:79) noted that it only takes a few minutes of true isolation before anxiety appears, and only a few hours before hallucinations begin and an individual may fall into a receptive state of metaprogramming. One of the authors of this book (Wingate) can attest to this sort of experience while undergoing an extended period of time in a "dark room." By sitting in absolute darkness for a long enough time (2 weeks), the nervous system begins to produce hallucinations (due to endogenous DMT), creating a state of imprint vulnerability. Such states may also arise (for better or worse) in situations of relative isolation from normative cultural reality. These include long hospital stays (Leary, 1988:57), or time spent in vastly different cultural environments. These can include prison, the military, or travels to a very different culture in which returning to the original cultural environment can be disorienting, shocking, or difficult due to loosening or changes to initial imprints.

"Throughout human life, when the biosurvival brain flashes danger, all other mental activities cease." (Leary, 1988:54)

First circuit reimprinting involves accessing a state relative to that of initial imprinting (i.e., infancy, in which the basic somatic needs for survival and safety are directly experienced. Leary 1988:54). This may be facilitated by Circuit 5 neurosomatic bliss signal awareness.

Second circuit reimprinting involves accessing a state akin to that of a clumsy toddler in which personal autonomy, ownership, and territorial pecking-order power-dynamics are directly experienced (Leary, 1988:54). This may be facilitated by Circuit 6 neuroelectric self-defining awareness.

Third circuit reimprinting occurs when language, symbols, doctrines, and dexterity are experienced as incomplete or no longer of sufficient use, and new signals and skills become necessary. This is more efficient if it is also tied into C-1 survival needs and C-2 status needs (Leary, 1988:55). This may be facilitated by Circuit 7 neurogenetic meta-symbolic awareness.

Fourth circuit reimprinting occurs when the community, tribal, or sexual value-systems or identities are found to no longer be sufficient or beneficial. Like C-3 reimprinting, this becomes more efficient when further tied into survival/safety and status needs (Leary, 1988:56). For example, shipwrecked sailors who are isolated from social interactions may become afraid of human conversation because their imprints have faded and they may fear being thought insane should they speak of their experience (Leary, 1988:56). Alli recommends a 3-month period of abstinence (sexual isolation) to facilitate reimprinting unwanted sexual imprints or patterns. Circuit 4 re-imprinting may be facilitated by Circuit 8 nondual/non-local quantum awareness.

Leary (1988:57) professes that early life imprints to establish survival (C-1) and status (C-2) were established at the expense of the infinite possibilities of unconditioned consciousness. It is during the metaprogramming phase these infinite possibilities may once again become accessible.

BELIEF STRUCTURES & PSYCHEDELICS: REBUS, SEBUS & ALBUS

Leary (1988:59) states that *"neurotransmitter drugs such as psychedelics perform the same function as isolation, as they weaken or suspend the user's old imprints."* A 2023 paper published in the scientific journal *Nature* explored evidence of various psychedelics reopening "critical periods" (imprints) of development learning (Nardou et al., 2023). Twenty percent of the 65 protein-producing genes affected in these states regulate the maintenance and repair of the extracellular matrix located in the nucleus accumbens—an area of the brain associated with survival and reproductive drives, social learning, risk-taking, and reward (Salgado & Kaplitt, 2015). In this study, the time of the critical-period effects in mice varied depending on the substance given, with ketamine having a 48-hour duration, MDMA and psilocybin having a two-week duration, LSD three weeks, and ibogaine four weeks. They note these time periods parallel self-reports of acute effects of human psychedelic use that *"may be an opportunity for a post-treatment integration period to maintain the learning state."*

The concept of **Re**laxed **B**eliefs **U**nder Psychedelics (REBUS; Carhart-Harris, 2019) as it relates to metaprogramming was discussed in Chapter IX. Expanding on this, Dr. Adam Safron has proposed a broader model he calls "**Al**tered **B**eliefs **U**nder Psychedelics" (ALBUS; 2020), which includes REBUS phenomena, but also proposes the role of **S**trengthened **B**eliefs **U**nder Psychedelics (SEBUS). For the sake of work with the 8-Circuit Model, SEBUS may be thought to correlate to Circuit 5 activation, while REBUS may be thought to correlate to activation of the more complex circuits, 6–8.

Safron (2020) approaches this model *"within the context of understanding brains as hybrid computational systems (e.g., posterior cortices as autoencoding heterarchies; hippocampal/entorhinal-systems as high-level controllers and predictive sequence memories; frontal lobe striatal-cortical loops as metalearning systems, etc.)"* (p. 9). This system considers hierarchical predictive processing (HPP) to describe how free energy can be minimized within the brain (Ahmad & Scheinkman, 2019). In this context, REBUS may correspond to high levels of serotonin 2a (5-HT_{2a}) receptor agonism (as found with moderate to high doses of classical psychedelics) that results in relaxation of top-down pre-existing beliefs ("priors"), promotion of flexibility in learning, and attentional shifts that create less perceptual filtering (Parr & Friston, 2017). This allows for more bottom-up influence from the senses and *"asynchronous activation modes, and thereby relaxed beliefs through attenuated coherence"* (p. 22). SEBUS, on the other hand, correlates to low-to-moderate 5-HT_{2a} receptor stimulation (as found with micro or low psychedelic doses), and is proposed to account for experiencing a more acute clarity of one's reality including the "mind manifesting," "consciousness deviating" experiences that include imaginative planning and goal-oriented cognition. ALBUS then encompasses both of these dynamics as well as thalamic gating models (Preller et al., 2019) and cortico-striatal thalamo-cortico models (Doss et al., 2021), in which we *"might expect increased illusion susceptibility with lower doses of psychedelics, but potentially decreased illusion-susceptibility with higher doses"* (p. 23).

Safron describes a concept that seems rather similar to "the thinker and the prover," wherein *"perceptions correspond to the brain's internally-generated predictions, rather than constituting a faithful readout of incoming sense data."* He argues that each moment of experience corresponds to a top-down prediction of bottom-up observations, rather than actual incoming observations. Here "predictive coding" of incoming information is filtered and tends to bypass higher-order processing altogether for the sake of efficiency—except in cases in which expectations are violated. This allows for *"a surprising amount of cognition"* being explained in terms of inference (Safron, 2020a; 2021a). He cites Frith (2005) who characterizes one's subjective experience as a kind of *"controlled hallucination."*

> *"We may understand the stream of consciousness as the iterative estimation of likely sensory states, inferred according to a coherent model of the world." (Safron, 2020a; 2021a)*

Within this model, meditative and psychedelic-associated states of non-dual awareness and dissociation may be understood as stemming from a breakdown of this process (Ciaunica & Safron, 2022; Safron 2021b). Specific beliefs are thought to be generated through complexes of neural activity synchronized at beta frequencies. Alpha frequencies correspond to integration into egocentric reference frames/predictions/priors. Alpha rhythms have been associated with working memory (Kerr et al., 2013; Sato et al., 2018) and resting wakefulness (or consciousness), including that found in REM sleep (Cantero et al., 2002). It is speculated that such a partially dissociated state could allow for more absorption of both imagination and perception (Csikszentmihalyi, 1991; Ott et al., 2005). Gamma power—thought to encode prediction errors—from the primary visual cortex is inhibited with $5\text{-}HT_{2a}$ agonism (Michaiel et al., 2019)

Much of this work is focused on classical psychedelics/$5\text{-}HT_{2a}$ agonists. However, it is proposed that REBUS may be more straightforwardly applied to ketamine (Li et al., 2018), which may be associated with increased psychological and brain network flexibility (Braun et al., 2016). Bottom-up influences, including long-term revision, on high-level priors seem to be less evident with ketamine, and may not engage insightful processes the same way as classical psychedelics.

These processes seem non-linear. However, SEBUS effects may produce REBUS effects, which in turn produce more SEBUS effects, and so on— and *vice versa*. Safron (2020) explores several types of belief-updating that can occur under psychedelics within this model with SEBUS (low dose) and REBUS (high dose) specific actions:

- **Inference**—Via neural activity dynamics (set/setting dependent)
  Timescale of Belief Updating: 10s–100s of msec
  SEBUS: More precise predictions via increased activity levels
  REBUS: Less precise predictions via excitation-induced desynchronization

- **Learning**—Via synapse strengthening, synaptogenesis, neurogenesis
  Timescale of Belief Updating: minutes to days
  SEBUS: Increasing opportunities for enduring metabolic changes
  REBUS: Potential for enhanced learning if relaxed prior expectations are more easily modified/updated

- **Structure Learning**—via formation (and reformation) of compositional representations in the hippocampal/entorhinal system
  Timescale of Belief Updating: Days to weeks
  SEBUS: Accommodation/updating of schemas
  REBUS: Less rigidly held beliefs may be more easily modified/updated

- **Top-down attention**—via context-sensitive precision-weighting of predictions, transient emotional states, more enduring moods
  Timescale of Belief Updating: 100s of msec to hours
  SEBUS: Strengthening of policies over attentional selection (low-to-moderate 5-HT_{2a} agonism)
  REBUS: Relaxation of policies over attentional selection (moderate to high 5-HT_{2a} agonism)

Safron further explores various phenomena of the psychedelic experience through this model. A partial list of particularly relevant ones includes:

- **Feeling of unity and deep order**

    SEBUS: Strengthening of core socioemotional priors from early developmental stages

    REBUS: Reduced modeling of self as separate from world

- **Recovered memories**

    SEBUS: Increased conscious access

    REBUS: Reduced suppression from defense mechanisms (e.g., experiential avoidance patterns)

- **Personal transformation**

    SEBUS: Increased perceptual and imaginative abilities enhancing capacity for visualizing desired goals and undesired consequences of behavior patterns

    REBUS: Letting go of rigid beliefs via relation of internal models

- **Ego death**

    SEBUS: Potential consequences of extreme absorption causing a collapse of temporally deep and counterfactually-rich models by which extended selfhood is actively inferred/ constructed

    REBUS: Extreme relaxation of core beliefs related to both extended and embodied Selfhood

- **Ontological shock**

    SEBUS: Strong experiences causing extreme updating of core (and potentially stabilizing) beliefs (REBUS effects via SEBUS effects)

    REBUS: Difficulty integrating experiences not structured according to internal working models of self and world

- **Personality change**

    SEBUS: Increased ability to perceive and pursue new goals

    REBUS: Relaxation of internal working models, creating a space within which new characteristic adaptations may form

NAVIGATING THE METAPROGRAMMING PHASE

It is recommended that one review intentions and current state of mind, address/resolve concerns, and reaffirm that the journeyer agrees not to leave until after the medicine wears off. Before and throughout each session, one should always consider how to handle difficult experiences (e.g., abreactions versus adverse reactions; discussions about the journeyer's support system and potential issues; when to stay with a difficult experience; breathing techniques; movement), and best and safe practices, especially during psychedelic journeys. The setting should be safe and comfortable. An aesthetically designed room, or a safe outdoors setting in nature will facilitate a much better experience than a sterile-looking office. Moreover, when working with particular circuits, part of our approach encourages creating spaces that are representative in various ways of each circuit (e.g., a Circuit 1 space may resemble the archetypal mother through symbolism such as round objects—representing the breast—or warm, dark spaces—symbolizing the safety of the womb). We offer further instruction on how to perceptually represent such spaces for working with each circuit in our 8-Circuit Ascension Metaprogramming Certification Course.

The journeyer should have a comfortable place to lie down. To prevent injury when a journeyer wishes to stand while under the influence of any psychedelics, always remind them to stand up slowly; stand close to them in case they fall; and walk with them to wherever they wish to go. Rising too quickly can result in lowered blood pressure leading to lightheadedness, dizziness, or fainting. Blankets and temperature options should be available. Plenty of water and snacks should be available, and the journeyer should be reminded to stay hydrated throughout the journey.

At various points, the guide can check in with the journeyer regarding the optional use of music, eyeshades, supportive touch; or if they are largely turned attentionally inward, if they want to talk. (However, if the journeyer is having a largely inward process and does not wish to speak, they should be reminded that speaking is optional and should not be pressured to do so.) Eyeshades can be useful when the journeyer wants to go inwards to block out light, or if they have a hard time keeping their eyes closed. They may also wish to use them while speaking with the guide to block out unwanted external stimuli. However, because the guide is there for safety, support, and note-taking; and to provide a dedicated space and assistance in whatever way the journeyer needs, do not try to impose anything on the journeyer.

HERMIT PHASE (HP)

The importance of taking some alone time immediately after a journey—ideally, for several days after an important phase—is often underestimated; sometimes it is even bypassed altogether. An integration period should be applied to any significant life-event that you wish to maintain long-term—be it quitting smoking, going vegan, or completing a yoga training. If you do not sufficiently allow for this phase, you run the risk of losing some of the benefits or transformations that were experienced during the journey.

First, the journeyer should take some time soon after the journey to reflect upon and journal about the experience. Many details may be forgotten if too much time passes before these memories and insights are recorded. If the journeyer is unable to write or type, perhaps a sitter or trusted friend can assist with transcribing reflections, or a voice recorder could be used. Daily journaling can be an enjoyable activity, and can help expand and deepen your understanding of your experiences. Here are some suggestions for post-journey reflection prompts:

- What were your intention(s) for the journey? If you are familiar with the 8-Circuit Model, were you aware of areas in which you were treadmilling or lacked circuit integration?
- Describe the set and setting at the start of the session. What was your mindset like? Did you feel trust and comfort with your guide(s) and your environment?
- Describe the set and setting later on in the session. Were your guide(s) supportive? Would you have changed anything?
- Did you feel safe and comfortable? Is there anything that would have helped you to feel safer and/or more comfortable?

- How would you describe your journey? What details do you remember (imagery, symbolism, thoughts, feelings, emotions, insights, intuitions, memories, bodily sensations, etc.)?
- If you are familiar with the 8-Circuit Model, which circuit(s) were activated during your journey? Are you surprised by anything that came up during the journey? Do you feel that anything was resolved during the journey?
- Is there anything about your experience that you wish to integrate in your life? What is your plan to integrate your experience? Identify activities, practices, and exercises that will help to reinforce this integration and any desired changes.

Be gentle with yourself for several days after the journey. Ideally, you should allow for long periods of alone time to keep free from worldly distractions, falling back into previous patterns, or being influenced by others who might not be respectful or understanding of the healing or transformational process you are undergoing. Self-care should be practiced for several days. This can be defined in whatever ways best suit you; for example, meditation, walking/hiking, yoga, baths (or relaxing in a float tank if possible), or creative expressions such as drawing, painting, poetry, writing music, singing, dance, spending time in nature, the No-Form Zazen moving meditation, etc. In particular, the Zazen moving meditation can help to express and release somatic memories and trauma locked in various parts of the body. To better understand the nature of anxiety and trauma and how they become stored in the body, the following video—*Stress, Trauma and the Body* by Saj Razvi—may be helpful:

youtube.com/watch?v=q6M1FumqeyM&t=656s

Although not everyone has the luxury to take a week or two off from worldly responsibilities to engage in ongoing self-care practices, we encourage you to maintain this phase for as long as possible, and to remain mindful of this intention even while working, caring for family, or whatever has to be done. Mundane daily activities can be a living meditation when done with mindfulness and love. As eloquently stated by Jack Kornfield (2000),

"After the ecstasy, the laundry." Unless you are a monk secluded from society, healing and spiritual development does not take place in a vacuum. This post-journey phase is what you make of it. If that means returning to stressful responsibilities, relationships, etc., realize that these experiences are all filtered through your reality tunnel. While you might not be able to control all external factors, you do have power over the way that you experience the world around you and there are things you might be able to change or accept if you are able to view the situation from a different perspective. Do your best to stay committed to attending to your internal experience during this phase, setting an intention each morning, journaling each day, and making time for yourself. If you are unable to remain entirely alone for several days, at least try to observe your interactions and relationships with others. Be mindful of patterns (especially unwanted patterns), the re-emergence of undesired thoughts, feelings, or behaviors, and the emergence of new ones that may be healthful and positive to your life. Record reflections on these observations throughout the day, or at least once a day—ideally just before bed—so you can reflect on the entire day. (Reflections and affirmations in the morning and at other times during the day can also be helpful.)

INTEGRATION & REINFORCEMENT PHASE (IRP)

Along with the Hermit Phase, the post-journey Integration & Reinforcement Phase (IRP) is immensely important if you wish to maintain insights and changes in the long term. The purpose of this phase is to assist you with processing any insights attained during or since the journey, help you integrate these insights, implement any desired changes in your life, and to reinforce these transformations. An integration session should be offered as soon as possible after a journey—ideally, within a day or two (especially when working with ketamine as the experiences and insights tend to be forgotten more rapidly than with other psychedelic drugs), but no longer than a week later. At least one integration session is highly recommended, and additional sessions can be beneficial, especially if there is a lot of material to be processed, or if you require additional emotional support. If you are not a trained mental healthcare professional, and feel unequipped to properly support the journeyer through this phase, we strongly advise that you be honest with the journeyer about this so they can find someone who can better help them.

In this session, guides should invite journeyers to share their recollections, and any insights and changes they might have experienced since the journey. Conversely, if the guide(s) took notes during the journey, they should be reviewed with the journeyer. It is most helpful if the guide has already analyzed and mapped out these notes according to the 8-Circuit Model so this deeper understanding and follow-up exercises can be focused most effectively. If the journeyer is also already familiar with the 8-Circuit Model, it would be beneficial if they attempt to map out their experiences and reflections prior to the session as well, and bring these insights to discuss during integration sessions.

What were the journeyer's initial intentions as set in the PP and MP sessions? How, if at all, did the journeyer's experience reflect those intentions? Help the journeyer identify ways to incorporate insights and changes into their lives. (We have included a **SMART** goals worksheet at the end of this chapter to help guide this process. **SMART** is an acronym for outlining a practical approach to implementing changes and goals. It stands for **S**pecific, **M**easurable, **A**chievable, **R**ealistic, and **T**imely.) While helping the journeyer to outline their goals, also help them to identify any challenges that may interfere with realizing their goals, and how they can work through them. Additional exercises can be suggested for continued healing and transformation in particular circuit(s). Any additional IRP sessions can be an extension of the integration and reinforcement work done in the initial session, and if there have been new insights and/or challenges since the previous integration session, additional session(s) afford an opportunity to further help the journeyer update their plan.

If you do not have a professional mental healthcare license and emotional or traumatic clinical material emerges during a session, we can't emphasize enough the importance of staying in your lane and helping the journeyer find the level of professional support that they need. You may offer to speak with their therapist to provide collateral information if a

Release of Information (ROI) form is signed. Our persistent reminder to avoid working with clinical issues if you are not a licensed mental healthcare professional is not just a matter of liability, but a genuine concern for the safety and proper care for the journeyer. With psychedelic drugs being touted as a panacea for just about everything, there is a risk of reckless use/misuse by inexperienced journeyers and/or guides that we feel is important to address. NOSC, vulnerable states, and psychedelic medicines do have great potential to heal. This is an exciting time in which we are seeing widespread decriminalization efforts and research on clinical efficacy; however, using them irresponsibly could have serious adverse effects and impede this progress. We implore you to deeply consider your intentions before embarking on any such journey, and approach these types of experiences with the utmost respect, whether as journeyer or guide.

CHAPEL PERILOUS & SPIRITUAL EMERGENCE/SPIRITUAL EMERGENCY

We discussed Chapel Perilous in Chapter VII, but we feel it necessary to reference it again here in the context of spiritual emergence and spiritual emergency. Spiritual emergence is:

"...the process of personal awakening into a level of perceiving and functioning which is beyond normal ego functioning. At its peak, spiritual emergence is the experience of the ultimate unity of all things, a mystical experience, a merging with the Divine which transcends verbal description. Among the positive effects of this process are increased creativity, feelings of peace and an expanded sense of compassion." (Bragdon, 1988, p. 10)

And spiritual emergencies:

"...can be defined as critical and experientially difficult stages of a profound psychological transformation that involves one's entire being. They take the form of non-ordinary states of consciousness [enhanced states of awareness] and involve intense emotions, visions and other sensory changes, and unusual thoughts, as well as various physical mani-

festations. These episodes often revolve around spiritual themes; they include sequences of psychological death and rebirth, [experiences that transcend spatial/temporal boundaries], feelings of oneness with the universe, encounters with various mythological beings and other similar motifs." (Grof & Grof, 1989)

Although some people may find non-ordinary states of consciousness and/or spiritual awakening to be beautiful, fascinating, and awe-inspiring, others may find such experiences to be confusing, frightening, overwhelming, disorienting, isolating, or provoke other adverse reactions. It is important to be aware of this possibility so these types of challenging experiences can be recognized and properly supported. (We strongly encourage you to review Chapter VII to properly prepare for encountering these types of experiences.)

SUPERVISION & CONSULTING

Even licensed therapists working in the burgeoning field of psychedelic-assisted therapy receive supervision as they learn this skill. Moreover, licensed psychotherapists, in general, continue to consult with other mental healthcare professionals for guidance about difficult cases. Unless a Release of Information is signed, or the professionals work at the same institution, clients are always spoken about anonymously and with unidentifiable information. That said, if you intend to offer ongoing services as a guide, it is highly recommended that you connect with a network of others who are experienced in this field, who can supervise you, or with whom you can exchange consulting services. (Be careful not to consult with anyone who might know the person you are consulting about.)

The following is a list of various psychotherapeutic approaches that may lend themselves toward the integration of circuit-specific material. This list is not exhaustive, nor does it imply that one particular approach only lends itself to a particular circuit. It is instead meant as a broad stroke of considerations in approach or referral (see also the Recommended Reading section of this book for materials on these approaches):

- C-1: Somatic Therapies, Sensorimotor Psychotherapy, Trauma Release Exercises (TRE), EMDR
- C-2: Emotional Regulation Therapy, Desensitization, Primal Scream Therapy
- C-3: Cognitive Behavioral Therapy (CBT)/Talk Therapy
- C-4: Group Work, Support Groups
- C-5: Dialectical Behavior Therapy (DBT), Mindfulness-Based Stress Reduction
- C-6: Metaprogramming, NLP, Motivational Interviewing
- C-7: Internal Family Systems, Jungian Therapy
- C-8: Gestalt Therapy, Process Work, Intersubjectivity Theory

THE SMART GOALS WORKSHEET

S	**Specific** What am I going to do? Why is this important to me?
M	**Measurable** How will I measure my success? How will I know when I have achieved my goal?
A	**Attainable** What will I do to achieve this goal? How will I accomplish this goal?
R	**Relevant** Is this goal worthwhile? How will achieving it help me? Does this goal fit my values?
T	**Time-Bound** When will I accomplish my goal? How long will I give myself?

Table 19: *SMART Goals Worksheet*

BOOK III:
TRANSMIT

Chapter XIII

The Post-Common Era: Individual & Collective Healing & Engineering the Future

"The aim of human life is to know thyself. Think for yourself. Question authority. Think with your friends. Create, create new realities. Philosophy is a team sport. Philosophy is the ultimate, the ultimate aphrodisiac pleasure. Learning how to operate your brain, learning how to operate your mind, learning how to redesign chaos."
— Dr. Timothy Leary

Dr. Timothy Leary and Robert Anton Wilson often referred to the concept of "reality tunnels" (or "reality labyrinths"). That is to say, we are all the product of a combination of our genetic predispositions and environmental influences/sociocultural conditioning, and other types of external programming (e.g., family, religion, school, political ideology, media, cultural traditions, social norms, and a multitude of other indoctrinations, belief systems, and conditionings). Thus, we each see the world through a subjective lens— our "reality tunnel"—that has been largely shaped by forces outside of our conscious awareness and control. One of the authors (Turetzky) is a psychotherapist, and common themes she has encountered among a majority of clients are: overidentification with the collective/lack of individual identity; a need for external validation and/or difficulty with internal validation; motivation and behaviors driven by an external locus of control at the expense of an inner-defined sense of purpose, meaning, and self-fulfillment. A significant number of clients seem to have little-to-no sense of self or personal identity, and are compliant and conforming to their families, work environments, and other social groups, while all too often neglecting their own desires, thoughts, and feelings. That said, take a moment to consider who *you* are, and how do you know that is your true, authentic Self?

We are each born into a culture and social contract that we had no part in creating. We are taught history, customs, and traditions, and most people typically develop into roles that fit into contemporary social norms. Those who question these norms are often labeled deviants, outcasts, black sheep, or are marginalized or stigmatized in some way. The world progresses, but along tracks set in place by our ancestors, by powerful elites (e.g., government organizations, corporations/industries, billionaire investors, religious and other institutions), and indirectly by our families and communities. These influences reinforce and affect individual and collective development and the existing social structure. However, most people go through life without questioning their own inherited belief systems, values, and ideas about, and perceptions of, consensus reality upon which our world is built.

We are not taught to question the *status quo*. We are not encouraged to deeply explore, discover, and create ourselves. We are not taught the power of our imagination and that it is within our power to re-imagine the world in which we live and re-create it. In recent years, the world seems to be transforming at warp speed. Now, more than ever, it seems imperative for each individual to take responsibility for themselves, to recognize our individual and collective power, and to realize how we can intentionally influence the future of human evolution and society.

> *Status quo*
> *Is a multidimensional tapestry*
> *Of what has been*
> *And will never be again.*
> *It is, ipso facto,*
> *No longer existent*
>
> — Buckminster Fuller (1976:109)

We are bombarded by media with seemingly endless fears around public health, climate change, and scarcities of food, energy, and other resources. With these fears, we are given someone else's agendas to combat these crises—plans that seem to make certain people and institutions exponentially richer and more powerful, often at the expense of the rights, liberties, privacy, prosperity, and quality of life of the masses. However, we now have a unique opportunity to intercept the passive progression based on the unconscious forces that drive societal evolution, and instead take advantage of this transitional phase so we can consciously influence and restructure our world more willfully and proactively.

We contend that if each individual takes the initiative to heal themselves, question their Belief Systems ("BS"), and develop themselves to their highest potential, we would have the potential to co-create and re-build a new world based on love, compassion, and collaboration. A world that works for all of us, not just the billionaire elite, technocrats, corporations, politicians, and corrupt individuals and institutions that have been recklessly destroying our ecosystem and human civilization. It is with this intention that we envision the start of what we call the *Post-Common Era* (PCE). The world is not just ready for a new era; we require it if we are to survive.

We believe that the accessibility of conscious metaprogramming on a large-scale may act as a catalyst to bring about this vision. The first two parts of this book provided the tools for the intentional rewiring of the nervous system that allows for the re-imprinting of the circuits. By practicing techniques designed to initiate the alchemical maxim *"solve et coagula"* ("to dissolve and coagulate": something must be broken down before it can be rebuilt into something new), you can heal your past, transform your identity, and re-program self-hindering belief systems, behavioral/emotional/thought patterns, and responses. Further, metaprogramming not only allows for re-imprinting to occur, it also allows for the development of the upper circuits, of which many people remain unaware, underdeveloped, or altogether incredulous. It is precisely this type of self-exploration and development that may facilitate the further evolution of consciousness into increasingly expansive, complex, and creative states. Connections and communication among previously unconnected brain regions and systems of the body (e.g., physical, emotional, neuroendocrine, psychological, neuro-genetic, spiritual) allow for novel experiences.

As discussed in Chapter IX, we propose that the mechanism underlying synesthetic experience and its development may also be the underlying mechanism in the development of upper-circuit, non-ordinary experiences. In the past, initiations into esoteric traditions have often been reserved for an elite, with many traditions veiled in secrecy. This was especially true as Christianity spread across the globe throughout the Common Era (CE), and dissenters were punished with torture and/or death. However, spirituality and magickal practices (along with the use of psychedelics) have become increasingly available and acceptable in modern society. Moreover, we are at a point in history in which it seems imperative that humans must evolve, or we may end up destroying ourselves and our beautiful planet. That said, now more than ever, it is critical that every individual reflect on their belief structures and perform the Self Work to create increasingly higher versions of themselves. In this way, perhaps we can enter into the Post-Common Era, in which societies, both locally and globally, function compassionately and collaboratively rather than ruthlessly and competitively—where individuals and their unique natures and abilities are encouraged and nourished rather than thwarted by conformity and interpersonal judgment. Thus, metaprogramming may be one of the most important tools available to us as it is capable of being used to not only transform and improve your quality of life, but of the world and the future of humanity as a whole. Perhaps the answer is not about trying to change or fix or fight a broken system, but to build a more functional one alongside it so that it eventually becomes the dominant system. Dr. Terence McKenna proclaimed that what today's society needs most is an Archaic Revival—the integration of tribal values and shamanic technologies (Mckenna, 1991). We believe that large-scale change can be possible, and that it starts with each individual.

"I must create a system or be enslaved by another man's"

— William Blake

A New Subspecies of Human: *Homo ascendus*

We often think about evolution in terms of the past, and how we've evolved to our current state. Human civilization, cognitive abilities, and technology have all transformed over many millennia, yet we are still considered the same species. But where are we going next? What might we become? And what if we were able to consciously influence that?

Before discussing this idea further, we'd be remiss not to address the shadow side of this suggestion—namely, ideas like eugenics and transhumanism, neither of which are we in any way advocating for! The goal of eugenicists is to improve the human gene pool through selective breeding, scientifically selecting and/or altering genes, and at its worst, attempting genocide to wipe out what is believed to be "inferior" people—as happened in the Holocaust. Ideals and values are subjective and vulnerable to in-group/out-group racism, classism, ableism, ageism, and other "isms". Who gets to decide what is "superior"?

Transhumanism takes this a step further and aims to merge humans with various types of technology, even artificial intelligence. Despite the remarkable advances in human intelligence, we are nonetheless limited in knowledge, wisdom, and understanding of the deeper and broader workings of the universe, and we are naive to the potential consequences our ambitions may have on the natural order of things and what may actually be in our best interest.

On the other hand, we are promoting individual and collective healing and psychospiritual transformation that is available naturally to each individual who puts in the effort to explore and develop themselves to their highest potential. Unlike eugenics and transhumanism—which raise a broad spectrum of ethical questions around superiority/inferiority and exclusivity—it is our hope and ambition that this work is accessible to all, and that through this intentional and accelerated evolutionary process, humanity can flourish—on personal and societal levels, and as guardians of our beautiful, natural world.

"What we need in order to meet the crisis of the times, is a shared reality...psychedelic healing reveals something vital about cultural healing—that we must fearlessly move in two directions at once: deep into ourselves and out into the cosmos." (Beiner, 2023: xxiv)

Fortunately—as is described in the alchemical maxim, *"As above, so below; as within, so without"*—these two directions are really the same thing.

The 8-Circuit Model, being a meta-model, can be effectively applied by people of any background, and various systems and philosophies can be mapped onto it. It challenges you to bring into question your sense of reality and belief systems, and in realizing the relative and subjective nature of your maps and models of the world, encourages increased tolerance and acceptance of others different from yourself. Through balancing, healing, and transcending the lower circuits, you may become more likely to act from an internally-driven place with little-to-no concern over the external judgment of others while, conversely, respecting the rights of others to act from a similar place. Imagine the dynamic of an emotionally mature, self-aware, and self-responsible society that nurtured you to reach your highest potential, and where people act in virtuous ways for the sake of itself—a concept the Ancient Greeks called *arête*. Individuals would be more likely to act in genuinely altruistic and compassionate ways. We propose that the value would shift from the belief that evolution is based on competition ("survival of the fittest") to that of collaboration, which seems imperative to a more advanced, peaceful, and prosperous civilization.

"When we come together with the intention of having honest, open, compassionate conversations, we can go beyond our own opinions to a much deeper level of shared human connection. And when we really lean in, we can create a collective intelligence between us that is more than the sum of its parts, and that contains within it vast possibilities and creative solutions to our problems." Beiner (2023:131)

In a talk given by mycologist Paul Stamets (2022), he asserts the necessity that humans evolve into a new species, which he calls *Homo ascendus*. Dr. Mona Sobhani (2022) describes this talk:

" 'We are facing an extinction event'—losing biodiversity, polluting the environment, spreading disease, and inciting war—but **psilocybin can help us reinvent the human species.** He made the case for psilocybin, arguing that it reduces violence (in prisons, psilocybin has been associated with reduction in crime), helps us overcome addiction (is associated with lower odds of opium use disorder) ... We should use the mushrooms to elevate our intelligence with the purpose of creating innovations capable of overcoming the impending calamity. **Homo ascendus awaits.**" (para. 6)

Stamets' vision of *Homo ascendus* is aligned with our vision for the Post-Common Era. Perhaps by synchronicity, even the species name he chose—*ascendus*—is aligned with our own work, 8-Circuit *Ascension*. Stamets also refers to using *"mushrooms to elevate our intelligence,"* which is also aligned with Leary's goal—as well as our own—of using the 8-Circuit Model of Consciousness for what he called *"intelligence increase."*

"One way to ensure that these animistic awakenings lead to real systems change is to combine psychedelic insights with biology and policy. As mycologist Paul Stamets has argued, fungi can give us a blueprint for a much deeper pattern in nature—a pattern of interconnected, supportive networks." (Beiner, 2023:217)

Although we agree that psilocybin can most certainly be a tool in facilitating this evolution, they are just one means of getting there along with various psychospiritual practices such as spirituality, yoga, meditation, breathwork, magick, mysticism, and other methods included in this text for attaining higher/altered/non-ordinary states of consciousness. Applying the 8-Circuit Model to the use of these tools, we propose that the effectiveness of these methods can be optimized with respect to understanding which circuit they are affecting, and when and how using a particular tool or method would be most appropriate—what Dr. John Vervaeke has described as an *"ecology of practices"* available to us to see the bigger picture more fully (Vervaeke, 2019b).

In addition to intelligence increase, Leary referred to what he called *hedonic engineering* and Wilson referred to as **HEAD** (Hedonic Engineering And Development; Wilson, 1980). Hedonic engineering is *"The art and science of reimprinting one's own nervous system for more ecstatic or intelligent functioning. Serial reincarnation in one body"* (Wilson, 1980, Glossary p. 1). In the first stage of entering into this upper realm of the intentional and transcendent evolution of our nervous system through Circuit 5, we realize that our existence need not be robotic, mundane, and filled with psychological strife (e.g., anxiety/fear, sadness/depression, anger), but joyful, curiosity-filled, interesting, pleasurable, and fun! This is what hedonic engineering is all about.

> *"Hedonic Engineering—The human nervous system studying and improving itself: intelligence studying and improving intelligence. Why be depressed, dumb, and agitated when you can be happy, smart, and tranquil?" (Wilson 1980:1)*

As proposed earlier, the intentional rewiring of the nervous system can result in the development of new types of experiences and abilities. These include parapsychological experiences and abilities. As more people experience this psychic shift in consciousness through meditation/spirituality, psychedelics, natural ability/evolution, or other means, the 8-Circuit Model offers a framework for a better understanding and navigation of these experiences.

IMAGINING THE POST-COMMON ERA SOCIAL STRUCTURE

> *"Perhaps the most radical revolution we can enact is to embody some part of this love in our day-to-day lives; in how we show up with one another; in how we treat ourselves; in how we care for the sacred land we all share." (Beiner 2023:233)*

If you zoom out and look at the human world as a whole through the lens of the 8-Circuit Model, the dominant zeitgeist and political milieu generally reflect an adolescent/young adult stage that is stuck in the lower mundane circuits, and has not yet realized the potential beyond this. More-over, there are cultural circuit imbalances and traumas playing out on the world stage resulting in wars, violence, famine, greed, and myriad atrocities. In this final section, we invite you to imagine a world beyond this, and what a future "utopian" society might look like to you. What would it be like to live in a world in which you—and everyone else—could just be your true, authentic Self? Imagine that expression came from a place of health and self-responsibility rather than a place of ego defenses, traumatic wounding, and unconscious patterns/conditioning. What would it be like if you—and the majority of the humans around you—dedicated themselves to raising their consciousness from the robotic determinism of habit and identity, to increasing degrees of free will and expansive consciousness?

Imagine finding joy in your life's work and play. Imagine seeing the world through a lens of infinite possibility and love. Imagine recognizing and honoring the Divine in all things and each other. How differently might we feel about ourselves and each other? How differently might we co-exist—both with other humans as well as other species and our natural world, in general?

> *"True revolution is born not from changing what we do, but changing how we see ourselves. Widening the frame of what we understand our-selves to be at the very deepest level of existence is a process not just of chang-ing our own personal or even cultural cognition, but of changing how we relate—how we relate to one another as individuals, as well as how our whole species relates to the wider ecosystem of the planet and the cosmos."*
> *(Beiner 2023:215)*

DEFINING CHARACTERISTICS OF *HOMO ASCENDUS*

Although we can't speak for how Stamets envisions the defining features of *Homo ascendus*, we describe our vision of a new subspecies and the social dynamics of the PCE. The ascended human—who has worked through and activated/balanced each circuit—is independent, secure, and self-stable. They generally feel safe in the world, and are able to appropriately set healthy boundaries and trust. They are emotionally stable and confident in their identity. They do not feel a need to dominate others, nor are they submissive. They are able to create models and maps of their experiences and ideas, and they are able to update them as new information becomes available. They are not dogmatic and rigid in their beliefs and belief systems. They are individuals, yet interpersonally cooperative in their participation in society. They are not worried about how they are perceived, or what others think of them, and conversely, they are respectful and non-judgmental of others. These features alone would make for a healthier and more functional society, yet this description only touches upon the activation and balancing of the lower four mundane, terrestrial circuits.

With activation and balancing of the higher, transcendental/post-terrestrial circuits comes an increase in feelings of empathy, spirituality, aesthetic appreciation, creativity, open-mindedness, curiosity, and connection with nature—similar enhancements often described from psychedelic experiences, especially with psilocybin and LSD. Visions of some of the higher aspects of Classical and Renaissance culture come to mind, such as the value of learning, and creating for the sake of itself. In this state of mind, the root of hedonism is the ability to find intrinsic pleasure in experience and imagination itself, rather than the overindulgent addiction to things that help to distract and remove us from unwanted experiences and memories. It is rooted in pleasure and love, rather than escapism.

The more you enjoy being in your own body and can appreciate the experiences of embodiment, the more you may feel inspired to pay more attention to it, to take better care of this vehicle of earthly existence, and to explore how to use it in more creative ways. You become more open to questioning your perceptions, your interpretations of your perceptions, your assumptions, your conditionings, your limitations, and so on. When looking at the proverbial glass and see it as half empty or half full, may you instead see it as entirely full: half filled with water, half filled with air—a perspective we refer to as positive realism. With this approach, you are open to see the full picture of possibility and potential, both the "good" and the "bad"—then choosing to operate and make decisions based on the probabilities of engineering the most desirable outcomes possible, yet with a surrender and acceptance of outcome, even if it's not the most desired.

You become increasingly free to experience yourself and the world in novel ways, which can further open you up to various types of non-ordinary states of consciousness. These may include: Circuit 7 experiences of astral projection, discarnate entities (e.g., ancestral spirits, astral entities [such as the fae and other elementals], archetypal beings, gods and goddesses), psi phenomena (e.g., telepathy, precognition, mediumship and other psychic abilities, telekinesis, the ability to see auras), magickal abilities, and synchronicity; Circuit 8 experiences of non-duality (e.g., ego dissolution/henosis [feelings of oneness with everything]), near-death experiences, and out-of-body experiences, including lucid dreaming.

DEFINING CHARACTERISTICS OF THE POST-COMMON ERA

"Consciousness interfacing with biology empowers us to evolve from passive victims to responsible co-creators of the world to come."
— Bruce Lipton

Now that we have an idea of what our prototypical ascended human may have the potential to become, let's imagine what a whole society of this type of person might look like, and how that may affect how it functions. We currently live in a world driven by competition, corruption, greed, ignorance, fear, trauma, and so many types of ego-defenses. We envision a world in which each individual takes responsibility for their own lives—even when the world has wronged them—and chooses to heal and grow beyond their past circumstances and evolutionary limitations. Moreover, rather than living robotically in traditions, customs, and other influences of the past, we recognize ourselves as the ancestors of our descendants and creators of the future.

To be clear, we are not against tradition or culture *per se,* and there is much to be celebrated and honored in our personal and collective histories. However, we also recognize our place in the present, and the power to more consciously recognize and choose how much we want to let the past dictate our present and future. We see determinism and free will as a spectrum. The more robotic among us (e.g., the addict or religious zealot) have a lower degree of free will, whereas those more aware of these automatonistic tendencies have more psychospiritual freedom to transcend pre-programmed beliefs and behaviors. Doing so allows for thinking, acting, feeling, and intuiting more mindfully, and based on ever-evolving perceptual and conceptual abilities.

How do *you* imagine this Post-Common Era world might look? When people live and act from a place of security, love, and compassion (rather than scarcity, fear, and competition), there can exist a foundation of genuine altruism and cooperation. The entire structure of society and how its functions can be reconsidered and transformed to be more beneficial, not only for humans, but also for the living world all around us. We can choose to be destroyers or guardians of the natural world.

> *"The way we see the world shapes the way we treat it. If a mountain is a deity, not a pile of ore; if a river is one of the veins of the land, not potential irrigation water; if a forest is a sacred grove, not timber; if other species are biological kin, not resources; or if the planet is our mother, not an opportunity—then we will treat each other with greater respect. Thus is the challenge, to look at the world from a different perspective."*
> — David Suzuki

With this in mind, we encourage you to work toward healing yourself, and exploring and developing your psychospiritual potential. We invite you to question everything you think you know, and to explore and define your own inner and moral compasses. Consider how your current beliefs and belief systems affect the way that you show up in your family, your friendships and relationships, at work, in your community, etc. Consider how playing with your reality tunnel and experimenting with the neurorelativity of your experiences can change how you experience and show up in the world.

What do you observe about the way the world currently works that feels dysfunctional to you? How do you think you contribute to this? Everything we do is a decision, and has an effect on our participation in "reality"—even inaction or avoiding a decision is a decision, which leaves things increasingly up to chance, the less responsibility (i.e., "response-ability"—the ability to respond) we choose to take. So, what do you feel in this world needs healing, and what do you think you can bring to the process of transformation? Imagine from a place where anything is possible. Imagine from a place of love. What do you envision?

The authors of this book are certainly not claiming authority, or that we have all of the answers. Yet we can envision this new era as a participatory co-creation of and by individuals and communities. Let us consider the universal values that ultimately respect the integrity and liberties of each individual. How can you fully individuate and realize your fullest potential if your life is under the control of some "other"—be it another person or an institution? Thus, we place the value for individual freedom and personal sovereignty as the cornerstone of the PCE.

> *"Do what thou Wilt shall be the whole of the Law; Love is the Law, Love under Will."*
>
> — Aleister Crowley

> *"And ye harm none; do what ye will."*
>
> — *Wiccan Rede*

However, we are not advocating for selfishness. We imagine a place comprised of our prototypical ascended humans who act from a place of psychospiritual healthfulness and mutual self/other respect and consideration. Thus, we imagine the PCE can be about exploring and developing new ways of sharing and distributing resources that allow for goods and services to be available to all. As you progress in your psychospiritual development, the desire for ego-driven goals and materialistic objects wanes, while a genuine altruistic value for the well-being of others grows. The ascended human becomes increasingly immune to marketing and advertising by profit-driven agencies who appeal to our weaknesses and unintegrated parts of self for the sake of selling their products. In the PCE, however, goods and services can be exchanged based on its true value, whether it is something of survival necessity, lifestyle enhancement, or sheer hedonic appreciation.

It is beyond the scope of this book and the authors' expertise to attempt to propose a comprehensive plan for a future era. Our intention has been to present a means to healing both the individual and the collective. That is, to encourage individuals and communities to reclaim their personal power, and to re-imagine and transform their own lives and their immediate environments, communities, relationships to self/others and the world around them, and how they show up in the world. We believe that when enough people choose to heal, to evolve, and to consciously show up in the world with greater awareness, love, and vision of the infinite possibilities before them, an evolution into a new way of life becomes inevitable.

"You are a powerful, unlimited and eternal soul who is here to enjoy the experience of creativity and contribute to humanity's evolution."
— Dr. Timothy Leary

"Your head's like mine, like all our heads; big enough to contain every god and devil there ever was. Big enough to hold the weight of oceans and the turning stars. Whole universes fit in there! But what do we choose to keep in this miraculous cabinet? Little broken things, sad trinkets that we play with over and over. The world turns our key and we play the same little tune again and again and we think that tune's all we are."
— Grant Morrison

"Try living forever with the metaprogram, 'Everything works out more perfectly than I plan it.'"
— Robert Anton Wilson

Epilogue

Certification Courses

This book began with the objective of bringing the 8-Circuit Model of Consciousness into the mainstream realms of academia, clinical practice, and psychospiritual development. Dr. Timothy Leary—nicknamed "Theory Leary"—was a highly respected scholar and professor at Harvard with many notable academic works, writings, and theories prior to becoming the infamous counterculture acid guru he is most associated with. With the "psychedelic renaissance" upon us, along with the increasing interest in spirituality and non-ordinary states of consciousness (NOSC), we recognized the value of this model in its utility to account for the inevitable increase in transcendent experiences that often result from the use of psychedelics and other spiritual practices

We wrote this book with the intention of making the model accessible for individuals to explore the topics in enough detail that it may be personally applied; however, it lies beyond our scope to address all of the complexities that can arise, and clinical approaches used when working with others. If you wish to study further for either personal or professional applications, we offer in-depth coursework through 8-Circuit Ascension

8circuitascension.com

and The Metaprogramming Institute

metaprogramminginstitute.com.

The material in each program is similar, but varies slightly in its focus and objective. **8-Circuit Ascension** is the branch of our organization that may be more suitable for psychonauts, occultists, spiritual aspirants, and laypeople seeking personal psychospiritual development or skills that may assist them in working with friends, families, or spiritual communities *outside* of academia, clinical practices, or other more formal mental health/healing/personal development professions.

On the other hand, **The Institute of Applied Metaprogramming (I AM)** takes a more academic and scholarly approach to the dissemination of this information to professionals who wish to utilize this model with an increased level of rigor in their clinical practices, research, or other more formal institutions. We made this distinction to be mindful of our various audiences, and how we can offer this material in a way that may be most beneficial to the varying needs and interests of all.

Two levels of courses/training are offered:

• **Certified Metaprogrammer (CMPr)**

This level of coursework is applicable for those wishing to directly explore and gain a thorough understanding of working with the 8-Circuit Model for personal use, as well as for mental health professionals, coaches, and other guides/healers wishing to integrate its use into their practice.

• **Master Practitioner Metaprogrammer (MP-MPr)**

This deeper level of coursework is applicable for those wishing to gain a more in-depth understanding of working with the 8-Circuit Model, mental health professionals, coaches, and other guides/healers wishing to integrate its use into their clinical practice, as well as receiving certification and additional proprietary resources to teach and offer official trainings of the course material.

In addition to our certification courses, we have several books and projects in the works. If you would like to stay informed about our upcoming projects, please sign up for our mailing list at the above-mentioned websites.

RECOMMENDED READING

8-CIRCUIT MODEL OF CONSCIOUSNESS

Prometheus Rising — Robert Anton Wilson

Info-Psychology — Timothy Leary

The Game of Life — Timothy Leary

Angel Tech: A Modern Shaman's Guide to Reality Selection — Antero Alli

The Eight Circuit Brain: Navigational Strategies for the Energetic Body — Antero Alli

Circuits and Shen: Models of the Evolution of Consciousness and Chinese Medicine — Douglas S. Wingate

Nonlocal Nature: The Eight Circuits of Consciousness — James A. Heffernan

The Shamanic Path to Quantum Consciousness — Laurent Huguelitt

Freud, Jung, and a Platypus Get an MRI — Mike Gathers (Online)

CONSCIOUS SELF-CHANGE/METAPROGRAMMING

Programming and Metaprogramming in the Human Biocomputer: Theory and Experiments — John C. Lilly

Games People Play: The Psychology of Human Relationships — Eric Berne

Psychomagic: The Transformative Power of Shamanic Psychotherapy — Alejandro Jodorowsky

ALTERED STATES OF CONSCIOUSNESS

Altering Consciousness: Multidisciplinary Perspectives [2 Volume Set] —
Etzel Cardeña (Editor), Michael J. Winkelman (Editor)

HYPNOSIS/NLP

*Creative Choice in Hypnosis: The Seminars, Workshops and Lectures of
Milton H. Erickson* — Milton Erikson

The Structure of Magic, Vol. 1: A Book About Language and Therapy —
Richard Bandler & John Grinder

The Structure of Magic II: A Book About Communication and Change —
Richard Bandler & John Grinder

Monsters & Magical Sticks: There's No Such Thing as Hypnosis? — Steven
Heller & Terry Steele

Energized Hypnosis: A Non-Book for Self-Change — Christopher Hyatt &
Calvin Iwema

MAGICK

Magick: Liber ABA, Book 4 — Aleister Crowley

Condensed Chaos — Phil Hine

S.S.O.T.B.M.E Revised: An Essay on Magic — Ramsey Dukes

The Golden Dawn: A Complete Course in Practical Ceremonial Magic —
Israel Regardie

*Low Magick: It's All In Your Head...You Just Have No Idea How Big Your
Head Is* — Lon Milo DuQuette

*Llewellyn's Complete Book of Ceremonial Magick: A Comprehensive Guide
to the Western Mystery Tradition* — Lon Milo DuQuette, David
Shoemaker, et al.

PRE/PERINATAL EXPERIENCES

Realms of the Human Unconscious: Observations from LSD Research —
Stanislav Grof

The Holotropic Mind — Stanislav Grof

POLYVAGAL THEORY

The Polyvagal Theory: Neurophysiological Foundations of Emotions, Attachment, Communication, Self-Regulation — Stephen Porges

Polyvagal Exercises for Safety and Connection — Deb Dana

INTERPERSONAL NEUROBIOLOGY

Pocket Guide to Interpersonal Neurobiology — Daniel Siegel

Interpersonal Neurobiology and Clinical Practice — Daniel Siegel, Allen Shore, Louis Cozollino

The Developing Mind: How Relationships and the Brain Interact to Shape Who We Are — Daniel Siegal

ATTACHMENT THEORY

Adult Attachment Styles — R.C. Fraley & P.R. Saver

Attachment and Trauma — Diane Heller (lectures)

The Attachment Theory Workbook: Powerful Tools to Promote Understanding, Increase Stability & Build Lasting Relationships — Annie Chen

SOMATIC PSYCHOTHERAPY

The Body Keeps the Score — Bessel van der Kolk

Waking the Tiger: Healing Trauma — Peter Levine

Complex PTSD: From Surviving to Thriving: A Guide and Map for Recovering from Childhood Trauma — Pete Walker

SENSORIMOTOR PSYCHOTHERAPY

Trauma and the Body: A Sensorimotor Approach to Psychotherapy — Pat Ogden et al.

Sensorimotor psychotherapy: Interventions for Trauma and Attachment — Pat Ogden

REICHIAN THERAPY

Character Analysis — Wilhelm Reich

The Function of the Orgasm — Wilhelm Reich

Reichian Therapy: The Technique, for Home Use — Jack Willis

NEO-REICHIAN APPROACHES

Undoing Yourself with Energized Meditation & Other Devices
 — Christopher Hyatt

Radical Undoing: The Complete Course for Undoing Yourself
 Volumes 1–6 (video) — Christopher Hyatt

Energized Hypnosis: A 'Non-Book' for Self-Change — Christopher Hyatt &
 Calvin Iwema

Energized Hypnosis: A Program for Self-Development & Power
 Volumes 1–4 (video) — Christopher Hyatt

HAKOMI

The Hakomi Way: Consciousness & Healing — Ron Kurtz

Hakomi Mindfulness-Centered Somatic Psychotherapy: A Comprehensive
 Guide to Theory & Practice — Halko Weiss et al.

TRAUMA RELEASE EXERCISES (TRE)

Trauma Releasing Exercises — David Berceli

BIOENERGETICS

Bioenergetics: The Revolutionary Therapy That Uses the Language of the
 Body to Heal the Problems of the Mind — Alexander Lowen

The Voice of the Body: The Role of the Body in Psychotherapy — Alexander
 Lowen

EMDR

Eye Movement Desensitization and Reprocessing (EMDR) Therapy: Basic
 Principles, Protocols, and Procedures — Francine Shapiro

Emdr As an Integrative Psychotherapy Approach: Experts of Diverse
 Orientations Explore the Paradigm Prism — Francine Shapiro

Cultural Competence and Healing Culturally Based Trauma with EMDR
  Therapy: Innovative Strategies and Protocols
  — Mark Nickerson

EMOTION REGULATION THERAPY

Emotion Regulation in Psychotherapy: A Practitioner's Guide
  — Robert Leahy, Dennis Tirch, et al.

Emotion Regulation in Children and Adolescents: A Practitioner's Guide
  — Michael A. Southam-Gerow

PLAY THERAPY

Creative Play Therapy with Adolescents and Adults: Moving from Helping
  to Healing — Denis A. Thomas, Melanie H. Morris

Creative Arts and Play Therapy for Attachment Problems — Cathy A.
  Malchiodi, David A. Crenshaw

Play Therapy with Traumatized Children — Paris Goodyear-Brown

DESENSITIZATION

Prolonged Exposure Therapy for PTSD: Emotional Processing of Traumatic
  Experiences—Therapist Guide — Edna Foa et al.

Reclaiming Your Life from a Traumatic Experience: A Prolonged Exposure
  Treatment Program—Workbook — Barbara Olasov Rothbaum et al.

OPERANT CONDITIONING

The Essentials of Conditioning and Learning —Michael Domjan

COGNITIVE BEHAVIORAL THERAPY (CBT)

Cognitive Behavior Therapy: Basics and Beyond — Judith S. Beck

The CBT Workbook for Mental Health: Evidence-Based Exercises to
  Transform Negative Thoughts and Manage Your Well-Being — Sarah
  Fader & Simon Rego

GROUP THERAPY

The Theory and Practice of Group Psychotherapy — Irvin D. Yalom & Molyn Leszcz

How to Create and Sustain Groups that Thrive: Therapist's Workbook and Planning Guide — Ann Steiner

Working More Creatively with Groups — Jarlath F. Benson

Trauma-Informed Principles in Group Therapy, Psychodrama, and Organizations Action Methods for Leadership — Scott Giacomucci

DIALECTICAL BEHAVIORAL THERAPY (DBT)

DBT Skills Training Manual — Marsha M. Linehan

Radical Acceptance — Tara Brach

Mindful Compassion — Paul Gilbert

The Mindful Self-Compassion Workbook — Kristin Neff

MOTIVATIONAL INTERVIEWING (MI)

Motivational Interviewing: Helping People Change — William Miller & Stephen Rollnick

Building Motivational Interviewing Skills: A Practitioner Workbook — David Rosengren

The Motivational Interviewing Workbook: Exercises to Decide What You Want and How to Get There — Angela Wood

PSYCHOSYNTHESIS

Psychosynthesis, A Manual of Techniques — Roberto Assagioli

Transpersonal Development: The Dimension Beyond Psychosynthesis — Roberto Assagioli

Psychosynthesis: A Psychology of the Spirit — John Firman & Ann Gila

Unfolding the Self: The Practice of Psychosynthesis — Molly Young Brown

JUNGIAN PSYCHOLOGY

Modern Man in Search of a Soul — C.G. Jung

Jung's Map of the Soul: An Introduction — Murray Stein

Jung and the Alchemical Imagination — Jeffrey Raff

Re-Visioning Psychology — James Hillman

INTERNAL FAMILY SYSTEMS

No Bad Parts: Healing Trauma and Restoring Wholeness — Richard Schwartz

Somatic Internal Family Systems Therapy: Awareness, Breath, Resonance, Movement, and Touch in Practice — Susan McConnell & Richard Schwartz

The Mosaic Mind: Empowering the Tormented Selves of Child Abuse Survivors — Regina A. Goulding & Richard C. Schwartz

ART THERAPY

Existential Art Therapy: The Canvas Mirror — Bruce L. Moon

Imagination in Action: Secrets for Unleashing Creative Expression — Shaun McNiff

Jungian Art Therapy: Images, Dreams, and Analytical Psychology — Nora Swan-Foster

A Jungian Approach to Spontaneous Drawing: A Window on the Soul — Patricia Elwood

INTERSUBJECTIVITY THEORY

The Empathic Ground: Intersubjectivity and Nonduality in the Psychotherapeutic Process — Judith Blackstone

Contexts of Being: The Intersubjective Foundations of Psychological Life — Robert D. Stolorow, George E. Atwood

Working Intersubjectively: Contextualism in Psychoanalytic Practice — Donna M. Orange, George E. Atwood, Robert D. Stolorow

GESTALT THERAPY

Gestalt Therapy: A Guide to Contemporary Practice — Philip Brownell

Human Interaction and Emotional Awareness in Gestalt Therapy: Exploring the Phenomenology of Contacting and Feeling — H. Peter Dreitzel

Reclaiming Reality: A Therapist's Guide to Conquering Depersonalization: A Journey from Sufferer to Healer — Tidal Grace

PROCESS-ORIENTED PSYCHOLOGY (PROCESS WORK)

River's Way: The Process Science of the Dreambody — Arnold Mindell

Quantum Mind: The Edge Between Physics and Psychology — Arnold Mindell

ProcessMind: A User's Guide to Connecting with the Mind of God — Arnold Mindell

DREAMWORK

Dreaming Wide Awake: Lucid Dreaming, Shamanic Healing, and Psychedelics — David Jay Brown

Dreambody: The Body's Role in Healing the Self — Arnold Mindell

Working with the Dreaming Body — Arnold Mindell

TRANSPERSONAL PSYCHOLOGY

Changes of Mind: A Holonomic Theory of the Evolution of Consciousness — Jenny Wade

The Ego and the Dynamic Ground: A Transpersonal Theorey of Human Development — Michael Washburn

Integral Psychology — Ken Wilbur

Shadow, Self, Spirit: Essays in Transpersonal Psychology — Michael Daniels

The Transpersonal: Spirituality in Psychotherapy and Counseling — John Rowan

PSYCHEDELICS

Handbook of Medical Hallucinogens — Charles S. Grob & Jim Grigsby

The Psychedelic Handbook — Rick Strassman

Huberman Lab (podcast) — Andrew Huberman

The Microdosing Guidebook: A Step-by-Step Manual to Improve Your Physical and Mental Health through Psychedelic Medicine
— C.J. Spotswood

KETAMINE

The Ketamine Papers: Science, Therapy, and Transformation
— Phil Wolfson M.D. & Glenn Hartelius Ph.D.

Ketamine: Dreams and Realities — Emanuel Sferios and Karl L.R. Jansen

The Ketamine Handbook: A Beginner's Guide to Ketamine-Assisted Therapy for Depression, Anxiety, Trauma, PTSD, & More
— Janelle Lassalle

MDMA

Ecstasy: The Complete Guide: A Comprehensive Look at the Risks and Benefits of MDMA — Julie Holland

Listening to Ecstasy: The Transformative Power of MDMA
— Charles Wininger

CANNABIS

Cannabis and Spirituality: An Explorer's Guide to an Ancient Plant Spirit Ally — Stephen Gray

Elevated: Cannabis as a Tool for Mind Enhancement
— Sebastián Marincolo

PSILOCYBIN

The Psilocybin Connection: Psychedelics, the Transformation of Consciousness, and Evolution on the Planet — Jahan Khamsehzadeh

The Psilocybin Solution: The Role of Sacred Mushrooms in the Quest for Meaning — Simon G. Powell

Sacred Mushroom of Visions: Teonanácatl: A Sourcebook on the Psilocybin Mushroom — Ralph Metzner

LSD

LSD and the Mind of the Universe: Diamonds from Heaven —
Christopher M. Bache

*LSD My Problem Child: Reflections on Sacred Drugs, Mysticism and
Science* — Albert Hofmann

Realms of the Human Unconscious: Observations from LSD Research
— Stanislav Grof

DMT

*DMT: The Spirit Molecule: A Doctor's Revolutionary Research into the
Biology of Near-Death and Mystical Experiences* — Rick Strassman

*The Illustrated Field Guide to DMT Entities: Machine Elves, Tricksters,
Teachers, and Other Interdimensional Beings* — David Jay Brown &
Sara Phinn Huntley

DMT Dialogues: Encounters with the Spirit Molecule — David Luke &
Rory Spowers

METAPHYSICS/QUANTUM PHILOSOPHY

A New Science of Life: Morphic Resonance — Rupert Sheldrake

*Conversations on the Edge of the Apocalypse: Contemplating the Future with
Noam Chomsky, George Carlin, Deepak Chopra, Rupert Sheldrake, and
Others* — David Jay Brown

Quantum Psychology — Robert Anton Wilson

GLOSSARY

Anchors: Circuits 1–4 provide stabilizing "anchors" for upper circuit dynamics that may become too chaotic or disorienting

Archetypes (Jungian): A concept from psychology that refers to a universal, inherited idea, pattern of thought, or image that is present in the "collective unconscious" of all human beings

Astral Projection: An experience in which a person's consciousness is said to leave their physical body for a period of time and travel in the "astral plane"

Chapel Perilous: An existential state of limbo, usually full of confusion and disorientation for the ego. A psychological state in which an individual's ego may feel confused, displaced, uncentered, or uncertain whether some course of events was affected by a supernatural force, or was a product of their own imagination. This state may be experienced anytime, though one may be more prone to experiencing it during activation of a transpersonal circuit experience.

Circuit 0: Prenatal and perinatal experiences

Circuit 1: Basic needs, survival, physical security/safety, attachment style (Freud's "oral stage"; Bowlby's "attachment theory")

Circuit 2: Emotional needs, role in the social hierarchy/territorial politics, power dynamics in relationships (submissive versus dominant, autonomy versus dependence; Freud's "anal stage")

Circuit 3: Logic, symbolic thought, language/semantics, writing, mathematics, development of representational mental maps, cognitive processes, executive functions (Piaget's "concrete operational stage")

Circuit 4: Social groups, cultural norms, tribal behaviors, religious/other rites of passage into adulthood, sexuality, morality/superego development, social proscriptions/prescriptions (puberty/adolescence; Piaget's "formal operational stage")

Circuit 5: Pleasure for the sake of itself; ecstatic states (e.g., as attained through yoga, cannabis, ecstatic dance, tantric sex)

Circuit 6: Questioning of one's identity and the influences of conditioning on personality and sense of self; metaprogramming (the conscious and intentional deprogramming and reprogramming of the self in accordance with more internally/transpersonally-defined constructs of personality/psychospiritual identity and individual will (e.g., Crowley's concept of the HGA [Holy Guardian Angel]); conscious and intentional self-transformation and self-actualization

Circuit 7: Astral plane/astral projection; experiences with non-physical/discarnate entities, paranormal/psi experiences, telepathy, the archetypes; psychoid space, synchronicity, inter-generational heredity/genetic memory encoded in one's DNA; accessing past lives, the Akashic records

Circuit 8: Non-dual states, ego dissolution, dream states, near-death experiences (NDE), oneness with the universe or "God"

Co-Regulation: A psychological term describing the continuous and dynamic interaction of two or more individuals who influence each other's emotions and behaviors

Collective Unconscious: A term introduced by psychiatrist Carl Jung to represent a form of the unconscious—the part of the mind containing memories and impulses of which the individual is not aware—common to mankind as a whole and originating in the inherited structure of the nervous system

Critical Periods: Refers to a specific timeframe within which a child "must" acquire certain skills, because if this does not happen, the child cannot easily attain these skills outside this time frame

Cybernetics: The science of communication and control theory that is especially concerned with the comparative study of automatic control systems (such as the nervous system and brain and mechanical-electrical communication systems)

Epigenetics: The science of how environmental influences change the expression of genes

Experiential Metaprogramming Phase (EMP): The acute phase in which an individual undergoes or experiences altered/non-ordinary/ transpersonal states of consciousness by a variety of means outlined in this text, or other practices which may induce such a state and allow for a greater ability for conscious metaprogramming, re-imprinting, or self-change.

Hedonic Engineering: Methods of using incoming sensory signals and somatic sensations as a means of experiencing heightened pleasure for pleasure's own sake are discovered and developed

Henosis: A classical Greek word for mystical "oneness", "union", or "unity"

Hermit Phase: A short period of time following the induction or experiencing of a transpersonal or psychedelic state where one is encouraged to reflect on, journal about, and settle back into ordinary consciousness to maximize effective integration or metaprogramming

Holonomic: A system is called "holonomic" if, in a certain sense, one can recover global information from local information. Wherein the whole is contained, to some degree, within the individual part. Derived from "holos" and "nomos", the law of wholeness. Dr. Jenny Wade cites physicist David Bohm's concept of the simultaneous inter-relatedness and interpenetration of all phenomena to her use of the term in her holonomic model of the evolution of consciousness

Holotropic Breathwork: A breathing practice developed by Dr. Stanislav Grof based on his research with psychedelics and non-ordinary states of consciousness to emulate or achieve these states through deeper and accelerated breathing patterns, evocative music, and facilitation of energy release through a specific form of bodywork

Hypoxia: A state in which oxygen is not available in sufficient amounts at the tissue level to maintain adequate homeostasis

Imprinting: The concept that life-events at particular stages of development set patterns that continue to resonate throughout one's lifetime

Imprint Vulnerability: A period or state lending itself to the nervous system or psyche taking on an imprint which it may perpetuate or act as a filter or bias when processing future experiences or states

Inner Healer/Inner Healing Intelligence: The tendency, ability, knowledge, and power within oneself to move towards wholeness and wellbeing

Integration & Reinforcement Phase (IRP): The phase following an altered/non-ordinary/transpersonal state of consciousness and the Hermit Phase in which the individual performs or receives guidance in effectively integrating and reinforcing insights, metaprograms, or re-imprinting

Kundalini: In yogic traditions, the life force that is said to lie coiled at the base of the spine until it is aroused and sent to the head to trigger enlightenment

Lower Circuits (see also: Mundane Circuits): Circuits 1–4 in the original 8-Circuit Model of Consciousness—or Circuits 0–4 in the 8-Circuit Ascension model—relating to personal egoic human development

Lucid Dream: The experience of achieving conscious awareness of dreaming while still asleep

Metamodel: A model of a model or which may encompass multiple models simultaneously

Metaprogramming: Programming or re-programming beliefs, habits, and thought patterns through the action of applied metacognition—thinking about or reflecting on how and why one has certain thought or behavior patterns and the development of the ability to consciously alter these for one's benefit

Morphic Field: Proposed organizing fields of resonance responsible for Morphogenesis of living entities, that memory is inherent in nature, and that most of the so-called laws of nature tend to be more like habits; best known through the works of Dr. Rupert Sheldrake

Morphic Resonance: A proposal by Rupert Sheldrake that morphogenetic fields may be transmitted from past members of the species through a non-local resonance wherein the patterns of activity in self-organizing systems are influenced by similar patterns in the past, giving each species and each kind of self-organizing system a collective memory

Morphogenesis: The origin and development of morphological characteristics

Mundane Circuits (see also: Lower Circuits): Circuits 1–4 in the original 8-Circuit Model of Consciousness (Circuits 0–4 in the 8-Circuit Ascension version) relating to personal egoic human development

Near Death Experience (NDE): An experience wherein one comes very close to dying and has memories of a spiritual experience (such as meeting dead friends and family members, out-of-body experiences, or seeing a white light) during the time when death was near

Non-Duality: A state or experience of unity with all things wherein duality and plurality, and separation of self from all else, becomes experienced as phenomenal illusion. An awareness of matter as materialized energy, and the temporal manifestation of an eternal incorporeal essence constituting the innermost self of all things

Non-Locality: In physics, the concept of action-at-a-distance—that an object's state can be affected by another object without being in physical contact with it; that is, the non-local interaction of objects that are separated in space. In quantum physics, quantum non-locality refers to the phenomenon by which the measurement statistics of a multipartite quantum system do not allow an interpretation with local realism

Parapsychology: A field of study concerned with the investigation of evidence for paranormal psychological phenomena such as telepathy, clairvoyance, and psychokinesis

Pranayama: A Sanskrit word formed by the conjunction of *"prana"* (breath of life/vital energy), and *"ayama"* (expansion/regulation/control). A yogic art of breathing consisting of the deliberate modifications of the breathing process, such as rapid diaphragmatic breathing, slow/deep breathing, alternate nostril breathing, and breath holding/retention, which are usually done in a seated posture

Precognition: Knowledge of a future event, especially when this comes from a direct message to the mind (such as in a dream), rather than by reason

Preprogramming Phase (PP): First phase of metaprogramming. Assessing relevant background information about the journeyer, establishing rapport, assessing the journeyer's prior knowledge about and experience with psychedelics/therapy/coaching and their expectations, addressing safety issues and concerns, providing education, setting intentions, creating a map of the circuits and any imbalances to be worked with, identifying and understanding current reality tunnels and beliefs systems (including mental health history), and setting a plan for metaprogramming. These guidelines can be applied by individuals doing their own circuit work to consider and reflect upon before embarking on their metaprogramming journeys. This approach can be effectively utilized in methods with or without psychedelic drugs

Psi Phenomena: The phenomena (or alleged phenomena) studied in parapsychology, including extrasensory perception, precognition, and psychokinesis

Out-of-Body Experience (OBE): A phenomenon in which a person perceives the world from a location outside their physical body. A form of autoscopy

Re-imprinting: The process of re-coding specific belief structures, memories, or behavioral patterns within your neurology

Shocks: Circuits 5–8 may act as stimulating "shocks" toward development, evolution, or reprogramming within the egoic circuits

Spiritual Emergence: *"The movement of an individual to a more
expanded way of being that involves enhanced emotional and psychosomatic health, greater freedom of personal choices, and a sense of deeper
connection with other people, nature, and the cosmos"* (Grof & Grof,
1989)

Spiritual Emergency: A form of crisis in which one may experience
drastic changes to their meaning system (i.e., their unique purposes,
goals, values, attitudes and beliefs, identity, and focus), often as a result
of a spontaneous spiritual or transpersonal experience. These may
include psychiatric complications related to existential crisis, mystical
experience, near-death experiences, kundalini, paranormal experiences,
ecstatic states, or other spiritual practices

Synchronicity: The simultaneous occurrence of events which appear
significantly related, but have no discernible causal connection.
"Meaningful coincidence"

Telekinesis: The production of motion in objects (as by a spiritualistic
medium) without contact or other physical means

Telepathy: Communication from one mind to another by extrasensory
means

Transpersonal Circuits (see also: Upper Circuits): Circuits 5–8
relating to non-ordinary states of consciousness (NOSC)/transpersonal
experiences

Transpersonal Psychology: A branch of psychology focused on studying the spiritual, transcendental, and non-ordinary aspects of human
experience

Treadmilling: An instance in which a person becomes rigidly stuck or
locked into narrowly operating within a particular circuit

Uncertainty Threshold: How much ambiguity, uncertainty, and change
that a person can tolerate; a low uncertainty threshold can result in

increased adverse reactions to environmental stimuli (e.g., anxiety, depression, compulsive behaviors)

Upper Circuits (see also: Transpersonal Circuits): Circuits 5–8 relating to non-ordinary states of consciousness (NOSC)/transpersonal experiences

Verticality: Interdynamics and relationship between the personal and transpersonal circuits, wherein the personal circuits may act as "anchors" for transpersonal circuits, while transpersonal circuit experiences may act as "shocks" to imprints or belief structures of personal circuit experience. These relationships are: Circuit 1 anchor with Circuit 5 shock; Circuit 2 anchor with Circuit 6 shock; Circuit 3 anchor with Circuit 7 shock; Circuit 4 anchor with Circuit 8 shock

References

Chapter 1

Alli, A. (1987). *Angel Tech: A modern shaman's guide to reality selection.* Falcon Press.

Alli, A. (2014). *The eight-circuit brain: Navigational strategies for the energetic body.* Falcon Press.

Bacon, F. *Novum Organum.* P.F. Collier, 1620.

Bartholomew, R.E. (2001). *Little Green Men, Meowing Nuns and Head-hunting Panics: A Study of Mass Psychogenic Illnesses and Social Delusion.* McFarland.

Beiner, A. (2023). *Bigger picture, the.* Penguin.

Bruer, J.T., & Mcdonnell, J.S. (2011). *Revisiting "The Myth of the First Three Years".* Centre for Parenting Culture Studies.

Conkbayir, M. (2021). *Early childhood and neuroscience theory, research and implications for practice.* Bloomsbury Publishing.

Dishion, T.J., & Tipsord, J.M. (2011). "Peer contagion in child and adolescent social and emotional development." *Annual review of psychology,* 62, 189–214. doi.org/10.1146/annurev.psych.093008.100412

Fields R.D. (2008). "White matter in learning, cognition and psychiatric disorders." *Trends in neurosciences,* 31(7), 361–370. doi.org/10.1016/j.tins.2008.04.001

Galván, A. (2017). *The neuroscience of adolescence.* Cambridge University Press.

Garfinkel, H. (1967). *Studies in Ethnomethodology.* Polity.

Khamsehzadeh, J. (2022). *The Psilocybin Connection: Psychedelics, the transformation of consciousness, and evolution on the planet.* North Atlantic Books.

Leary, T. (1978). *The Game of Life.* Peace Press.

Leary, T. (1994). *Info-psychology: A manual on the use of the human nervous system according to the instructions of the manufacturers and a navigational guide for piloting the evolution of the human individual.* Falcon Press.

Leary, T., Wilson, R.A., & Koopman, G.A. (2006). *Neuropolitique.* Falcon Press.

Lerner, I., Bentin, S., & Shriki, O. (2012). "Spreading activation in an attractor network with latching dynamics: automatic semantic priming revisited." *Cognitive science,* 36(8), 1339–1382. doi.org/10.1111/cogs.12007

Mckenna, T., & Mckenna, D.J. (1975). *Invisible landscape.* HarperCollins (USA).

Perry, B.D. (2009). *The Neuroarcheology of Childhood Maltreatment: The Neurodevelopmental Costs of Adverse Childhood Events.*

Peters, U. "What Is the Function of Confirmation Bias?" *Erkenn 87,* 1351–1376 (2022). doi.org/10.1007/s10670-020-00252-1

Piaget, J. (1964). *The early growth of logic in the child.* London: Routledge and Kegan Paul Ltd.

Russell, P. (1995). *The Global Brain Awakens: our next evolutionary step.* Brain.

Scheffer, M., Borsboom, D., Nieuwenhuis, S., & Westley, F. (2022). "Belief traps: Tackling the inertia of harmful beliefs." *Proceedings of the National Academy of Sciences of the United States of America,* 119(32), e2203149119. doi.org/10.1073/pnas.2203149119

Sheldrake, R. (1981). *A new science of life: The hypothesis of formative causation.* Icon Books.

Siegler, R.S. (2005). *Children's thinking* (4th ed). Prentice-Hall.

Wilson, R.A. (1983). *Prometheus Rising.* Falcon Press.

Wilson, R.A. (1986). *The new inquisition: Irrational rationalism and the citadel of science.* Falcon Press.

Wilson, R.A., & Higgs, J. (2020). *The Starseed Signals: Link Between Worlds: A Raw Perspective on Timothy Leary, Ph.D.* Hilaritas Press

CHAPTER II (C-O)

Ackerman S. (1992). *Discovering the Brain.* Washington (DC): National Academies Press (US); 6, The Development and Shaping of the Brain. *ncbi.nlm.nih.gov/books/NBK234146/*

Conkbayir, M. (2021). *Early childhood and neuroscience theory, research and implications for practice.* Bloomsbury Publishing

Doi, M., Usui, N., & Shimada, S. (2022). "Prenatal Environment and Neurodevelopmental Disorders". *Frontiers in endocrinology,* 13, 860110. doi.org/10.3389/fendo.2022.860110

Fitzgerald, E., Hor, K., & Drake, A.J. (2020). "Maternal influences on fetal brain development: The role of nutrition, infection and stress, and the potential for intergenerational consequences". *Early human development,* 150, 105190. doi.org/10.1016/j.earlhumdev.2020.105190

Fox, N., Shonkoff, J. (2011). "How persistent fear and anxiety can affect young children's learning, behaviour and health". *Early Childhood Matters.* Bernard van Leer Foundation. pp. 8–14

Gerhardt, S. (2015). *Why love matters: How affection shapes a baby's brain.* Routledge.

Grof, S. (1975). *Realms of the Unconscious.* Viking, Reprinted by Condor Books, 1995.

Grof, S. (1985). *Beyond the brain.* State Univ. of New York Press.

Leary, T. (1994). *Info-psychology: A manual on the use of the human nervous system according to the instructions of the manufacturers and a navigational guide for piloting the evolution of the human individual.* Falcon Press.

McGowan P.O., Kato T. (2008). "Epigenetics in mood disorders". *Environmental Health and Preventive Medicine.* 13: 16–24. doi:10.1007/s12199-007-0002-0

McGowan, P.O., Sasaki, A., D'Alessio, A.C., Dymov, S., Labonté, B., Szyf, M., Turecki, G., & Meaney M.J. (2001). "Maternal care, gene expression, and the transmission of individual differences in stress reactivity across generations." *Annual review of neuroscience,* 24, 1161–1192. doi.org/10.1146/annurev.neuro.24.1.1161

Meaney, M.J. (2009). "Epigenetic regulation of the glucocorticoid receptor in human brain associates with childhood abuse". *Nature neuroscience,* 12(3), 342–348. doi.org/10.1038/nn.2270

Pahnke, W. (1963). *Drugs and Mysticism: an analysis of the relationship between psychedelic drugs and the mystical consciousness.* [Doctoral dissertation, Harvard University]

Prado, E.L., & Dewey, K.G. (2014). "Nutrition and brain development in early life". *Nutrition reviews,* 72(4), 267–284. doi.org/10.1111/nure.12102

Wade, J. (1996). *Changes of mind: A holonomic theory of the evolution of consciousness.* State University of New York Press.

Weaver, I.C., Cervoni, N., Champagne, F.A., D'Alessio, A.C., Sharma, S., Seckl, J.R., Dymov, S., Szyf, M., & Meaney, M.J. (2004). "Epigenetic programming by maternal behavior". *Nature neuroscience,* 7(8), 847–854. doi.org/10.1038/nn1276

Chapter III (C-1)

Alli, A. (2014). *The eight-circuit brain: Navigational strategies for the energetic body.* Falcon Press.

Bartlett, J.& Steber, K. (2019). "How to Implement Trauma-informed Care to Build Resilience to Childhood Trauma". *Child Trends.* 10.13140/RG.2.2.11496.01284.

Berceli, D. (2005). *Trauma releasing exercises (TRE): A revolutionary new method for stress/trauma recovery.* BookSurge.

Berman, R.M., Cappiello, A., Anand, A., Oren, D.A., Heninger, G.R., Charney, D.S., & Krystal, J.H. (2000). "Antidepressant effects of ketamine in depressed patients". *Biological psychiatry*, 47(4), 351–354. doi.org/10.1016/s0006-3223(99)00230-9

Bowlby, J., Fry, M., & Salter, A.M.D. (1953). *Childcare & the growth of Love.* Penguin.

Brennan, K.A., & Shaver, P.R. (1995). "Dimensions of adult attachment, affect regulation, and romantic relationship functioning." *Personality and Social Psychology Bulletin*, 21(3), 267–283. doi.org/10.1177/0146167295213008

Brown, D.W., Anda, R.F., Tiemeier, H., Felitti, V.J., Edwards, V.J., Croft, J.B., & Giles, W.H. (2009). "Adverse childhood experiences and the risk of premature mortality." *American journal of preventive medicine*, 37(5), 389–396. doi.org/10.1016/j.amepre.2009.06.021

Carlson, J.S., Yohannan, J., Darr, C.L., Turley, M.R., Larez, N.A., & Perfect, M.M. (2020). "Prevalence of adverse childhood experiences in school-aged youth: A systematic review (1990–2015)". *International Journal of School & Educational Psychology*, 8 (Suppl 1), 2–23. doi.org/10.1080/21683603.2018.1548397

Chugani, H.T., Behen, M.E., Muzik, O., Juhász, C., Nagy, F., & Chugani, D.C. (2001). "Local brain functional activity following early deprivation: a study of postinstitutionalized Romanian orphans". *NeuroImage*, 14(6), 1290–1301. doi.org/10.1006/nimg.2001.0917

Churches, R., Dommett, E., & Devonshire, I. (2017). *Neuroscience for teachers: Applying research evidence from brain science.* Crown House Publishing Limited.

Conger, J.P. (1998). *Jung & Reich: The body as shadow.* North Atlantic Books.

Conkbayir, M. (2021). *Early childhood and neuroscience theory, research and implications for practice.* Bloomsbury Publishing.

Dowling, J.E. (2004). *The Great Brain Debate: Is it nature or nurture?* Joseph Henry Press.

Epstein H.T. (2001). "An outline of the role of brain in human cognitive development." *Brain and cognition,* 45(1), 44–51. doi.org/10.1006/brcg.2000.1253

Felitti, V.J., Anda, R.F., Nordenberg, D., Williamson, D.F., Spitz, A.M., Edwards, V., Koss, M.P., & Marks, J.S. (1998). "Relationship of childhood abuse and household dysfunction to many of the leading causes of death in adults. The Adverse Childhood Experiences (ACE) Study". *American journal of preventive medicine,* 14(4), 245–258. doi.org/10.1016/s0749-3797(98)00017-8

Felitti V.J. (2002). "The Relation Between Adverse Childhood Experiences and Adult Health: Turning Gold into Lead". *The Permanente journal,* 6(1), 44–47. doi:10.7812/TPP/02.994

Fraley, R.C., & Shaver, P.R. (2000). "Adult romantic attachment: Theoretical developments, emerging controversies, and unanswered questions". *Review of General Psychology,* 4(2), 132–154. doi.org/10.1037/1089-2680.4.2.132

Galván, A. (2017). *The neuroscience of adolescence.* Cambridge University Press.

Gálvez V, Li A, Huggins C, et al. "Repeated intranasal ketamine for treatment-resistant depression—the way to go? Results from a pilot randomised controlled trial". *Journal of Psychopharmacology.* 2018;32(4):397407. doi:10.1177/0269881118760660

Gathers, M. (2020). *Freud, Jung, and a platypus get an MRI.* Online. rawilsonfans.org/wp-content/uploads/2020/07/8C-Mike-Gathers.pdf

Gray, P. (2011). "The decline of play and the rise of psychopathology in children and adolescents". *American Journal of Play,* 3(4), 443–463.

Grob, C.S., & Grigsby, J. (2022). *Handbook of Medical hallucinogens.* The Guilford Press.

Hess, E.H. (1958). "Imprinting in animals. *Scientific American,* 198, 81–90.

Hess, E.H. (1973). *Imprinting: Early experience and the developmental psychobiology of attachment.* Van Nostrand Reinhold Company.

Holcomb, H.H., Lahti, A.C., Medoff, D.R., Weiler, M., & Tamminga, C.A. (2001). "Sequential regional cerebral blood flow brain scans using PET with H2(15)O demonstrate ketamine actions in CNS dynamically". *Neuropsychopharmacology: official publication of the American College of Neuropsychopharmacology,* 25(2), 165–172. doi.org/10.1016/S0893-133X(01)00229-9

Hughes, D.A., & Baylin, J.F. (2012). *Brain-based parenting: The neuroscience of caregiving for Healthy Attachment.* W.W. Norton.

Kinlein, S.A., Wilson, C.D., & Karatsoreos, I.N. (2015). "Dysregulated hypothalamic-pituitary-adrenal axis function contributes to altered endocrine and neurobehavioral responses to acute stress". *Frontiers in psychiatry,* 6, 31. doi.org/10.3389/fpsyt.2015.00031

Koita, K., Long, D., Hessler, D., Benson, M., Daley, K., Bucci, M., Thakur, N., & Burke Harris, N. (2018). "Development and implementation of a pediatric adverse childhood experiences (ACEs) and other determinants of health questionnaire in the pediatric medical home: A pilot study". *PloS one,* 13(12), e0208088. doi.org/10.1371/journal.pone.0208088

Kolp, E.; Friedman, H.L.; Krupitsky, E.; Jansen, K.; Sylvester, M; Young, M.S.; and Kolp, A., "Ketamine Psychedelic Psychotherapy: Focus on its Pharmacology, Phenomenology, and Clinical Applications" (2016). *Mental Health Law & Policy Faculty Publications.* 885. digitalcommons.usf.edu/mhlp_facpub/885

Krzywkowski, P., Penna, B., & Gross, C.T. (2020). "Dynamic encoding of social threat and spatial context in the hypothalamus". *eLife,* 9, e57148. doi.org/10.7554/eLife.57148

Kuhl P.K. (2010). Brain mechanisms in early language acquisition. *Neuron,* 67(5), 713–727. doi.org/10.1016/j.neuron.2010.08.038

Lampl, M., & Emde, R.N. (1983). "Episodic growth in infancy: A preliminary report on length, head circumference, and behavior". *New Directions for Child Development,* 21, 21–36. doi.org/10.1002/cd.23219832104

Leary, T. (1957). *Interpersonal diagnosis of personality: A functional theory and methodology for personality evaluation.* Resource Publications.

Leary, T. (1994). *Info-psychology: A manual on the use of the human nervous system according to the instructions of the manufacturers and a navigational guide for piloting the evolution of the human individual.* Falcon Press.

LeDoux, J. (2016). *Anxious: Using the brain to understand and treat fear and anxiety.* Penguin Books.

Martial, C., Cassol, H., Charland-Verville, V., Pallavicini, C., Sanz, C., Zamberlan, F., Vivot, R.M., Erowid, F., Erowid, E., Laureys, S., Greyson, B., & Tagliazucchi, E. (2019). "Neurochemical models of near-death experiences: A large-scale study based on the semantic similarity of written reports". *Consciousness and cognition, 69,* 52–69. doi.org/10.1016/j.concog.2019.01.011

Ogden, P., Pain, C., & Minton, K. (2014). *Trauma and the body: A sensorimotor approach to psychotherapy.* Nota.

Ogden, P., Fisher, J., Minton, K., & Pain, C. (2015). *Sensorimotor psychotherapy: interventions for trauma and attachment.* W.W. Norton & Company.

Porges, S.W., Porges, S.W., & Porges, S.W. (2011). *The polyvagal theory: Neurophysiological foundations of emotions, attachment, communication, and self-regulation.* First Edition; the pocket guide to the polyvagal theory: The transformative power of feeling safe. first edition. W.W. Norton & Company.

Poulin-Dubois, D., Blaye, A., Coutya, J., & Bialystok, E. (2011). "The effects of bilingualism on toddlers' executive functioning". *Journal of experimental child psychology, 108*(3), 567–579. doi.org/10.1016/j.jecp.2010.10.009

Rogers, K. (2011). *The brain and the nervous system.* Britannica Educational Pub. in association with Rosen Educational Services.

Siegel, D.J. (2012). *The developing mind: How relationships and the brain interact to shape who we are.* The Guilford Press.

Shanker, S., Hopkins, S. and Davidson, S. (2015). *Self-Regulation: A Discussion Paper for Goodstart Early Learning in Australia.* Canada: The Mehrit Centre Ltd.

Shanker, S., & Barker, T. (2018). *Self-reg: How to help your child (and you) break the stress cycle and successfully engage with life.* Penguin Books.

Shanker, S. (2020). *Reframed: Self-reg for a just society.* University of Toronto Press.

Tarullo, A.R., & Gunnar, M.R. (2006). "Child maltreatment and the developing HPA axis". *Hormones and behavior,* 50(4), 632–639. doi.org/10.1016/j.yhbeh.2006.06.010

Thompson, R.A., & Goodvin, R. (2005). "The Individual Child: Temperament, Emotion, Self, and Personality". In M.H. Bornstein & M.E. Lamb (Eds.), *Developmental science: An advanced textbook* (pp. 391–428). Lawrence Erlbaum Associates Publishers.

Vollenweider, F., Kometer, M. "The neurobiology of psychedelic drugs: implications for the treatment of mood disorders". *Nat Rev Neurosci* 11, 642–651 (2010). doi.org/10.1038/nrn2884

Vygotsky, L.S., & Cole, M. (1978). *Mind in society: The development of Higher Psychological Processes.* Harvard Univ. Press.

Wade, J. (1996). *Changes of mind: A holonomic theory of the evolution of consciousness.* State University of New York Press.

Warneken, F., & Tomasello, M. (2006). "Altruistic helping in human infants and young chimpanzees". *Science* (New York, N.Y.), 311(5765), 1301–1303. doi.org/10.1126/science.1121448

Whitebread, D., Larkin, S., Robson, S., O'Sullivan, L., Zachariou, A. (2016). "Self-regulation". *Early Education Journal.* 80:1–20

Wilber, K. (1994). *Integral psychology: Consciousness, spirit, psychology, therapy.* Shambhala.

Wilson, R.A. (1983). *Prometheus Rising.* Falcon Press.

Wilson, R.A., & Higgs, J. (2020). *The Starseed Signals: Link Between Worlds: A Raw Perspective on Timothy Leary, Ph.D.* Hilaritas Press.

Wolfson, P. (2016). *Ketamine papers: Science, therapy, and transformation.* Multidisciplinary Assn Fo.

Zanos P., Gould T.D. (2018). "Mechanisms of ketamine action as an antidepressant". *Mol Psychiatry.* 2018 Apr;23(4):801–811. doi:10.1038/mp.2017.255. Epub 2018 Mar 13.

Chapter IV (C-2)

Abdissa, D. (2020). "Review Article on adult neurogenesis in humans". *Translational Research in Anatomy.* 20. 100074. 10.1016/j.tria.2020.100074.

Alli, A. (2014). *The eight-circuit brain: Navigational strategies for the energetic body.* Falcon Press.

Babakr, Z.H., Mohamedamin, P., & Kakamad, K.K. (2019). "Piaget's cognitive developmental theory: Critical review." *Education Quarterly Reviews.*

Bernstein, D.A., Clarke-stewart, A., & Roy, E.J. (2008). *Psychology.* Houghton Mifflin.

Choi, K.W., Na, E.J., Hong, J.P., Cho, M.J., Fava, M., Mischoulon, D., Cho, H., & Jeon, H.J. (2018). "Alcohol-induced disinhibition is associated with impulsivity, depression, and suicide attempt: A nationwide community sample of Korean adults." *Journal of affective disorders,* 227, 323–329. doi.org/10.1016/j.jad.2017.11.001

Conkbayir, M. (2021). *Early childhood and neuroscience theory, research and implications for practice.* Bloomsbury Publishing.

Cooper, M.L. (2006). "Does Drinking Promote Risky Sexual Behavior?: A Complex Answer to a Simple Question." *Current Directions in Psychological Science,* 15(1), 19–23. doi.org/10.1111/j.0963-7214.2006.00385.x

Dick, D.M., Smith, G., Olausson, P., Mitchell, S.H., Leeman, R.F., O'Malley, S.S., & Sher, K. (2010). "Understanding the construct of impulsivity and its relationship to alcohol use disorders." *Addiction biology,* 15(2), 217–226. doi.org/10.1111/j.1369-1600.2009.00190.x

Eldar, E. Cohen, J.D., Niv, Y. "The effects of neural gain on attention and learning." *Nat. Neurosci.* 16, 1146–1153 (2013).

Epstein H.T. (2001). An outline of the role of brain in human cognitive development. *Brain and cognition,* 45(1), 44–51. doi.org/10.1006/brcg.2000.1253

Galván, A. (2017). *The neuroscience of adolescence.* Cambridge University Press.

Gathers, M. (2020). *Freud, Jung, and a platypus get an MRI.* Online. rawilsonfans.org/wp-content/uploads/2020/07/8C-Mike-Gathers.pdf

Graham, K., Leonard, K.E., Room, R., Wild, T.C., Pihl, R.O., Bois, C., & Single, E. (1998). "Current directions in research on understanding and preventing intoxicated aggression". *Addiction* (Abingdon, England), 93(5), 659–676. doi.org/10.1046/j.1360-0443.1998.9356593.x

Holley C. Allen, Mark T. Fillmore, (2023). "Cognitive preoccupation with drinking and behavioral effects of alcohol as predictors of current consumption patterns". *Drug and Alcohol Dependence.* Vol 248. doi.org/10.1016/j.drugalcdep.2023.109899.

Kegan, R. (1982). *The evolving self: Problem and process in human development.* Harvard University Press.

Leary, T. (1957). *Interpersonal diagnosis of personality: A functional theory and methodology for personality evaluation.* Resource Publications.

Menkes, D.B., & Herxheimer, A. (2014). "Interaction between antidepressants and alcohol: signal amplification by multiple case reports". *The International journal of risk & safety in medicine,* 26(3), 163–170. doi.org/10.3233/JRS-140632

Mieda, T., Taku, K., Oshio, A. "Dichotomous thinking and cognitive ability". *Pers. Individ. Dif.* 169, 110008 (2021).

Oshio, A., Mieda, T., Taku, K. "Younger people, and stronger effects of all-or-nothing thoughts on aggression: Moderating effects of age on the relationships between dichotomous thinking and aggression". *Cogent Psychol.* 3, 1244874 (2016).

Piaget, J. (1970). *Science of education and the psychology of the child.* Trans. D. Coltman.

Rose, A.K., & Duka, T. (2007). "The influence of alcohol on basic motoric and cognitive disinhibition". *Alcohol and alcoholism* (Oxford, Oxfordshire), 42(6), 544–551. doi.org/10.1093/alcalc/agm073

Rzepecki-Smith C.I., Meda S.A., Calhoun V.D., et al. (2010). "Disruptions in functional network connectivity during alcohol intoxicated driving". *Alcoholism: Clinical and Experimental Research.* 34(3):479–487. doi:10.1111/j.1530-0277.2009.01112.x.

Santrock, J.W. (2011). *Child Development.* McGraw-Hill International.

Shaffer, D.R., & Kipp, K. (2010). *Developmental Psychology: Childhood and Adolescence.* Wadsworth

Tobore, O.T. (2020). "On alcohol disinhibition and inhibition: The intricate relationship between oxidative stress and behavior". *Aggression and Violent Behavior.* 51. 101378. 10.1016/j.avb.2020.101378.

Vygotsky, L. (1962). *Thought and language.* (E. Hanfmann & G. Vakar, Eds.). MIT Press. doi.org/10.1037/11193-000

Wade, J. (1996). *Changes of mind: A holonomic theory of the evolution of consciousness.* State University of New York Press.

Weafer, J., & Fillmore, M.T. (2012). "Comparison of alcohol impairment of behavioral and attentional inhibition". *Drug and alcohol dependence,* 126(1-2), 176–182. doi.org/10.1016/j.drugalcdep.2012.05.010

Weafer, J. & Fillmore, M. (2016). "Low-Dose Alcohol Effects on Measures of Inhibitory Control, Delay Discounting, and Risk-Taking". *Current Addiction Reports.* 3. 10.1007/s40429-016-0086-y.

Wilson, R.A. (1983). *Prometheus Rising.* Falcon Press.

Wilson, R.A., & Higgs, J. (2020). *The Starseed Signals: Link Between Worlds: A Raw Perspective on Timothy Leary, Ph.D.* Hilaritas Press.

Zheng, H., Kong, L., Chen, L., Zhang, H., Zheng, W. (2015). "Acute effects of alcohol on the human brain: a resting-state FMRI study". *Biomed Res Int.* 2015:947529. doi:10.1155/2015/947529.

Chapter V (C-3)

Alli, A. (1987). *Angel Tech: A modern shaman's guide to reality selection.* Falcon Press.

Alderson-Day B, Fernyhough C. "Inner Speech: Development, Cognitive Functions, Phenomenology, and Neurobiology". *Psychol Bull.* 2015 Sep;141(5):931-65. doi:10.1037/bul0000021.

Cho, H., Godwin, C., Geisler, M., Morsella, E. (2014). "Internally Generated Conscious Contents: Interactions between Sustained Mental Imagery and Involuntary Subvocalizations". *Frontiers in psychology.* 5. 1445. 10.3389/fpsyg.2014.01445.

Devlin, M.J., Walsh, B.T., Katz, J.L., Roose, S.P., Linkie, D.M., Wright, L., Vande Wiele, R., & Glassman, A.H. (1989). "Hypothalamic-pituitary-gonadal function in anorexia nervosa and bulimia". *Psychiatry research,* 28(1), 11–24. doi.org/10.1016/0165-1781(89)90193-5

Dorn, L.D., Dahl, R.E., Woodward, H.R., & Biro, F. (2006). "Defining the boundaries of early adolescence: A user's guide to assessing pubertal status and pubertal timing in research with adolescents". *Applied Developmental Science,* 10(1), 30–56. doi.org/10.1207/s1532480xads1001_3

Ellis B.J. (2004). "Timing of pubertal maturation in girls: an integrated life history approach". *Psychological bulletin,* 130(6), 920–958. https://doi.org/10.1037/0033-2909.130.6.920

Epstein H.T. (2001). "An outline of the role of brain in human cognitive development". *Brain and cognition,* 45(1), 44–51. doi.org/10.1006/brcg.2000.1253

Fiani, B., Zhu, L., Musch, B.L., Briceno, S., Andel, R., Sadeq, N., & Ansari, A.Z. (2021). "The Neurophysiology of Caffeine as a Central Nervous System Stimulant and the Resultant Effects on Cognitive Function". *Cureus,* 13(5), e15032. doi.org/10.7759/cureus.15032

Galván, A. (2017). *The neuroscience of adolescence.* Cambridge University Press.

Giedd, J.N., Raznahan, A., Alexander-Bloch, A., Schmitt, E., Gogtay, N., & Rapoport, J.L. (2015). "Child psychiatry branch of the National Institute of Mental Health longitudinal structural magnetic resonance imaging study of human brain development". *Neuropsychopharmacology: official publication of the American College of Neuropsychopharmacology*, 40(1), 43–49. doi.org/10.1038/npp.2014.236

Graber J.A. (2013). Pubertal timing and the development of psychopathology in adolescence and beyond. *Hormones and behavior*, 64(2), 262–269. doi.org/10.1016/j.yhbeh.2013.04.003

Korzybski, A. (1958). *Science and sanity: An introduction to non-Aristotelian Systems and general semantics*. Institute of General Semantics in Komm.

Leary, T. (1977). *Info-psychology: A manual on the use of the human nervous system according to the instructions of the manufacturers and a navigational guide for piloting the evolution of the human individual*. Falcon Press.

Mendle, J., Leve, L.D., Van Ryzin, M., Natsuaki, M.N., & Ge, X. (2011). "Associations Between Early Life Stress, Child Maltreatment, and Pubertal Development Among Girls in Foster Care". *Journal of research on adolescence: the official journal of the Society for Research on Adolescence*, 21(4), 871–880. doi.org/10.1111/j.1532-7795.2011.00746.x

Monteleone, P., Luisi, M., Colurcio, B., Casarosa, E., Monteleone, P., Ioime, R., Genazzani, A.R., & Maj, M. (2001). "Plasma levels of neuroactive steroids are increased in untreated women with anorexia nervosa or bulimia nervosa". *Psychosomatic medicine*, 63(1), 62–68. https://doi.org/10.1097/00006842-200101000-00008

Newmeyer, A.J., Grether, S., Grasha, C., White, J., Akers, R., Aylward, C., Ishikawa, K., & Degrauw, T. (2007). "Fine motor function and oral-motor imitation skills in preschool-age children with speech-sound disorders". *Clinical pediatrics*, 46(7), 604–611. doi.org/10.1177/0009922807299545

Nguyen, T.V., McCracken, J., Ducharme, S., Botteron, K.N., Mahabir,
M., Johnson, W., Israel, M., Evans, A.C., Karama, S., & Brain
Development Cooperative Group (2013). "Testosterone-related
cortical maturation across childhood and adolescence". *Cerebral cortex*
(New York, N.Y.: 1991), 23(6), 1424–1432.
doi.org/10.1093/cercor/bhs125

Piaget, J. (1970). *Science of education and the psychology of the child.* Trans.
D. Coltman.

Redle, E., Vannest, J., Maloney, T., Tsevat, R.K., Eikenberry, S., Lewis, B.,
Shriberg, L.D., Tkach, J., & Holland, S.K. (2015). "Functional MRI
evidence for fine motor praxis dysfunction in children with persistent
speech disorders". *Brain research,* 1597, 47–56.
doi.org/10.1016/j.brainres.2014.11.047

Reese, H.W. (2000). "Thinking as the behaviorist views it". *Behavioral
Development Bulletin,* 9(1), 10–12. doi.org/10.1037/h0100531

Sisk, C.L., & Foster, D.L. (2004). "The neural basis of puberty and
adolescence". *Nature neuroscience,* 7(10), 1040–1047.
doi.org/10.1038/nn1326

Wilson, R.A. (1983). *Prometheus rising.* Falcon Press.

Wilson, R.A., & Higgs, J. (2020). *The Starseed Signals: Link Between
Worlds: A Raw Perspective on Timothy Leary, Ph.D.* Hilaritas Press.

CHAPTER VI (C-4)

Adamson, S., Metzner, R. (1988). "The nature of the MDMA experience
and its role in healing, psychotherapy, and spiritual practice". *The
Journal of Consciousness and Change.* 10(4), 59–72

Alli, A. (1987). *Angel Tech: A modern shaman's guide to reality selection.*
Falcon Press.

Amodio, D., Frith, C. (2006). "Meeting of minds: the medial frontal
cortex and social cognition". *Nat Rev Neurosci* 7, 268–277.
doi.org/10.1038/nrn1884

Bruner, J.S. (1972). "Nature and uses of immaturity". *American Psychologist, 27*(8), 687–708. doi.org/10.1037/h0033144

Burklund, L.J., Eisenberger, N.I., & Lieberman, M.D. (2007). "The face of rejection: rejection sensitivity moderates dorsal anterior cingulate activity to disapproving facial expressions". *Social neuroscience, 2*(3–4), 238–253. doi.org/10.1080/17470910701391711

Burnett, S., Sebastian, C., Cohen Kadosh, K., & Blakemore, S.J. (2011). "The social brain in adolescence: evidence from functional magnetic resonance imaging and behavioural studies". *Neuroscience and biobehavioral reviews, 35*(8), 1654–1664. doi.org/10.1016/j.neubiorev.2010.10.011

Carhart-Harris, R.L., Murphy, K., Leech, R., Erritzoe, D., Wall, M.B., Ferguson, B., et al. (2015). "The Effects of Acutely Administered 3,4-Methylenedioxymethamphetamine on Spontaneous Brain Function in Healthy Volunteers Measured with Arterial Spin Labeling and Blood Oxygen Level-Dependent Resting State Functional Connectivity". *Biological psychiatry, 78*(8), 554–562. doi.org/10.1016/j.biopsych.2013.12.015

Carlson, S.M., Koenig, M.A., & Harms, M.B. (2013). "Theory of mind". *Wiley interdisciplinary reviews. Cognitive science, 4*(4), 391–402. doi.org/10.1002/wcs.1232

Casey, B.J., Galván, A., & Somerville, L.H. (2016). "Beyond simple models of adolescence to an integrated circuit-based account: A commentary". *Developmental cognitive neuroscience, 17*, 128–130. doi.org/10.1016/j.dcn.2015.12.006

Chambers, R.A., Taylor, J.R., & Potenza, M.N. (2003). "Developmental neurocircuitry of motivation in adolescence: a critical period of addiction vulnerability". *The American journal of psychiatry, 160*(6), 1041–1052. doi.org/10.1176/appi.ajp.160.6.1041

Chein, J., Albert, D., O'Brien, L., Uckert, K., & Steinberg, L. (2011). "Peers increase adolescent risk taking by enhancing activity in the brain's reward circuitry". *Developmental science, 14*(2), F1–F10. doi.org/10.1111/j.1467-7687.2010.01035.x

de la Torre, R., Farré, M., Ortuño, J., Mas, M., Brenneisen, R., Roset, P.N., Segura, J., & Camí, J. (2000). "Non-linear pharmacokinetics of MDMA ('ecstasy') in humans". *British journal of clinical pharmacology, 49*(2), 104–109. doi.org/10.1046/j.1365-2125.2000.00121.x

Diamond A. (2012). "Activities and Programs That Improve Children's Executive Functions". *Current directions in psychological science, 21*(5), 335–341. doi.org/10.1177/0963721412453722

Downing, J. (1985). "Testimony of Joseph J. Downing, M.D. In the matter of MDMA Scheduling". Docket No. 84-48. United States Department of Justice, Drug Enforcement Administration. Received from erowid.org/chemicals/mdma/mdma_law2.shtml

Drury, S., Theall, K., Gleason, M. *et al.* "Telomere length and early severe social deprivation: linking early adversity and cellular aging". *Mol Psychiatry* 17, 719–727 (2012). doi.org/10.1038/mp.2011.53

Ernst M. (2014). "The triadic model perspective for the study of adolescent motivated behavior". *Brain and cognition, 89*, 104–111. doi.org/10.1016/j.bandc.2014.01.006

Galván, A. (2017). *The neuroscience of adolescence*. Cambridge University Press.

Gathers, M (2021). *Two's Company, Eight's a Fnord: A 2021 relational gestalt for Leary's eight circuit model of consciousness*. Online. rawilsonfans.org/wp-content/uploads/2024/06/Relational-8CM-Gathers.pdf

Giedd, J.N., & Rapoport, J.L. (2010). "Structural MRI of pediatric brain development: what have we learned and where are we going?" *Neuron, 67*(5), 728–734. doi.org/10.1016/j.neuron.2010.08.040

Giedd, J.N., Raznahan, A., Alexander-Bloch, A., Schmitt, E., Gogtay, N., & Rapoport, J.L. (2015). "Child psychiatry branch of the National Institute of Mental Health longitudinal structural magnetic resonance imaging study of human brain development". *Neuropsychopharmacol-ogy: official publication of the American College of Neuropsychopharma-cology, 40*(1), 43–49. doi.org/10.1038/npp.2014.236

Golarai, G., Ghahremani, D.G., Whitfield-Gabrieli, S., Reiss, A., Eberhardt, J.L., Gabrieli, J.D., & Grill-Spector, K. (2007). "Differential development of high-level visual cortex correlates with category-specific recognition memory". *Nature neuroscience, 10*(4), 512–522. doi.org/10.1038/nn1865

Golarai, G., Liberman, A., Yoon, J.M., & Grill-Spector, K. (2010). "Differential development of the ventral visual cortex extends through adolescence". *Frontiers in human neuroscience, 3*, 80. doi.org/10.3389/neuro.09.080.2009

Greer, G. (1985). "Using MDMA in psychotherapy". *Advances*, 2(2), 57–59

Grob, C.S., & Grigsby, J. (2022). *Handbook of Medical hallucinogens*. The Guilford Press.

Gweon, H., Dodell-Feder, D., Bedny, M., & Saxe, R. (2012). "Theory of mind performance in children correlates with functional specialization of a brain region for thinking about thoughts". *Child development, 83*(6), 1853–1868. doi.org/10.1111/j.1467-8624.2012.01829.x

Haber, S.N., & Knutson, B. (2010). "The reward circuit: linking primate anatomy and human imaging". *Neuropsychopharmacology: official publication of the American College of Neuropsychopharmacology*, 35(1), 4–26. doi.org/10.1038/npp.2009.129

Hartley, C.A., Fischl, B., & Phelps, E.A. (2011). "Brain structure correlates of individual differences in the acquisition and inhibition of conditioned fear". *Cerebral cortex* (New York, N.Y.: 1991), 21(9), 1954–1962. doi.org/10.1093/cercor/bhq253

Hysek, C.M., Schmid, Y., Simmler, L.D., Domes, G., Heinrichs, M., Eisenegger, C., Preller, K.H., Quednow, B.B., & Liechti, M.E. (2014). "MDMA enhances emotional empathy and prosocial behavior". *Social*

cognitive and affective neuroscience, 9(11), 1645–1652.
doi.org/10.1093/scan/nst161

Jones, P. (2013). Adult mental health disorders and their age at onset. *The British Journal of Psychiatry, 202*(S54), S5-S10.
doi:10.1192/bjp.bp.112.119164

Leary, T. (1977). *Info-psychology: A manual on the use of the human nervous system according to the instructions of the manufacturers and a navigational guide for piloting the evolution of the human individual.* Falcon Press.

Metzner, R. (1983). *Psychedelics and Spirituality*. Lecture presented at Psychedelics and Spirituality, Santa Barbara, CA.

Miller, E.K., & Cohen, J.D. (2001). "An integrative theory of prefrontal cortex function". *Annual review of neuroscience, 24*, 167–202.
doi.org/10.1146/annurev.neuro.24.1.167

Nichols, D.E. (1986). "Differences between the mechanism of action of MDMA, MBDB, and the classic psychedelics: Identification of a new therapeutic class: Entactogens". *Journal of Psychoactive Drugs, 18*(4), 305–313

Oberman, L., & Pascual-Leone, A. (2013). "Changes in plasticity across the lifespan: cause of disease and target for intervention". *Progress in brain research, 207*, 91–120. doi.org/10.1016/B978-0-444-63327-9.00016-3

Olesen, P.J., Macoveanu, J., Tegnér, J., & Klingberg, T. (2007). "Brain activity related to working memory and distraction in children and adults". *Cerebral cortex* (New York, N.Y.: 1991), 17(5), 1047–1054.
doi.org/10.1093/cercor/bhl014

Pfeifer, J.H., Iacoboni, M., Mazziotta, J.C., & Dapretto, M. (2008). "Mirroring others' emotions relates to empathy and interpersonal competence in children". *NeuroImage, 39*(4), 2076–2085.
doi.org/10.1016/j.neuroimage.2007.10.032

Paus T. (2013). "How environment and genes shape the adolescent brain". *Hormones and behavior*, 64(2), 195–202. doi.org/10.1016/j.yhbeh.2013.04.004

Schlegel, A. (2000). "The global spread of adolescent culture". In L.J. Crockett & R.K. Silbereisen (Eds.), *Negotiating adolescence in times of social change* (pp. 71–88). Cambridge University Press.

Qu, Y., Galván, A., Fuligni, A.J., Lieberman, M.D., & Telzer, E.H. (2015). "Longitudinal Changes in Prefrontal Cortex Activation Underlie Declines in Adolescent Risk Taking". *The Journal of neuroscience: the official journal of the Society for Neuroscience*, 35(32), 11308–11314. doi.org/10.1523/JNEUROSCI.1553-15.2015

Scherf, K.S., Smyth, J.M., & Delgado, M.R. (2013). "The amygdala: an agent of change in adolescent neural networks". *Hormones and behavior*, 64(2), 298–313. doi.org/10.1016/j.yhbeh.2013.05.011

Sisk, C.L., & Zehr, J.L. (2005). "Pubertal hormones organize the adolescent brain and behavior". *Frontiers in neuroendocrinology*, 26(3–4), 163–174. doi.org/10.1016/j.yfrne.2005.10.003

Somerville, L.H., Heatherton, T.F., & Kelley, W.M. (2006). "Anterior cingulate cortex responds differentially to expectancy violation and social rejection". *Nature neuroscience*, 9(8), 1007–1008. doi.org/10.1038/nn1728

Somerville, L.H., & Casey, B.J. (2010). "Developmental neurobiology of cognitive control and motivational systems". *Current opinion in neurobiology*, 20(2), 236–241. doi.org/10.1016/j.conb.2010.01.006

Steinberg, L. (2014). *Age of opportunity: Lessons from the new science of adolescence.* Mariner Books, Houghton Mifflin Harcourt.

Steinberg, L., Albert, D., Cauffman, E., Banich, M., Graham, S., & Woolard, J. (2008). "Age differences in sensation seeking and impulsivity as indexed by behavior and self-report: evidence for a dual systems model". *Developmental psychology*, 44(6), 1764–1778. doi.org/10.1037/a0012955

Van Duijvenvoorde, A.C., Jansen, B.R., Bredman, J.C., & Huizenga, H.M. (2012). "Age-related changes in decision making: comparing informed and noninformed situations". *Developmental psychology*, 48(1), 192–203. doi.org/10.1037/a0025601

Wade, J. (1996). *Changes of mind: A holonomic theory of the evolution of consciousness.* State University of New York Press.

Wager, T.D., Davidson, M.L., Hughes, B.L., Lindquist, M.A., & Ochsner, K.N. (2008). "Prefrontal-subcortical pathways mediating successful emotion regulation". *Neuron*, 59(6), 1037–1050. doi.org/10.1016/j.neuron.2008.09.006

Wilson, R.A. (1983). *Prometheus rising.* Falcon Press.

Wilson, R.A., & Higgs, J. (2020). *The Starseed Signals: Link Between Worlds: A Raw Perspective on Timothy Leary, Ph.D.* Hilaritas Press.

CHAPTER VII (CHAPEL PERILOUS)

Alli, A. (1987). *Angel Tech: A modern shaman's guide to reality selection.* Falcon Press.

Commons, M. & Richards, F. (2002). Four Postformal Stages. *Handbook of Adult Development.* 10.1007/978-1-4615-0617-1_11.

Grof, C. (1993). *Thirst for wholeness: Attachment, addiction and the spiritual path.* Harper San Francisco.

Grof, S., & Grof, C. (1989). *Spiritual emergency: When pastoral transformation becomes a crisis.* Tarcher/Putnam.

Wade, J. (1996). *Changes of mind: A holonomic theory of the evolution of consciousness.* State University of New York Press.

Washburn, M. (1988). *The ego and the dynamic ground: A transpersonal theory of human development.* State University of New York Press.

Wilson, R.A. (1977). *Cosmic trigger.* Falcon Press.

Wilson, R.A. (1983). *Prometheus rising.* Falcon Press.

Chapter VIII (C-5)

Alli, A. (1987). *Angel Tech: A modern shaman's guide to reality selection.* Falcon Press.

Austin, J.H. (1998). *Zen and the brain: Toward an understanding of meditation and consciousness.* MIT Press.

Bering, J.M. (2002). "The Existential Theory of Mind". *Review of General Psychology,* 6, 24–3.

Boccia, M., Piccardi, L., & Guariglia, P. (2015). "The Meditative Mind: A Comprehensive Meta-Analysis of MRI Studies". *BioMed research international,* 2015, 419808. doi.org/10.1155/2015/419808

Csikszentmihalyi, M. (1990). *Flow: The psychology of optimal experience.* Harper and Row.

Deyoung, C.G., Cicchetti, D., Rogosch, F.A., Gray, J.R., Eastman, M., & Grigorenko, E.L. (2011). "Sources of Cognitive Exploration: Genetic Variation in the Prefrontal Dopamine System Predicts Openness/Intellect". *Journal of research in personality,* 45(4), 364–371. doi.org/10.1016/j.jrp.2011.04.002

Dietrich A. (2003). "Functional neuroanatomy of altered states of consciousness: the transient hypofrontality hypothesis". *Consciousness and cognition,* 12(2), 231–256. doi.org/10.1016/s1053-8100(02)00046-6

Dietrich A. (2004). "Neurocognitive mechanisms underlying the experience of flow". *Consciousness and cognition,* 13(4), 746–761. doi.org/10.1016/j.concog.2004.07.002

Doyle, R. (2011). *Darwin's pharmacy: Sex, plants, and the evolution of the noösphere.* University of Washington Press.

Forstmann M., Kettner H.S., Sagioglou C., Irvine A., Gandy S., Carhart-Harris R.L., Luke D. (2023). "Among psychedelic-experienced users, only past use of psilocybin reliably predicts nature relatedness". *J Psychopharmacol.* 37(1):93–106. doi:10.1177/02698811221146356.

Fromm, E. (1973). *The Anatomy of Human Destructiveness.* Fawcett.

Graves, C.W. (1970). "Levels of existence: An open system theory of values". *Journal of Humanistic Psychology*, 10(2), 131–155. doi.org/10.1177/002216787001000205

Irvine, A., Luke, D., Harrild, F., Gandy, S., Watts, R. (2023). "Transpersonal Ecodelia: Surveying Psychedelically Induced Biophilia". *Psychoactives*. 2. 174–194. 10.3390/psychoactives2020012

Keltner, D., & Haidt, J. (2003). "Approaching awe, a moral, spiritual, and aesthetic emotion". *Cognition & emotion*, 17(2), 297–314. doi.org/10.1080/02699930302297

Khamsehzadeh, J. (2022). *The Psilocybin Connection: Psychedelics, the transformation of consciousness, and evolution on the planet.* North Atlantic Books.

Lazar, S.W., Kerr, C.E., Wasserman, R.H., Gray, J.R., Greve, D.N., Treadway, M.T., McGarvey, M., Quinn, B.T., Dusek, J.A., Benson, H., Rauch, S.L., Moore, C.I., & Fischl, B. (2005). "Meditation experience is associated with increased cortical thickness". *Neuroreport*, 16(17), 1893–1897. doi.org/10.1097/01.wnr.0000186598.66243.19

Leary, T. (1977). *Info-psychology: A manual on the use of the human nervous system according to the instructions of the manufacturers and a navigational guide for piloting the evolution of the human individual.* Falcon Press.

Lifshitz, M., van Elk, M., & Luhrmann, T.M. (2019). "Absorption and spiritual experience: A review of evidence and potential mechanisms". *Consciousness and Cognition* 73:102760.

Lovelock, J.E. (1979). *Gaia. A New Look at Life on Earth.* Oxford University Press.

Mechoulam, R. (2019). "The discovery of the endocannabinoid system: Centuries in the making". *International League Against Epilepsy*

Newberg, A., Newberg, S. (2005). *The neuropsychology of religious and spiritual experience. Handbook of the psychology of religion and spirituality.* pp. 199–215

Pacher, P., & Kunos, G. (2013). "Modulating the endocannabinoid system in human health and disease--successes and failures". *The FEBS journal*, 280(9), 1918–1943. doi.org/10.1111/febs.12260

Rivera, E. (2022). *William Shatner experienced profound grief in space. It was the 'overview effect'.* Online. npr.org/2022/10/23/1130482740/william-shatner-jeff-bezos-space-travel-overview-effect.

van Elk, M., Arciniegas Gomez, M.A., van der Zwaag, W., van Schie, H.T., & Sauter, D. (2019). "The neural correlates of the awe experience: Reduced default mode network activity during feelings of awe". *Human brain mapping*, 40(12), 3561–3574. doi.org/10.1002/hbm.24616

Wade, J. (1996). *Changes of mind: A holonomic theory of the evolution of consciousness.* State University of New York Press.

White, F. (1987). *The overview effect: Space exploration and human evolution.* Multiverse Publishing.

Wilson, R.A. (1983). *Prometheus Rising.* Falcon Press.

Wilson, R.A., & Higgs, J. (2020). *The Starseed Signals: Link Between Worlds: A Raw Perspective on Timothy Leary, Ph.D.* Hilaritas Press.

Yaden, D., & Newberg, A. (2022). *The Varieties of Spiritual Experience: 21st century research and perspectives.* Oxford University Press.

CHAPTER IX (C-6)

Alli, A. (2014). *The eight-circuit brain: Navigational strategies for the energetic body.* Falcon Press.

American Psychological Association (APA). (2006, July 15). *The APA dictionary of psychology.* Gary R. Vandenbos. archive.org/details/apadictionaryofp00vand

Bangasser, D.A., Waxler, D.E., Santollo, J., & Shors, T.J. (2006). "Trace conditioning and the hippocampus: the importance of contiguity". *The Journal of neuroscience: the official journal of the Society for*

Neuroscience, 26(34), 8702–8706.
doi.org/10.1523/JNEUROSCI.1742-06.2006

Blackwood, N., Ffytche, D., Simmons, A., Bentall, R., Murray, R., & Howard, R. (2004). "The cerebellum and decision making under uncertainty. Brain research". *Cognitive brain research,* 20(1), 46–53. doi.org/10.1016/j.cogbrainres.2003.12.009

Carhart-Harris, R.L., Leech, R., Hellyer, P.J., Shanahan, M., Feilding, A., Tagliazucchi, E., Chialvo, D.R., & Nutt, D. (2014). "The entropic brain: a theory of conscious states informed by neuroimaging research with psychedelic drugs". *Frontiers in human neuroscience,* 8, 20. doi.org/10.3389/fnhum.2014.00020

Carhart-Harris, R.L., & Friston, K.J. (2019). "REBUS and the Anarchic Brain: Toward a Unified Model of the Brain Action of Psychedelics". *Pharmacological reviews,* 71(3), 316–344. doi.org/10.1124/pr.118.017160

Cassilhas, R.C., Tufik, S. & de Mello, M.T. (2016). "Physical exercise, neuroplasticity, spatial learning and memory". *Cell. Mol. Life Sci.* 73, 975–983. doi.org/10.1007/s00018-015-2102-0

Catlow, B.J., Song, S., Paredes, D.A., Kirstein, C.L., & Sanchez-Ramos, J. (2013). "Effects of psilocybin on hippocampal neurogenesis and extinction of trace fear conditioning". *Experimental brain research,* 228(4), 481–491. doi.org/10.1007/s00221-013-3579-0

de Vos CMH, Mason NL, Kuypers KPC. (2021). "Psychedelics and Neuroplasticity: A Systematic Review Unraveling the Biological Underpinnings of Psychedelics". *Front Psychiatry.* 2021 Sep 10;12:724606. doi:10.3389/fpsyt.2021.724606.

Demanuele, C., Kirsch, P., Esslinger, C., Zink, M., Meyer-Lindenberg, A., & Durstewitz, D. (2015). "Area-specific information processing in prefrontal cortex during a probabilistic inference task: a multivariate fMRI BOLD time series analysis". *PloS one,* 10(8), e0135424. doi.org/10.1371/journal.pone.0135424

El-Sayes, J., Harasym, D., Turco, C.V., Locke, M.B., & Nelson, A.J. (2019). "Exercise-Induced Neuroplasticity: A Mechanistic Model and Prospects for Promoting Plasticity". *The Neuroscientist*, 25, 65–85.

Esser, A.H. (1978). "Designed communality: A synergic context for community and privacy". *Design for Communality and Privacy*, 9–49. doi.org/10.1007/978-1-4613-2853-7_3

Froemke, R., Young, L. (2021*).* "Oxytocin, Neural Plasticity, and Social Behavior". *Annual Review of Neuroscience.* 44:1, 359–381

Hötting, K., & Röder, B. (2013). "Beneficial effects of physical exercise on neuroplasticity and cognition". *Neuroscience & Biobehavioral Reviews.* Volume 37:9 Part B, 2243–2257. doi.org/10.1016/j.neubiorev.2013.04.005.

Khamsehzadeh, J. (2022). *The Psilocybin Connection: Psychedelics, the transformation of consciousness, and evolution on the planet.* North Atlantic Books.

Klöbl, M., et al (2021). "Serotonin modulates learning content-specific neuroplasticity of functional brain networks". *bioRxiv* 2021.01.15.426779. doi.org/10.1101/2021.01.15.426779

Leary, T. (1994). *Info-psychology: A manual on the use of the human nervous system according to the instructions of the manufacturers and a navigational guide for piloting the evolution of the human individual.* Falcon Press.

Lepow, L., Morishita, H., & Yehuda, R. (2021). "Critical Period Plasticity as a Framework for Psychedelic-Assisted Psychotherapy". *Frontiers in neuroscience*, 15, 710004. doi.org/10.3389/fnins.2021.710004

Lilly, J. (1978). *The Deep Self: consciousness exploration in the isolation tank.* Warner Books.

Lilly, J. (2014). *Programming and Metaprogramming in the human Biocomputer: Theory and experiments.* Coincidence Control Publishing.

Lukasiewicz, K., Baker, J.J., Zuo, Y., & Lu, J. (2021). "Serotonergic Psychedelics in Neural Plasticity". *Front Mol Neurosci.* Oct 12;14:748359. doi:10.3389/fnmol.2021.748359.

Maslow, A.H. (1954). *Motivation and Personality.* Harper & Rowe.

Mateos-Aparicio P., & Rodríguez-Moreno, A. (2019). "The Impact of Studying Brain Plasticity". *Front Cell Neurosci.* Feb 27;13:66. doi:10.3389/fncel.2019.00066. PMID: 30873009; PMCID: PMC6400842.

Miller, W.R., & Rollnick, S. (2013). *Motivational Interviewing: Preparing People for Change* (3rd ed.). Guildford Press.

Olson, D.E. (2018). "Psychoplastogens: A Promising Class of Plasticity-Promoting Neurotherapeutics". *J Exp Neurosci.* Sep 19;12:1179069518800508. doi:10.1177/1179069518800508. PMID: 30262987; PMCID: PMC6149016.

Paul, L.A. (2016). *Transformative experience.* Oxford University Press.

Petri, G., Expert, P., Turkheimer, F., Carhart-Harris, R., Nutt, D., Hellyer, P.J., & Vaccarino, F. (2014). "Homological scaffolds of brain functional networks". *Journal of the Royal Society, Interface, 11*(101), 20140873. doi.org/10.1098/rsif.2014.0873

Shao L.X., Liao C., Gregg I., Davoudian P.A., Savalia N.K., Delagarza K., & Kwan, A.C. (2021). "Psilocybin induces rapid and persistent growth of dendritic spines in frontal cortex in vivo". *Neuron.* Aug 18;109(16):2535-2544.e4. doi:10.1016/j.neuron.2021.06.008.

Sheldrake, R., McKenna, T.K., & Abraham, R. (1992). *Chaos, creativity, and Cosmic Consciousness.* Park Street Press.

Tosey, P., & Mathison, J. (2003). "Neuro-linguistic Programming and Learning Theory: a Response". *Organisational Behaviour,* HRM and Health Care Management. 14. 10.1080/0958517032000137667.

Turetzky, R. (2018). *Idiovisual-empathic synaesthesia.* Unpublished manuscript.

Wade, J. (1996). *Changes of mind: A holonomic theory of the evolution of consciousness.* State University of New York Press.

Wilson, R.A. (1983). *Prometheus Rising.* Falcon Press.

Wilson, R.A., & Higgs, J. (2020). *The Starseed Signals: Link Between Worlds: A Raw Perspective on Timothy Leary, Ph.D.* Hilaritas Press.

Xing, L., Kalebic, N., Namba, T., Vaid, S., Wimberger, P., & Huttner W.B. (2020). "Serotonin Receptor 2A Activation Promotes Evolutionarily Relevant Basal Progenitor Proliferation in the Developing Neocortex". *Neuron.* Dec 23;108(6):1113-1129.e6. doi:10.1016/j.neuron.2020.09.034. Epub 2020 Oct 19. PMID: 33080227.

Yaden, D., & Newberg, A. (2022). *The Varieties of Spiritual Experience: 21st century research and perspectives.* Oxford University Press

Chapter X (C-7)

Alli, A. (1987). *Angel Tech: A modern shaman's guide to reality selection.* Falcon Press.

Barrett, F., Krimmel, S., Griffiths, R., Seminowicz, D., Mathur, B. (2020). "Psilocybin acutely alters the functional connectivity of the claustrum with brain networks that support perception, memory, and attention". *NeuroImage.* Vol 218. doi.org/10.1016/j.neuroimage.2020.116980

Beiner, A. (2023). *Bigger picture, the.* Penguin.

Brown, D.J. (2013). *The new science of psychedelics: At the Nexus of Culture, consciousness, and spirituality.* Park Street Press.

Grof, S. (1975). *Realms of the human unconscious: Observations from LSD research.* Souvenir Press.

Grof, S. (1998). *The cosmic game: Explorations of the frontiers of human consciousness.* State University of New York Press.

Heffernan, J. (2017). *Nonlocal nature: The eight circuits of Consciousness.* New Falcon Publications

Jablonka E, Raz G. "Transgenerational epigenetic inheritance: prevalence, mechanisms, and implications for the study of heredity and evolution". *Quarterly Review of Biology.* 2009 Jun;84(2):131-76. doi:10.1086/598822.

Jacobi, J., Manheim, R., & Jacobi, J. (1959). *Complex, archetype, symbol in the psychology of C.G. Jung.* Pantheon Books.

Jung C.G. (1963). *Memories, dreams, reflections.* Routledge & Kegan Paul.

Jung, C.G., & Main, R. (1997). *On synchronicity and the paranormal.* Princeton University Press.

Kaufman, S.B. (2012). *Must One Risk Madness to Achieve Genius?.* scottbarrykaufman.com/must-one-risk-madness-to-achieve-genius/

Kellermann NP. "Epigenetic transmission of Holocaust trauma: can nightmares be inherited?" *Israel Journal of Psychiatry and Related Sciences.* 2013;50(1):33-9. PMID: 24029109.

Kent, J.L. (2010). *Psychedelic information theory: Shamanism in the age of reason.* PIT Press.

Khamsehzadeh, J. (2022). *The Psilocybin Connection: Psychedelics, the transformation of consciousness, and evolution on the planet.* North Atlantic Books.

Koestler, A. (1967). *The Ghost in the Machine.* Hutchinson.

Lau, E., McClintock, C., Graziosi, M., Nakkana, A., Garcia, A., & Miller, L. (2020). "Content analysis of spiritual life in Contemporary USA, India, and China". *Religions,* 11(6), 286. doi.org/10.3390/rel11060286

Leary, T. (1994). *Info-psychology: A manual on the use of the human nervous system according to the instructions of the manufacturers and a navigational guide for piloting the evolution of the human individual.* Falcon Press.

Luan, L.X., Eckernäs, E., Ashton, M., Rosas, F., Uthaug, M., Bartha, A., ... Timmermann, C. (2023, April 13). *Psychological and physiological effects of extended DMT.* doi.org/10.31234/osf.io/vg4dp

Maslow, A.H. (1971). *The farther reaches of human nature.* Penguin Books.

Miller, M.E., & Cook-Greuter, S.R. (1994). *Transcendence and mature thought in adulthood: The further reaches of adult development.* Rowman & Littlefield.

Murphy, T.R. (2014). *Sacred pathways: The brains role in religious and mystic experiences.* CreateSpace.

Persinger, M., & Healey, F. (2002). "Experimental facilitation of the sensed presence: possible intercalation between the hemispheres induced by complex magnetic fields". *The Journal of Nervous and Mental Disease.* 190 (8): 533–41. doi:10.1097/00005053-200208000-00006

Samuels, A. (1986). *Critical dictionary of Jungian analysis.* Routledge.

Švorcová J. "Transgenerational Epigenetic Inheritance of Traumatic Experience in Mammals". *Genes.* 2023; 14(1):120. doi.org/10.3390/genes14010120

Turetzky, R.L. (2021). *A hermeneutic phenomenology of the N,N-dimethyltryptamine experience* (Doctoral dissertation). Available from ProQuest Dissertation and Theses Database.

Vaughan, F. (1989). "Characteristics of Mysticism". *ReVision.* 12(2):23

Wade, J. (1996). *Changes of mind: A holonomic theory of the evolution of consciousness.* State University of New York Press.

Washburn, M. (1988). *The ego and the dynamic ground: A transpersonal theory of human development.* State University of New York Press.

Wilber, K. (1980). *The atman project.* The Theosophical Publishing House.

Wilber, K., & Wachowski, L. (1996). *A brief history of everything.* Shambhala Publications, Inc.

Wilson, R.A. (1983). *Prometheus Rising.* Falcon Press.

Wilson, R.A., & Higgs, J. (2020). *The Starseed Signals: Link Between Worlds: A Raw Perspective on Timothy Leary, Ph.D.* Hilaritas Press

Yaden, D., & Newberg, A. (2022). *The Varieties of Spiritual Experience: 21st century research and perspectives.* Oxford University Press.

Yeats, W.B. (1928). *The tower.* Penguin Classics.

Chapter XI (C-8)

Blanke, O., Ortigue, S., Landis, T., & Seeck, M. (2002). "Stimulating illusory own-body perceptions". *Nature, 419*(6904), 269–270. doi.org/10.1038/419269a

Blanke, O., Mohr, C., Michel, C.M., Pascual-Leone, A., Brugger, P., Seeck, M., Landis, T., & Thut, G. (2005). "Linking out-of-body experience and self processing to mental own-body imagery at the temporoparietal junction". *The Journal of neuroscience: the official journal of the Society for Neuroscience, 25*(3), 550–557.

Bohm, D. & Weber, R. (1983). 'Of matter and meaning: the super-implicate order. A conversation between David Bohm and Renee Weber', *ReVision 6*, 34–44. Photocopy of published conversation.

Cleary, T.F. (1993). *The Flower Ornament Scripture: A translation of the Avatamsaka Sutra.* Shambhala.

Grob, C.S., & Grigsby, J. (2022). *Handbook of Medical hallucinogens.* The Guilford Press.

Grof, S. (1975). *Realms of the human unconscious: Observations from LSD research.* Souvenir Press.

Grof, S. (1998). *The cosmic game: Explorations of the frontiers of human consciousness.* State University of New York Press.

Huguelit, L. (2014). *The shamanic path to quantum consciousness: The eight circuits of Creative Power.* Bear & Company.

Josipovic Z. (2014). "Neural correlates of nondual awareness in meditation". *Annals of the New York Academy of Sciences, 1307*, 9–18. doi.org/10.1111/nyas.12261

Khamsehzadeh, J. (2022). *The Psilocybin Connection: Psychedelics, the transformation of consciousness, and evolution on the planet.* North Atlantic Books.

Koplowitz, H. (1984). "A projection beyond Piaget's formal-operations stage: A general system stage and a unitary stage". In M.L. Commons, F.A. Richards, & C. Armon (Eds.), *Beyond formal operations* (pp. 272–295). New York: Praeger.

Leary, T. (1994). *Info-psychology: A manual on the use of the human nervous system according to the instructions of the manufacturers and a navigational guide for piloting the evolution of the human individual.* Falcon Press.

Lilly, J. (1975). *Simulations of god the science of belief.* Ronin Publishing.

Merrell-Wolff, F. (1973). *The philosophy of consciousness without an object: Reflections on the nature of Transcendental Consciousness.* Julian Press.

Millière, R., Carhart-Harris, R.L., Roseman, L., Trautwein, F.M., & Berkovich-Ohana, A. (2018). Psychedelics, Meditation, and Self-Consciousness. *Frontiers in psychology, 9,* 1475. doi.org/10.3389/fpsyg.2018.01475

Newberg, A., & d'Aquili, E.G. (2018). *Why God won't go away: Brain science and the biology of belief.* Ballantine Books.

Reinoso-Suárez, F., de Andrés, I., Rodrigo-Angulo, M.L., & Garzón, M. (2001). "Brain structures and mechanisms involved in the generation of REM sleep". *Sleep medicine reviews, 5*(1), 63–77. doi.org/10.1053/smrv.2000.0136

Solms M. (2000). "Dreaming and REM sleep are controlled by different brain mechanisms". *The Behavioral and brain sciences, 23*(6), 843–1121. doi.org/10.1017/s0140525x00003988

Stolorow, R.D., & Atwood, G.E. (1992). *Contexts of being: The Intersubjective Foundations of Psychological Life.* Taylor and Francis.

Wade, J. (1996). *Changes of mind: A holonomic theory of the evolution of consciousness.* State University of New York Press.

Wilson, R.A., & Higgs, J. (2020). *The Starseed Signals: Link Between Worlds: A Raw Perspective on Timothy Leary, Ph.D.* Hilaritas Press.

Yaden, D., & Newberg, A. (2022). *The Varieties of Spiritual Experience: 21st century research and perspectives.* Oxford University Press.

Yamada, R.G., & Ueda, H.R. (2020). "Molecular Mechanisms of REM Sleep". *Frontiers in neuroscience, 13,* 1402. doi.org/10.3389/fnins.2019.01402

Yuan, C. (1987). *Practice and attain sudden enlightenment.* Sutra Translation Committee of the United States and Canada

CHAPTER XII

Ahmad, S., & Scheinkman, L. (2019). "How Can We Be So Dense? The Benefits of Using Highly Sparse Representations". *ArXiv Prepr.* ArXiv190311257.

Alli, A. (1987). *Angel Tech: A modern shaman's guide to reality selection.* Falcon Press.

Alli, A. (2014). *The eight-circuit brain: Navigational strategies for the energetic body.* Falcon Press.

Alper, K.R., Lotsof, H.S., Frenken, G.M.N., Luciano, D.J., & Bastiaans, J. (1999). "Treatment of acute opioid withdrawal with ibogaine." *American Journal on Addictions,* 8(3), 234–242.

Attali, E., de Anna, F., Dubois, B., & Dalla Barba, G. (2009). "Confabulation in Alzheimer's disease: poor encoding and retrieval of over-learned information". *Brain: a journal of neurology,* 132 Pt 1, 204-12.

Bogenschutz, M.P., & Johnson, M.W. (2016). "Classic hallucinogens in the treatment of addictions". *Progress in neuro-psychopharmacology & biological psychiatry,* 64, 250–258. doi.org/10.1016/j.pnpbp.2015.03.002

Bouso, J.C., & Riba, J. (2014). "Ayahuasca and the treatment of drug addiction". In *The therapeutic use of ayahuasca* (pp. 95–109). Springer, Berlin, Heidelberg.

Bragdon, E. (1988). *A Sourcebook for Helping People with Spiritual Problems* (1st ed.). Lightening Up Press.

Braun, U., Schäfer, A., Bassett, D.S., Rausch, F., Schweiger, J.I., Bilek, E., et al. (2016). "Dynamic brain network reconfiguration as a potential schizophrenia genetic risk mechanism modulated by NMDA receptor function". *Proc. Natl. Acad. Sci.* 113, 12568–12573. doi:10.1073/pnas.1608819113

Bugliosi, V., & Gentry, C. (1994). *Helter Skelter: The true story of the manson murder.* Norton.

Cantero, J.L., Atienza, M., & Salas, R.M. (2002). "Human alpha oscillations in wakefulness, drowsiness period, and REM sleep: different electroencephalographic phenomena within the alpha band". *Neurophysiologie clinique = Clinical neurophysiology,* 32(1), 54–71. doi.org/10.1016/s0987-7053(01)00289-1

Carhart-Harris, R.L. (2018). "The entropic brain—revisited". *Neuropharmacology,* 142, 167–178. doi.org/10.1016/j.neuropharm.2018.03.010

Carhart-Harris, R.L., Leech, R., Hellyer, P.J., Shanahan, M., Feilding, A., Tagliazucchi, E., Chialvo, D.R., & Nutt, D. (2014). "The entropic brain: A theory of conscious states informed by neuroimaging research with psychedelic drugs". *Frontiers in Human Neuroscience,* 8, 20.

Carhart-Harris, R.L., & Friston, K.J. (2019). "REBUS and the Anarchic Brain: Toward a Unified Model of the Brain Action of Psychedelics". *Pharmacological reviews,* 71(3), 316–344. doi.org/10.1124/pr.118.017160

Ciaunica, A., Charlton, J., & Farmer, H. (2021). "When the Window Cracks: Transparency and the Fractured Self in Depersonalisation". *Phenomenol. Cogn. Sci.* 20, 1–19. doi:10.1007/s11097-020-09677-z.

Csíkszentmihályi, M. (1991). *Flow.* Harper Collins.

Doss, M.K., Madden, M.B., Gaddis, A., Nebel, M.B., Griffiths, R.R., Mathur, B.N., & Barrett, F.S. (2022). "Models of psychedelic drug action: modulation of cortical-subcortical circuits". *Brain: a journal of neurology,* 145(2), 441–456. doi.org/10.1093/brain/awab406

Eagle, M.N. (2000). "A critical evaluation of current conceptions of transference and countertransference". *Psychoanalytic Psychology,* 17(1), 24–37. doi.org/10.1037/0736-9735.17.1.24

Frith C. (2005). "The neural basis of hallucinations and delusions". *Comptes rendus biologies,* 328(2), 169–175. doi.org/10.1016/j.crvi.2004.10.012

Gasser, P., Holstein, D., Michel, Y., Doblin, R., Yazar-Klosinski, B., Passie, T., & Brenneisen, R. (2014). "Safety and efficacy of lysergic acid diethylamide-assisted psychotherapy for anxiety associated with life-threatening diseases". *The Journal of nervous and mental disease,* 202(7), 513.

Grof, C., & Grof, S. (Eds.). (1989). *Spiritual emergency: When personal transformation becomes a crisis.* Jeremy P. Tarcher

Hartogsohn, I. (2015). *The psycho-social construction of LSD: How set and setting shaped the American psychedelic experience 1950–1970.* Ph.D. Dissertation, Bar Ilan University, Israel.

Hartogsohn, I. (2017)." Constructing drug effects: A history of set and setting". *Drug Science, Policy and Law.* 3. doi:10.1177/2050324516683325

Hofmann, A. (2009). *LSD: My problem child.* Multidisciplinary Association for Psychedelic Studies (MAPS).

Kerr, C.E., Sacchet, M.D., Lazar, S.W., Moore, C.I., & Jones, S.R. (2013). "Mindfulness starts with the body: somatosensory attention and top-down modulation of cortical alpha rhythms in mindfulness meditation". *Front. Hum. Neurosci.* 7, 12. doi:10.3389/fnhum.2013.00012.

Kornfield, J. (2001). *After the ecstasy, the laundry: How the heart grows wise on the spiritual path.* Bantam Books.

Leary, T. (1977). *The Game of Life.* Peace Press.

Lee, M.A., & Shlain, B. (1992). *Acid dreams: The Complete Social History of LSD.* Grove Press.

Li, M., Woelfer, M., Colic, L., Safron, A., Chang, C., Heinze, H.-J., et al. (2018). "Default mode network connectivity change corresponds to ketamine's delayed glutamatergic effects". *Eur. Arch. Psychiatry Clin. Neurosci.* doi:10.1007/s00406-018-0942-y

Liester, M.B., & Prickett, J.I. (2012). "Hypotheses regarding the mechanisms of ayahuasca in the treatment of addictions". *Journal of psychoactive drugs,* 44(3), 200–208.

Lilly, J. (1975). *Simulations of god the science of belief.* Ronin Publishing.

MacLean, K.A., Johnson, M.W., & Griffiths, R.R. (2011). "Mystical experiences occasioned by the hallucinogen psilocybin lead to increases in the personality domain of openness". *Journal of psychopharmacology (Oxford, England),* 25(11), 1453–1461. doi.org/10.1177/0269881111420188

Michaiel, A.M., Parker, P.R.L., & Niell, C.M. (2019). "A Hallucinogenic Serotonin-2A Receptor Agonist Reduces Visual Response Gain and Alters Temporal Dynamics in Mouse V1". *Cell Rep.* 26, 3475-3483.e4. doi:10.1016/j.celrep.2019.02.104.

MK-ULTRA/Mind control experiments. (2005, December 20). From cia.gov/library/readingroom/document/cia-rdp91-00901r000500150005-5

Nardou, R., Sawyer, E., Song, Y.J., et al. "Psychedelics reopen the social reward learning critical period". *Nature* 618, 790–798 (2023). doi.org/10.1038/s41586-023-06204-3

Nayak, S.M., Gukasyan, N., Barrett, F.S., Erowid, E., Erowid, F., & Griffiths, R.R. (2021). "Classic Psychedelic Coadministration with Lithium, but Not Lamotrigine, is Associated with Seizures: An Analysis of Online Psychedelic Experience Reports". *Pharmacopsychiatry,* 54(5), 240–245. https://doi.org/10.1055/a-1524-2794

Ogden, T. (2004). "On holding and containing, on being and dreaming". *International Journal of Psychoanalysis,* 85, 1349–1364.

Ott, U., Reuter, M., Hennig, J., & Vaitl, D. (2005). "Evidence for a common biological basis of the Absorption trait, hallucinogen effects, and positive symptoms: epistasis between 5-HT2a and COMT polymorphisms". *Am. J. Med. Genet. Part B Neuropsychiatr. Genet. Off. Publ. Int. Soc. Psychiatr. Genet.* 137B, 29–32. doi:10.1002/ajmg.b.30197.

Parr, T., & Friston, K.J. (2017). "Working memory, attention, and salience in active inference". *Sci. Rep.* 7, 14678. doi:10.1038/s41598-017-15249-0.

Pollan, M. (2019). *How to change your mind: What the new science of psychedelics teaches us about consciousness, dying, addiction, depression, and transcendence.* Penguin Books.

Preller, K.H., Razi, A., Zeidman, P., Stämpfli, P., Friston, K.J., & Vollenweider, F.X. (2019). "Effective connectivity changes in LSD-induced altered states of consciousness in humans". *Proc. Natl. Acad. Sci. U.S.A.* 116, 2743–2748. doi:10.1073/pnas.1815129116.

Richards, W.A. (2017). "Psychedelic Psychotherapy: Insights From 25 Years of Research". *Journal of Humanistic Psychology,* 57(4), 323–337. doi.org/10.1177/0022167816670996

Safron, A. (2020a). "An Integrated World Modeling Theory (IWMT) of Consciousness: Combining Integrated Information and Global Neuronal Workspace Theories with the Free Energy Principle and Active Inference Framework; Toward Solving the Hard Problem and Characterizing Agentic Causation". *Frontiers in Artificial Intelligence* 3. doi.org/10.3389/frai.2020.00030

Safron, A. (2021a). "Integrated World Modeling Theory (IWMT) Expanded: Implications for Theories of Consciousness and Artificial Intelligence". *PsyArXiv.* doi.org/10.31234/osf.io/rm5b2

Safron, A. (2020, November 30). *On the Varieties of Conscious Experiences: Altered Beliefs Under Psychedelics (ALBUS).* doi.org/10.31234/osf.io/zqh4b Version 12 May 14, 2023

Salgado, S., & Kaplitt, M.G. (2015). "The Nucleus Accumbens: A Comprehensive Review". *Stereotactic and functional neurosurgery,* 93(2), 75–93. doi.org/10.1159/000368279

Sato, J., Mossad, S.I., Wong, S.M., Hunt, B.A.E., Dunkley, B.T., Smith, M.L., et al. (2018). "Alpha keeps it together: Alpha oscillatory synchrony underlies working memory maintenance in young

children". *Dev. Cogn. Neurosci.* 34, 114–123.
doi:10.1016/j.dcn.2018.09.001.

Schwartz, R.C. (1995). *Internal family systems therapy.* Guilford Press.

Stevens, J. (1998). *Storming heaven: LSD and the American Dream.* Grove
Press.

Strassman R.J. (1984). "Adverse reactions to psychedelic drugs. A review
of the literature". *The Journal of nervous and mental disease,* 172(10),
577–595. doi.org/10.1097/00005053-198410000-00001

Tarnas, R., & Kelly, S. (2021). *Psyche unbound: Essays in honor of
Stanislav Grof.* Multidisciplinary Association for Psychedelic Studies.

Turetzky, R.L. (2021). *A hermeneutic phenomenology of the N,N-
dimethyltryptamine experience* (Doctoral dissertation). Available from
ProQuest Dissertation and Theses Database.

Ungerleider, J.T., Fisher, D.D., & Fuller, M. (1966). "The dangers of LSD.
Analysis of seven months' experience in a university hospital's
psychiatric service". *JAMA,* 197(6), 389–392.
doi.org/10.1001/jama.197.6.389

Wilson, R.A. (1983). *Prometheus Rising.* Falcon Press.

Wilson, R.A. (2001). *Robert Anton Wilson Explains Everything: (or Old
Bob Exposes His Ignorance).* Audio CD. Sounds True.

CHAPTER XIII

Beiner, A. (2023). *Bigger picture, the.* Penguin.

Hendricks P.S., Crawford M.S., Cropsey K.L., et al. (2018). "The
relationships of classic psychedelic use with criminal behavior in the
United States adult population". *Journal of Psychopharmacology.*
32(1):37–48. doi:10.1177/0269881117735685

Khamsehzadeh, J. (2022). *The Psilocybin Connection: Psychedelics, the
transformation of consciousness, and evolution on the planet.* North
Atlantic Books.

Lepow, L., Morishita, H., & Yehuda, R. (2021). "Critical Period Plasticity as a Framework for Psychedelic-Assisted Psychotherapy". *Frontiers in neuroscience*, *15*, 710004. doi:10.3389/fnins.2021.710004

McKenna, T.K. (1991). *The archaic revival: Speculations on psychedelic mushrooms, the Amazon, virtual reality, ufos, evolution, shamanism, the rebirth of the goddess, and the end of history.* HarperSanFrancisco.

Rifkin, J. (2009). *The empathetic civilization: The race to Global Consciousness in a world in crisis.* Tarcher/Penguin.

Sobhani, M. (2022). *"Each time a medicine man dies, it's as though a library burned down."* Jun 2. psychedelicrenaissance.substack.com/p/each-time-a-medicine-man-dies-its?utm_source=%2Fprofile%2F68289684-mona-sobhani-phd&utm_medium=reader2

Vervaeke, J. (2019a). *Ep. 1—Awakening from the meaning crisis—Introduction* [internet] cited 2023 Jun 26. Available from youtube.com/watch?v=54l8_ewcOlY

Vervaeke, J. (2019b) *Ep. 37—Awakening from the meaning crisis—Reverse engineering enlightenment: part 2* [internet] cited 2023 Jun 26. Available from youtube.com/watch?v=2kQooMZzR7w

Wilson, R.A. (1980). *The illuminati papers.* And/Or Press.

Xing, L., Kalebic, N., Namba, T., Vaid, S., Wimberger, P., & Huttner, W.B. (2020). "Serotonin Receptor 2A Activation Promotes Evolutionarily Relevant Basal Progenitor Proliferation in the Developing Neocortex". *Neuron*, *108*(6), 1113–1129.e6. doi.org/10.1016/j.neuron.2020.09.034

About the Authors

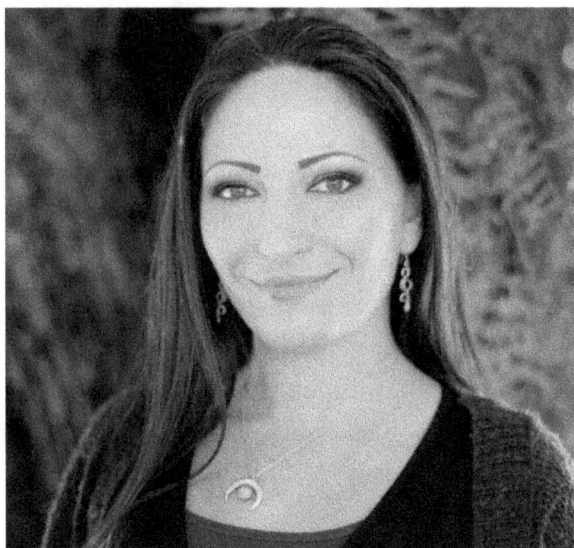

Dr. Rachel Turetzky has a Ph.D. in Clinical Psychology with an emphasis in Depth Psychology from *Pacifica Graduate Institute*. Her dissertation was an analysis of Rick Strassman M.D.'s bedside notes from his early 1990s DMT studies. She received her Master's degree in Psychology from *The New School*, and received additional research training working as Research Assistant in a cognitive neuroscience lab at *Icahn School of Medicine, Mount Sinai*. She has further training as a Psychedelic-Assisted Therapist through *Alchemy Community Therapy Center* (formerly called *Sage Institute*). Additionally, she has worked extensively with the *Multidisciplinary Association for Psychedelic Studies* (MAPS; now called *Lykos Therapeutics*) since 2012, and is currently working as an Adherence Rater on their clinical trials using

MDMA to treat PTSD. Dr. Turetzky is also a Certified Integrative Wellness & Life Coach through *Integrative Wellness Academy*, a Certified Yoga Teacher through *Marianne Wells Yoga School*, and Reiki Healer through the *Usui System of Natural Healing*. She had the honor of studying the 8-Circuit Model of Consciousness with Antero Alli in his 8-Circuit Brain course. She studies and practices herbalism, and offers holistic health and lifestyle guidance. Dr. Turetzky offers psychedelic integration and psychonautic guidance through her organization *Eleusia Psychedelic Integration Coaching* and Dr. Douglas Wingate's psilocybin service center, *7 Gates Sanctuary*, as well as metaprogramming instruction and guidance through *8-Circuit Ascension/The Institute of Applied Metaprogramming* with co-founder Dr. Douglas Wingate.

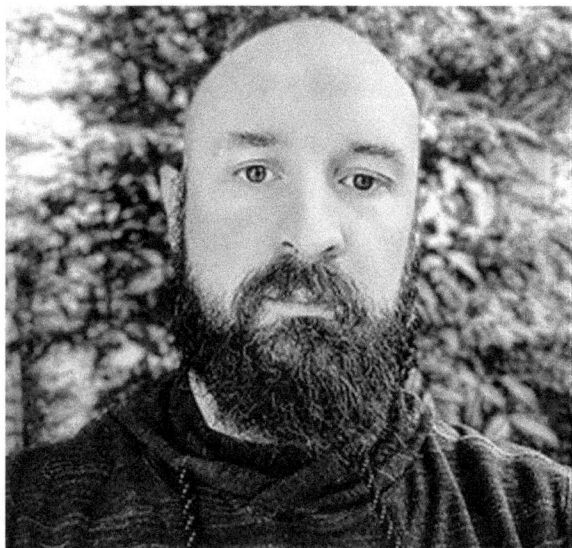

Dr. Douglas Wingate received his Doctorate in Traditional Chinese Medicine from *Five Branches University*, and his Masters from the *Oregon College of Oriental Medicine*. He has completed postdoctoral studies in clinical neuroscience from the *Carrick Institute*, as well as being a certified Functional Medicine Hyperbaric Clinician, Licensed Acupuncturist, herbalist, and is certified in somatic psychedelic integration. He was part of the first cohort of licensed psilocybin facilitators in his home state of Oregon, and co-owns one of the first licensed psilocybin service centers in the United States. He works with the *Integrative Psychiatry Institute's* psychedelic-assisted therapy program, as well as providing metaprogramming instruction and guidance through *8-Circuit Ascension/The Institute of Applied Metaprogramming* with co-founder Dr. Rachel Turetzky. He specializes in neurological, emotional, neuro-cognitive, and chronic pain conditions, including working as an adjunct professor at the National University of Natural Medicine, and in the neurology department of *Oregon Health & Science University Hospital*. He has written multiple books on the topics of brain health and consciousness including *Circuits and Shen: Models of the Evolution of Consciousness and Chinese Medicine*. He is a long-time practitioner of meditation, *qigong,* and Daoist internal alchemy *(neidan)*. He is also an alumnus of the *Maybe Logic Academy* where he had the honor of studying the Eight-Circuit Model of Consciousness under Robert Anton Wilson.

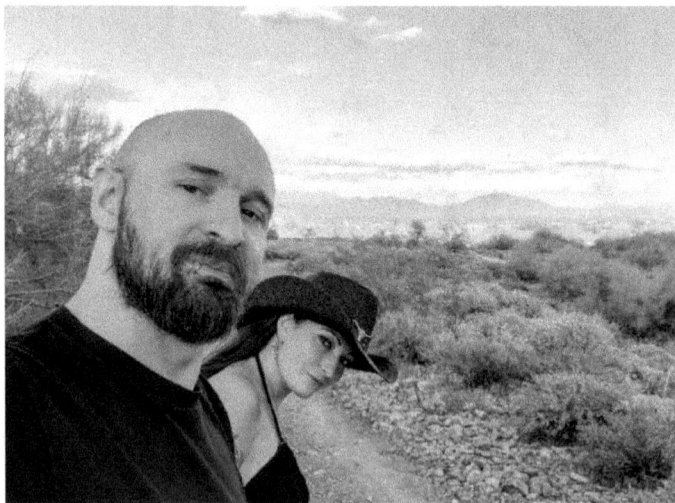

For more information, see:

8circuitascension.com

FROM ANTERO ALLI

ANGEL TECH
A Modern Shaman's Guide to Reality Selection

Angel Tech is a comprehensive compendium of insights and techniques for the direct application of Dr. Timothy Leary's Eight-Circuit Brain model for Intelligence Increase. What Dr. Leary posited as theory and Dr. Robert Anton Wilson brilliantly demonstrated in sociopolitical, mathematical and intellectual proofs, Antero Alli has extended into tangible tasks, exercises, rituals and meditations.

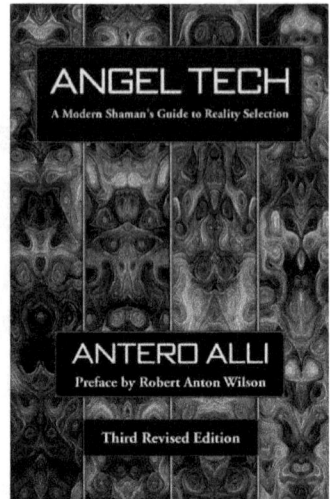

ANGEL TECH
A Modern Shaman's Guide to Reality Selection

ANTERO ALLI
Preface by Robert Anton Wilson

Third Revised Edition

THE EIGHT-CIRCUIT BRAIN
Navigational Strategies for the Energetic Body

The Eight-Circuit Brain advances and expands the material presented in *Angel Tech,* a compendium of techniques and practical applications based on Dr. Timothy Leary's 8-Circuit Brain model. After more than twenty years of research and experimentation, Antero's earlier findings are significantly updated and enriched.

From the Author of "Angel Tech" and "Towards an Archeology of the Soul"

THE EIGHT-CIRCUIT BRAIN

Navigational Strategies for the Energetic Body
ANTERO ALLI

FROM ANTERO ALLI

PARATHEATRE
A Ritual Technology for Self-Initiation

Since 1977, Antero Alli has been developing a ritual technology for Self-Initiation—Paratheatre—combining techniques of theatre, dance and zazen to access and express the internal landscape. Paratheatre is highly transformative, and has served as a critical source of inspiration for many of Antero's artistic endeavors, especially his films. (Audio)

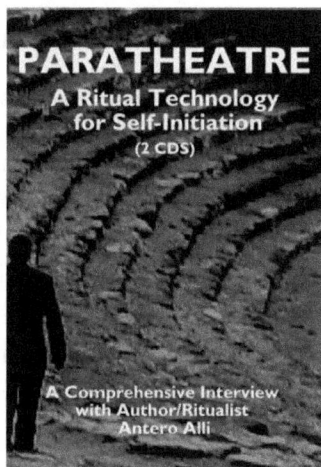

PARATHEATRE
A Ritual Technology
for Self-Initiation
(2 CDS)

A Comprehensive Interview
with Author/Ritualist
Antero Alli

8-CIRCUITS OF CONSCIOUSNESS

In this video, Antero Alli discusses his research results and a wide variety of perceptions on Timothy Leary's 8-Circuit Brain model for Intelligence Increase. Antero introduces the origin of this system, and how his interpretations differ from Dr. Leary's and Robert Anton Wilson's, along with his insights on the vertical connectivities between upper and lower circuits, the function and nature of shock, the first and second attentions, and much, much more.

THE EIGHT-CIRCUIT BRAIN
A Video Lecture by Antero Alli

THE *Original* FALCON PRESS

Invites You to Visit Our Website:
originalfalcon.com

At our website you can:

- Browse the online catalog of all of our great titles
- Find out what's available and what's out of stock
- Get special discounts
- Order our titles through our secure online server
- Find products not available anywhere else including:
  - One of a kind and limited availability products
  - Special packages
  - Special pricing
- Get free gifts
- Join our email list for advance notice of New Releases and Special Offers
- Find out about book signings and author events
- Send email to our authors
- Read excerpts of many of our titles
- Find links to our authors' websites
- Discover links to other weird and wonderful sites
- And much, much more

Visit us today at originalfalcon.com